OXFORD WORLD'S CLASSICS

# SIX TRAGEDIES

LUCIUS ANNAEUS SENECA was born some time between 1 BCE and 4 CE, in Corduba, in southern Spain, to a Roman equestrian family. Seneca's father ('Seneca the Elder') had a successful rhetorical career, and educated his sons in Rome, in rhetoric and philosophy. Seneca was a life-long adherent to Stoic philosophy.

In the year 41 CE Caligula was murdered, and Claudius took over as emperor. Soon after the new ruler's accession Caligula's sister, Julia, was accused of committing adultery with Seneca. They were tried before the Senate and sentenced to death, but Claudius altered the sentence to exile. Seneca was sent to Corsica, where he spent the next eight years, and where several of his prose works were probably written. Perhaps many or most of the tragedies were written on Corsica. Seneca was brought back to Rome in 49 CE through the intercession of Agrippina, who wanted a tutor for her son Nero.

On Nero's accession in 54 CE Seneca became a very powerful man. He was Nero's speechwriter, and perhaps political adviser. Along with the praetorian prefect Burrus, he may have been responsible for the relative restraint of Nero's early years as emperor. Their power diminished after 59 CE when they refused to help Nero kill his mother, Agrippina. In the early 60s CE Seneca officially retired from public life. In 65 CE there was a plan to assassinate the emperor (the 'Pisonian Conspiracy'). Nero accused Seneca of involvement in the plot and forced him to commit suicide; he died in a hot steam-bath.

EMILY WILSON is Associate Professor in Classical studies at the University of Pennsylvania. She is the author of *Mocked with Death: Tragic Overliving from Sophocles to Milton* (2004) and *The Death of Socrates: Hero, Villain, Chatterbox, Saint* (2007).

## OXFORD WORLD'S CLASSICS

*For over 100 years Oxford World's Classics have brought readers closer to the world's great literature. Now with over 700 titles—from the 4,000-year-old myths of Mesopotamia to the twentieth century's greatest novels—the series makes available lesser-known as well as celebrated writing.*

*The pocket-sized hardbacks of the early years contained introductions by Virginia Woolf, T. S. Eliot, Graham Greene, and other literary figures which enriched the experience of reading. Today the series is recognized for its fine scholarship and reliability in texts that span world literature, drama and poetry, religion, philosophy, and politics. Each edition includes perceptive commentary and essential background information to meet the changing needs of readers.*

OXFORD WORLD'S CLASSICS

SENECA

# Six Tragedies

*Translated with an Introduction and Notes by*
EMILY WILSON

OXFORD
UNIVERSITY PRESS

# OXFORD

UNIVERSITY PRESS

Great Clarendon Street, Oxford OX2 6DP

Oxford University Press is a department of the University of Oxford.
It furthers the University's objective of excellence in research, scholarship,
and education by publishing worldwide in

Oxford New York

Auckland Cape Town Dar es Salaam Hong Kong Karachi
Kuala Lumpur Madrid Melbourne Mexico City Nairobi
New Delhi Shanghai Taipei Toronto

With offices in

Argentina Austria Brazil Chile Czech Republic France Greece
Guatemala Hungary Italy Japan Poland Portugal Singapore
South Korea Switzerland Thailand Turkey Ukraine Vietnam

Oxford is a registered trade mark of Oxford University Press
in the UK and in certain other countries

Published in the United States
by Oxford University Press Inc., New York

British Library Cataloguing in Publication Data

Data available

Library of Congress Cataloging-in-Publication Data

Data available

Typeset by Cepha Imaging Private Ltd., Bangalore, India
Printed in Great Britain
on acid-free paper by
Clays Ltd., St Ives plc

ISBN 978-0-19-280706-9

1 3 5 7 9 10 8 6 4 2

# CONTENTS

*Introduction*     vii

*Note on the Text and Translation*     xxvii

*Select Bibliography*     xxix

*Chronology*     xxxiii

*Mythological Family Trees*     xxxiv

PHAEDRA     1

OEDIPUS     39

MEDEA     71

TROJAN WOMEN     103

HERCULES FURENS     139

THYESTES     179

*Explanatory Notes*     213

# INTRODUCTION

## Biography and History

SENECA's tragedies are intense. They show us people who push themselves too far, beyond the limits of ordinary behaviour and emotion. Passion is constantly set against reason, and passion wins out: as Seneca's Phaedra asks: 'What can reason do? Passion, passion rules' (184). Seneca's characters are obsessed and destroyed by their emotions: they are dominated by rage, ambition, lust, jealousy, desire, anger, grief, madness, and fear. The literary style of these plays, too, is intense: they use dense, witty, hyperbolic language and imagery to evoke an endless struggle for more and more absolute power.

Seneca's tragedies reflect the emotional and political intensity of the time in which they were written. Lucius Annaeus Seneca was a contemporary of Jesus, born some time between 1 BCE and 4 CE.[1] He lived in one of the most interesting and dangerous periods of Roman history, under the emperors Tiberius, Gaius (Caligula), Claudius, and Nero. The Roman Republic was long dead. Over the course of Seneca's lifetime the empire expanded, while Rome's rulers grew ever more corrupt.

Seneca was born in Corduba, in southern Spain, at a distance from Rome, the centre of imperial power, and both his parents had also been born in Spain. Seneca's tragedies have many passages that evoke the vast size of the Roman empire: lists of the most far-flung regions lying at or beyond the borders of Roman power. The fact that Seneca came from an outlying part of the empire may have made him particularly aware of the scale of Roman dominance in the western world of his time.

But Corduba was not a provincial backwater; it was an important centre of Roman culture. Moreover, Seneca came from a privileged, educated, and wealthy background. His family was upper class, belonging to the equestrian order. Equestrians (or 'knights'—the word literally suggests horse-rider or cavalryman) were traditionally

---

[1] The best overview of Seneca's life, and his interactions with the political circumstances of his times, is Miriam Griffin's *Seneca: A Philosopher in Politics* (Clarendon Press, 1976).

focused on business rather than politics—in contrast to senatorial families, but Seneca was to rise to enormous political prominence. According to Tacitus, one of our main sources for this period, Seneca expressed to Nero, towards the end of his life, his amazement at his own social rise: 'Am I, born of an equestrian father in the provinces, actually numbered among the leaders of the state? Has my newcomer presence achieved distinction amongst noblemen who can put on display a long series of glittering decorations?'[2] But there is some rhetorical disingenuousness in the implication that Seneca's rise to prominence from humble family origins was due entirely to the benevolence of the emperor Nero. In fact his success owed a great deal both to his own literary talent and to the influence of his family. Seneca did not come from nowhere.

Seneca's father ('Seneca the Elder') had a successful rhetorical career. He spent most of his life in Rome, studying oratory. He wrote a history of Rome (which has not survived), and also two sets of textbook examples of rhetorical exercises, called the *Suasoriae* (*Persuasions*) and *Controversiae* (*Controversial Issues*), sections of which are extant. These were written at the request of his sons, towards the end of his life.

Seneca the Elder had three sons; Lucius Annaeus was the middle child. Their father brought all three to Rome to be educated. All the brothers became intimately involved, in very different ways, with the workings of Roman imperial power. The elder brother, Annaeus Novatus, became the governor of southern Greece. He is mentioned in Acts (18: 12–16), since it was under his rule that the Jews brought an accusation against Paul for persuading people to 'worship God contrary to the law'. Annaeus Novatus, referred to in Acts under the name Gallio, dismissed the case, arguing that the issue was a matter of religious law, outside the realm of Roman legislation.

The youngest brother, Annaeus Mela, did not undertake an official political career. He became a successful businessman, and eventually helped to manage Nero's finances. He was the father of the poet Lucan—author of the *Civil War*, a great Republican epic poem about the war between Julius Caesar and Pompey.

We do not know much detail about the life of Lucius Annaeus Seneca, the middle brother, as a teenager and young man. These must have been the years in which he was educated in rhetoric.

[2] Tacitus, *Annals* 14. 53: trans. J. C. Yardley, Oxford World's Classics (Oxford University Press, 2008), 330.

The influence of Roman rhetorical training is evident in all of his work. He also trained with several different tutors in philosophy. A Stoic named Attalus emphasized the importance of ascetic habits: he recommended always sleeping on a hard bed, and avoiding luxurious foods such as oysters and mushrooms. Seneca became a life-long adherent to Stoic philosophy.[3] He also studied at the school of Quintus Sextus, another primarily Stoic philosopher. From Sextus he seems to have learnt the moral practice of daily self-examination. He also became a vegetarian, but was talked out of it after only a year by his father, who thought the meatless diet was weakening his son's health.

Seneca's health was certainly bad. He was a lifelong sufferer from chest problems, which may have been caused by cardiac asthma or angina. In his Epistle 78 to Lucilius, Seneca tells the story of how, in his early years, he was able to 'adopt a defiant attitude to sickness':

But eventually I succumbed to it altogether. Reduced to a state of complete emaciation, I had arrived at a point where the catarrhal discharges were virtually carrying me away with them altogether. On many an occasion I felt an urge to cut my life short there and then, and was only held back by the thought of my father, who had been the kindest of fathers to me and was then in his old age. Having in mind not how bravely I was capable of dying but how far from bravely he was capable of bearing the loss, I commanded myself to live. There are times when even to live is an act of bravery.[4]

After this episode, which perhaps took place when he was in his twenties, Seneca seems to have recuperated in Egypt. His aunt—his mother's stepsister—was the wife of the prefect of Egypt at this time, and probably cared for him in his illness.

Seneca returned to Rome in 31 CE. His father wanted him to begin a political career, and his aunt's connections were also useful in achieving this aim. At some point after his return to Rome—but perhaps as late as 37 CE, after several more years devoted to study—he took his first step on to the ladder of the traditional Roman political career (the *cursus*). He was appointed as a 'quaestor' (a financial officer), and enrolled in the Senate. It was a comparatively late start for a political career: Seneca's peers would have already begun to

---

[3] For more on Stoicism, see 'Stoicism and Seneca's Tragedies', below.
[4] Epistle 78. 1–2: *Letters from a Stoic*, trans. Robin Campbell (Penguin Books, 2004), 131.

climb the ladder in their twenties, while he had spent those years being ill and studying philosophy.

After his return to Rome Seneca quickly became a well-known public figure. His success was as much due to his literary and rhetorical skills as to his family background. He began writing: we know that during the reign of Tiberius he wrote the *Consolation to Marcia*, a philosophical work addressed to a woman whose son had died. Seneca puts Marcia's grief in the context of universal mortality, suggesting that if she can take a larger perspective she may be able to accept her individual loss. The treatise shows Seneca's conceptual and stylistic energy at work even at this early stage of his career.

Seneca became famous as an orator as well as a writer. But the growing admiration for Seneca among the Roman elite was not shared by the emperor himself. Gaius Caligula did not like him; perhaps he was wary of his influence among powerful people. The Greek historian Dio Cassius tells us that Caligula threatened to force Seneca to commit suicide, on the grounds that he had pleaded too well before the Senate. He was spared only because one of Caligula's mistresses argued that Seneca was tubercular and likely to die soon anyway.[5] The story may well be false, or at least exaggerated. But Seneca's rhetorical fluency does seem to have aroused the annoyance of Caligula, even if he did not threaten him with death. The Roman historian Suetonius tells us that the emperor had 'so much contempt for more subtle and refined kinds of writing' that he said of Seneca, 'then very much in fashion', that his compositions were 'mere school essays', and that his work was 'sand without lime'.[6] The implication of the metaphor is that there is no binding agent in Seneca's rhetoric to cement all the pointed witticisms together.

In the year 41 CE Caligula was murdered, and Claudius took over as emperor. Soon after the new ruler's accession the two sisters of Caligula who had been in exile, Julia and Agrippina, were allowed to return to Rome, but some months later Julia was accused of committing adultery with Seneca. They were tried before the Senate and sentenced to death, but Claudius altered the sentence to exile. Seneca was sent to Corsica, where he spent the next eight years. He had to leave behind his whole family, including his wife and young son.

---

[5] Dio, *Roman History*, 59. 19.

[6] Suetonius, *Lives of the Caesars*, 'Caligula', 53: trans. Catharine Edwards, Oxford World's Classics (Oxford University Press, 2000), 163.

It is not clear whether there was any truth in the accusations. One of our sources, Cassius Dio, suggests that the charges were trumped up by Claudius' wife Messalina, because she was jealous of Julia. Tacitus, on the other hand, implies that Seneca may have been guilty. But contemporary observers were probably as much in the dark as we are; the truth may never be known. For readers of Seneca's tragedies, the important thing about the affair is that Seneca had experienced, at first hand, exile, the anger of those in power, and the vicissitudes of fortune. He had been forced from his home as a criminal. Seneca's plays, which deal obsessively with the theme of tyranny and the destruction caused by lust for power, were written by a man who had experienced social degradation at the hands of an emperor.

While on Corsica Seneca presumably studied philosophy and got on with his writing: several of his prose works were almost certainly written in exile, and it is possible that many or most of the tragedies were also written on Corsica. The rhetorician and teacher Quintilian tells us that in his young days he heard Seneca debate whether a particular phrase was appropriate as tragic diction or not.[7] If Seneca was interested in this question at the time of Quintilian's youth, in the late 40s or early 50s, he had probably begun to write tragedy by this date. Seneca was brought back to Rome in 49 CE through the intercession of Agrippina. Agrippina wanted a tutor (*praeceptor*) for her son Nero. Seneca could repay her for her mercy by training the young man in politics, rhetoric, and philosophy.

Claudius died in 54 CE, probably poisoned, and Seneca, soon after the old emperor's death, wrote a satirical account of his deification called the *Pumpkinification of Claudius* (*Apocolocyntosis*). As well as showing Seneca's ability to poke fun at the pretensions of emperors, this work also provides an important clue to the dating of his tragedies, since a line from the *Pumpkinification* seems to be a comic rewriting of a passage of Seneca's own *Hercules Furens*.

On the accession of Nero, Seneca—as the old tutor and adviser of the new ruler—became a very powerful man. Tacitus tells us that he acted as Nero's speechwriter. But being close to Nero was never very safe. Seneca's role as adviser remained unofficial, and it is difficult to tell exactly how much power or influence he had over the young emperor. He may—as Tacitus suggests—have been responsible for the relative moderation of the early years of Nero's rule, along with Burrus, the head of the praetorian guard.

[7] *Institute of Oratory*, 8. 3. 31.

Many people, both contemporary and later, have been suspicious or critical of Seneca's relationship with Nero. It has often been suspected that Seneca, far from restraining the emperor or guiding him by ethical philosophy, in fact colluded with, or even encouraged, his excesses. This critique began in antiquity: we learn from the Greek historian Dio that some contemporaries accused Seneca of a hypocritical failure to live his life in accordance with his own philosophy:

> For while denouncing tyranny, he was making himself the teacher of a tyrant; while inveighing against the associates of the powerful, he did not hold aloof from the palace himself; and though he had nothing good to say of flatterers, he always fawned upon Messalina and the freedmen of Claudius, to such an extent, in fact, as actually to send them from the island of his exile a book containing their praises—a book which he afterwards suppressed out of shame. Though finding fault with the rich, he himself acquired a fortune of 300,000,000 sesterces; and though he had censured the extravagances of others, he had five hundred tables of citrus wood with legs of ivory, all identically alike, and he served banquets on them.[8]

But Tacitus, who is a more reliable source for the period, suggests that Seneca at least tried to give his pupil moral advice and train him to be a good man as well as a good emperor. In Tacitus' account, Seneca and Burrus competed with Nero's mother, Agrippina, for control of the uncontrollable young ruler. In 55 CE Nero arranged to have his stepbrother and main rival for imperial power, the fourteen-year-old Britannicus, murdered; Seneca failed to intervene, although his treatise addressed to the emperor, *On Mercy*, may have been a belated attempt to restrain Nero from further acts of violence.

By 59 CE Nero—who was married to Octavia—was desperately in love with a married woman called Poppaea. Agrippina opposed the match, and Nero decided that the only solution was to kill her. The first attempt failed, and he tried to persuade Seneca and Burrus to help him finish the job. They suggested that he should, instead, ask the freedman who had first proposed killing her by a supposed boating accident to complete the murder. Nero was irritated by this defection, and the two advisers' power over him waned from that point onwards.

In 62 CE Burrus died—probably assassinated—and Seneca's power declined still further. Seneca, according to Tacitus, tried to

---

[8] Dio, *Roman History*, 61. 10. 2–3; trans. Herbert B. Foster and Earnest Cary, Loeb Classical Library (Harvard University Press, 1968), viii. 57.

retire from the court at this point, responding in part to the criticisms of his enemies, who claimed that he had amassed too much private wealth for himself, that he was only interested in his own advancement, and that it was time for the adult emperor's tutor to retire. Seneca asked Nero for permission to withdraw from public life. Nero refused to allow any official retirement on the part of his old tutor, but Seneca probably took a less active role in policy-advising from this point onwards. In 64 CE Seneca made a further request to retire and offered to return some of the money the emperor had given him; Nero was by this time in great financial difficulties, and accepted the money.

In the following year, 65 CE, a group of prominent men plotted to kill Nero. The Pisonian Conspiracy—named after one of its instigators, Gaius Piso—involved a plan to assassinate the emperor during a festival in honour of the goddess Ceres at the public games, which were held in April. But Nero uncovered the plot and set about killing all those who seemed to have been in any way connected with it. Seneca's nephew, the poet Lucan, accused of being involved, was forced to kill himself, along with both of Seneca's brothers. Nero had no firm evidence connecting Seneca with the affair, but it provided a useful pretext to have him killed.

Tacitus provides a detailed account of his long-drawn-out and deliberately 'philosophical', Socratic suicide.[9] After making various speeches, Seneca—along with his wife, Paulina—cut his wrists, but found his blood was too desiccated for him to bleed to death. He tried poison, but that too failed. Eventually Seneca got into a hot bath and suffocated in the steam. His wife survived.

The dramatic events of Seneca's life, and the dramatic history of his times, are clearly relevant to a reading of his tragedies. But it is frustrating that we know very little about when exactly these plays were composed. The dating matters, because it makes a difference to our vision of the plays' political and moral context. If they were written under Nero, it is possible to read these presentations of passion overwhelming reason, and power gone horribly wrong, as nightmare presentations of life in Nero's court—or as warnings to the young emperor of what might happen if he allowed his evil tendencies to get out of control. But the evidence suggests that most, perhaps even all, of the tragedies were composed before Nero came to power. Stylistic analysis of the plays suggests that *Agamemnon*, *Phaedra*, and *Oedipus*

---

[9] Tacitus, *Annals*, 15. 60–5.

are probably among the earliest written, *Medea*, *Troades* (*Trojan Women*), and *Hercules Furens* (*Hercules Insane*) form a middle group, and *Thyestes* and the unfinished *Phoenissae* (*Phoenician Women*) are probably later than the rest.[10] If we accept this grouping, and if we also accept that the *Apocolocyntosis*—which was composed some time soon after the death of Claudius in 54 CE—parodies *Hercules Furens*, then it is likely that only *Thyestes* was composed under the reign of Nero.

Seneca's representations in the tragedies of ambition, tyranny, and cruelty reflect his own experiences under Tiberius, Caligula, and Claudius—as well as, in the case of *Thyestes*, Nero. As a provincial who rose to enormous influence, and who suffered exile as well as enjoying great wealth and prestige, he knew how quickly fortune can change, how easy it is for emperors to behave in cruel and savage ways, and how dependent people may be on the whims of those in power. Seneca's complex relationship with the politics of his own time is one of the many reasons why his work is relevant today.

## Stoicism and Seneca's Tragedies

Seneca was not only a writer of verse tragedies, but also a philosopher. He was a Stoic—like Epictetus and, later, Marcus Aurelius—and his prose works are the most extensive works of Stoic philosophy surviving from antiquity.[11]

The philosophical school of Stoicism was founded in Hellenistic Athens in the early third century BCE, by a Greek philosopher called Zeno. Zeno seems to have taught that the main path to tranquillity lies through indifference to pleasure and pain. After Zeno, most of the major doctrines of the Stoic school were developed by later leader of the school, Chrysippus, who lived in the later part of the third century BCE.

Stoicism was a complete world-view, encompassing not only moral philosophy and psychology but also physics, cosmology, and logic. But in all of these areas Stoics gave a central place to reason; rationality lies at the centre of the Stoic universe, and at the centre of the Stoics' ideal human life. The Stoics believed that the universe is

[10] See 'Sense-pauses and Relative Dating in Seneca, Sophocles and Shakespeare', *AJP* 102 (1981), 435–53.

[11] Recent introductions to Stoicism include John Sellars, *Stoicism* (California University Press, 2006), and M. Andrew Holowchak, *The Stoics: A Guide for the Perplexed* (Continuum, 2008).

controlled by a reasoning power: God or Nature. Fate, associated with primordial fire, causes everything that happens. Human and animal souls, too, are emanations of the primordial fire.

In modern popular usage being 'stoical' tends to mean suppressing one's feelings and keeping a stiff upper lip, but the attitude towards emotion of the ancient Stoics was somewhat more complex, and more appealing, than this. The Stoics did not believe that all emotions should be repressed, or that all emotions were wrong. Rather, they taught that most of the feelings that trouble and disturb us in daily life are the result of false beliefs. For instance, one may fear death under the false apprehension that death is the worst thing that can happen; or one may feel an intense desire for money, possessions, a particular sexual partner, or worldly power, under the false belief that these things are really good. From a Stoic perspective, though, none of these things is genuinely beneficial.

The Stoics took seriously Socrates' maxim that 'Virtue is knowledge'. They argued that the truly wise man is one whose feelings are in line with true belief: he will 'live in accordance with Nature'. (The wise person is almost always imagined, by Stoic philosophers, to be male.) He will not suppress his feelings; rather, he will not even feel the passions aroused by falsehoods. True joy and tranquillity will subsitute for the roller-coaster of emotions based on delusion.

The wise man's virtue is, they argued, both necessary and sufficient for his happiness. Within Stoicism there was some debate about whether anything other than virtue was good, and whether anything other than vice was bad. The Stoics developed the concept of 'indifferent things', which were neither good nor bad but which might nevertheless, according to at least some Stoic thinkers, be worthy either of choice or rejection. On these grounds, Stoics such as Seneca could justify their choice to enjoy, and even seek, wealth, worldly honour, and power, even though, strictly speaking, such things could not be classified as 'good'.

The central problem faced by all readers of Seneca is how to reconcile the Stoic philosophy of his prose writings either with his life or with his wild, gory tragedies. Should we—as some contemporaries certainly did—condemn him as a hypocrite, for combining a philosophical condemnation of material values and commitment to virtue with an intimate and very profitable relationship with the obviously un-virtuous emperor Nero? Even setting aside the biographical dilemma, what are we to make of someone who, in his prose writings, advocates moderation, life in accordance with nature, and control of the passions, but whose tragedies show us characters like the bloodthirsty Atreus, who are violently out of control?

It was once commonly believed that the tragedies and the philosophy must be by two different people, 'Seneca the tragedian' and 'Seneca the philosopher'. Scholars are now convinced that the same person wrote both prose and plays, but there is enormous disagreement about how to put the two together. Some have argued that, despite appearances, the tragedies are entirely reconcilable with orthodox Stoicism. According to this school of thought, the most manic tragic characters are presented to us as moral lessons, examples of all the nasty things that happen to you if you let your passions get out of control. Others suggest that the tragedies allow Seneca to play with the dark fears and possibilities that are repressed in his prose writings. One danger of the second type of interpretation is that it risks taking an oversimplified view of the prose, which contains its own contradictions and ambivalences.

It is clear, however, that in both his drama and his prose works Seneca had a particular concern with intense emotions, and especially with anger. Seneca wrote a prose treatise, *On Anger*, which argues that anger is the most intense and dangerous of all the passions. It is the one that may seize hold of anybody, rich or poor, Greek or barbarian, man or woman, young or old; and it is the passion which causes the most damage, both to the angry person's victims and to the one whose soul is maddened by this overwhelming emotion. Anger, Seneca tells us, is the feeling most likely to grow out of all measure, distorting rational judgement: 'it makes no difference how great the source is from which it springs; for from the most trivial origins it reaches massive proportions'.[12]

The tragedies show a whole range of out-of-control emotions: from Phaedra's incestuous lust, or Andromache's obsession with her dead husband, to the idleness and greed of Thyestes, the ambition of Hercules, the despair of Megara or Hecuba, or the cowardice of Jason. But anger is the passion that haunts each of these plays: all Seneca's tragedies are concerned in some way with the massive consequences of unrestrained human aggression. It is anger, unbridled by philosophy, that creates catastrophe. Medea, enraged at Jason's betrayal, is driven by her rage to kill her children; Atreus, furious at

---

[12] *Seneca: Dialogues and Essays*, trans. John Davie, Oxford World's Classics (Oxford University Press, 2007), 19.

the thought that his brother may have slept with his wife, plots to make Thyestes eat his own children; Juno, mad with rage at Jupiter's adulteries and Hercules' growing renown, fills him with madness and makes him kill his children. In *Phaedra* Theseus is overwhelmed by anger at his son, and calls down the god's curse upon him—not pausing to find out that he was innocent. Seneca's *Oedipus* shows us the consequences of the Theban king's anger at his father Laius, and also his unyielding anger at himself, which makes him gouge out his eyes from his sockets in a scene of unrelenting grossness: 'Greedily his nails dig into his eyeballs, | ripping and tearing out the jelly from the roots' (965–6). Seneca's characters show no mercy, either towards each other or to themselves. These plays create a world where forgiveness seems all but impossible.

Seneca wrote another prose treatise, *On Mercy*, addressed to the emperor Nero. In this work Seneca suggests that it is mercy (*clementia*) that distinguishes the just ruler from the tyrant. Conversely, Seneca's tragedies show us many terrible examples of figures who step over this line, refusing mercy in favour of greater and greater violence. *Trojan Women* provides the most thorough analysis of how a whole culture can refuse to show mercy on another. The Greeks, after their victory at Troy, insist that they must not only rape and enslave the women, and rob the Trojan treasure-houses and temples, but also kill the Trojan children. The Greek leader, Agamemnon, makes a case that sounds strikingly similar to that of Seneca in *On Mercy*: he tells Achilles' sadistic son Pyrrhus that human sacrifice is going too far: 'there is an etiquette to victory, a limit to defeat.| Those who abuse their power never stay powerful long' (257–8). But as always in Senecan tragedy, the moderate position loses. Calchas, the priest, recommends that the children be killed, and the Greek leaders comply: Polyxena, daughter of Priam and Hecuba, is slaughtered on Achilles' tomb, and Astyanax, baby son of Hector, is hurled from the city walls. The play is all the more troubling because this apparent brutality seems to be licensed by the gods.

Seneca's tragedies include many allusions to Stoic doctrines. But his tragic characters are never fully fledged representatives of a Stoic ideal. In several cases Stoic language and Stoic concepts are used in perverted ways. For instance, in *Phaedra* the Nurse tells Hippolytus, 'follow nature as your guide to life' (481). But to the Stoics life in accordance with nature implied conformity to natural reason—not yielding to lust and agreeing to have sex with one's stepmother.

Megara's resistance to the tyrant Lycus, in *Hercules Furens*, makes her look temporarily very much like a Stoic sage; she implies, for example, that the only real good in life is moral virtue (*virtus*, which also means courage): 'Courage means conquering what everybody fears' (435). But Megara's outspoken defence of true goodness seems undermined, in the dramatic context, by her fixation on death, and her inability to believe that her husband could ever return from the underworld. Rational philosophy, in this play, seems to come all too close to suicidal despair.

Hercules was one of the greatest heroes of the Stoics, who revered him for his courage and indifference to pain. But Seneca's tragic version of Hercules is hard to admire wholeheartedly as a philosophical hero. Seneca presents him in much less favourable terms than did Euripides in his version of the same myth, *Heracles*. Seneca's play throws doubt on the value of Hercules' achievements, even those performed when the hero is supposedly sane. Seneca's Hercules is less Superman—with his comforting Clark Kent persona—than Batman or Spiderman: a hero who can hardly bear to take off his mask, for fear of what it might reveal.

Those who try to advocate moderation in these plays are either overruled or shown to be misguided. The weak-willed Thyestes—who makes half-hearted and hypocritical gestures towards Stoic asceticism—is only a foil for his gloriously savage brother, while the Chorus and the ineffectual Attendant in the same play pose only short-lived and futile challenges to the tyrant Atreus. Plays like *Thyestes* show the folly of believing that passions can be controlled, or that extreme conflicts can be amicably resolved. Atreus murders his brother's children, feeds them to him, and exults in his triumph.

Most disturbingly of all, we, the readers and spectators of the play, are not only disgusted and horrified, but also seduced into sympathy and even admiration for the murderer. The emotional weight of Seneca's tragedies lies not with the moderates but with those consumed by monstrous passion. There is Atreus, with his insane desire for the most horrible possible revenge on his brother. There is Medea, the barbarian witch who will stop at nothing in her hatred of her former husband. There is Hippolytus, whose resistance to passion is itself a form of passion. We may shudder at these characters, but it is hard not to find oneself swept up by their energy.

## Literary Form

Seneca's tragedies are strikingly self-conscious about their own status as drama. Several of his most memorable characters—such as Atreus in *Thyestes*, and Medea—speak of their own plots in markedly dramatic terms, as if they are conscious of creating their own acts of theatre. The climactic scenes of these plays often draw attention to the notion of spectacle, and invite us, as readers or audience, to compare our own responses with those of the characters on stage. For example, Medea declares that she can achieve an even greater, and more pleasurable, act of revenge by killing the last child before Jason's own eyes: 'This was all I was missing, | that Jason should be watching' (992–3). Atreus, similarly, demands an appropriate audience as an essential element in his complete revenge: 'If only I could prevent the gods from leaving, | drag them down and force them all to watch | this vengeance feast!—But let the father see it, that is enough' (893–5). At the end of *Trojan Women* the Messenger emphasizes that the scene of Polyxena's murder is 'like a theatre', and describes the mixed motives of those who watch this act of savagery: some gleeful or full of *Schadenfreude*, some full of pity, but all unable to turn away their eyes: 'The fickle mob hates the crime, but watches anyway' (1129). The passage implicitly raises a question that applies to all of us, as readers or spectators of Senecan tragedy: what is it that drives us to watch or read about such horrors?

Those who dislike Senecan tragedy have tended to dismiss it as self-conscious—in contrast to the supposed naturalism of Greek tragedy; and, a related term, 'heavy', in contrast to the sweetness and light of the Greeks. 'Seneca cannot be too heavy, nor Plautus too light', says Hamlet,[13] and he is right that Senecan style is heavy. The word 'rhetorical' has often been flung at Seneca, as if it were obviously a bad thing to use dense, elevated, artificial language. Seneca's style was controversial already in antiquity. Quintilian saw Seneca's unusual language as a bad influence on aspiring young writers or speakers, commenting that 'he has many excellent *sententiae*, and much that is worth reading on moral grounds; but his style is for the most part decadent, and particularly dangerous because of the seductiveness of the vices with which it abounds. One could wish that he had used his own talents but other people's judgment.'[14]

[13] Shakespeare, *Hamlet*, II. ii. 395.
[14] *Institutes of Oratory* 10. 1. 129–30; trans. Donald A. Russell, Loeb Classical Library (Harvard University Press, 2001), 321.

Quintilian, like many subsequent critics, complained that Seneca's style is unnatural, both in his choice of expression and his fondness for witty epigrams.

But Seneca's combination of dramatic self-consciousness, bravura stylistic excess, and sharply pointed wit was never meant to sound natural. His language achieves something other than naturalism: a poetic and dramatic form in which to show what happens when people struggle against nature, and try to overcome all normal expectations by sheer force of will. Excess is Seneca's subject, as well as the primary characteristic of his style.

Seneca's plays share certain technical features with Greek tragedy. They are composed entirely in verse, and the rhythms—like those of most Latin poetry—are modelled on Greek metres. Most of the dialogue is in iambic trimeter, which is a fairly flexible pattern involving twelve alternating long and short syllables, conceived as three metrical building-blocks of two feet each—or some permitted variation of this structure. The choral metres, as in Greek tragedy, are much more varied, involving many different patterns and lengths of line, and were presumably designed for musical accompaniment. Seneca makes highly effective use of the Greek technique of *stichomythia*—where characters alternately speak a single line as they debate with one another—as well as *hemi-stichomythia*, where a single line may itself be divided up between different characters. Seneca's highly compressed style of writing produces a more pointed kind of *stichomythia* than we find in the Greek tragedians—more rich in quotable aphorisms.

There are also important formal differences between Senecan and Greek tragedy. Most influentially for later drama, Seneca—like earlier Latin dramatists—makes use of an implicit five-act structure in almost all his plays. He also employs Greek dramatic devices in a very different manner from the Greeks: for instance, his Choruses are usually far less involved in the action than the Chorus of an Athenian tragedy.

In terms of mood and tone Seneca's tragedies are strikingly unlike our surviving Greek tragedies. The comparison with Aeschylus, Sophocles, and Euripides draws attention to the stifling, claustrophobic atmosphere of Seneca's world. His people are trapped inside their own heads. Seneca has a far stronger obsession than any Greek tragedian with the possibility that the whole universe may be at a point of crisis, and a far greater interest in transgression and in physical disgust. For instance, the centrepiece of Seneca's *Oedipus* is an extensive account of gruesome attempts by Tiresias to find the source of the plague by disembowelling an ox, and then summoning the ghost of Laius, which has no counterpart in Sophocles' *Oedipus the King*.

Many of Seneca's tragedies have a parallel in Greek tragedy. Aeschylus, like Seneca, composed an *Agamemnon*; Sophocles, like Seneca, composed an *Oedipus*; Euripides, like Seneca, produced a *Trojan Women*, a *Phaedra* (= *Hippolytus*), and a *Hercules Furens*. Readers who come to Seneca fresh from Athenian tragedy may miss the lightness, the irony, the possibility of open-ended dialogues between one character and another, or between human beings and the gods. Above all, we miss the sense of community. Seneca's tragedies focus less on the relationships of people to one another, and more on the relationship of individuals to their own passions.

These plays are far darker, but also often much funnier, than their Athenian equivalents. *Oedipus* is, again, a good example. Seneca's play, like that of Sophocles on the same subject, plots the slow, painful process by which Oedipus finds out the truth about his past. But the atmosphere of Seneca's play is very different. Sophocles' Oedipus is, at the start of the play, self-confident and sure of his own powers as a thinker and a king. By contrast, Seneca evokes, from the very start of the play, a king uncomfortable with his own power and frightened of dark forces he knows he cannot understand. Sophocles' Oedipus is, at the end of the play, led off stage by Creon to begin his exile from the city of Thebes; we are left with the image of Oedipus as a loving father losing his children, and a loving king losing his city. Seneca, by contrast, ends with a solitary man who staggers off alone, with gruesomely bleeding eye-sockets, from a city which has been ruined by plague since the very start of the play. Seneca pushes against the limits of good taste by making his Oedipus warn himself: 'Be careful, do not fall upon your mother' (1051); the son risks yet another blind sexual encounter with his mother's corpse.

In comparison with Athenian tragedy, Seneca's plays focus less on the workings of the divine in human life and more on the conflicts within human nature itself. For example, Seneca's *Phaedra* is based on the same story as Euripides' *Hippolytus*. Euripides' play is framed by two goddesses: Aphrodite, goddess of love and sex, who speaks the prologue; and Artemis, goddess of the hunt and of chastity, who appears to the dying Hippolytus in the penultimate moments of the play. It suggests that Phaedra's incestuous passion and Hippolytus' excessive chastity are two extreme sides of the same spectrum.

Seneca removes the divine machinery, to create a drama about the conflict between passion and self-control within the human psyche.

Seneca was writing at a period of cultural 'belatedness': the citizens of Neronian Rome were often led to suspect that the time of Roman moral and literary greatness was already past. The great historians of the period—such as Tacitus and Suetonius—present the time of Nero in terms of decline and degeneracy from the lost glory days of the Roman Republic. Seneca's characters constantly seem to express the fear that the time of greatness may be over, and that their culture may be bankrupt. The Chorus in *Thyestes* ask in despair: 'Will the last days come in our time?' (878). *Trojan Women* evokes the despair of a city with no future left. In contrast with Euripides' plays on the same mythic moment—his *Trojan Women* and *Hecuba*—Seneca's drama is less an analysis of the workings of a cruel or indifferent set of gods than of the depths of human despair.

Although Seneca's are the only surviving examples of Roman tragedy, we know that there was a fairly extensive Roman tragic tradition which must certainly have informed Seneca's understanding of his own dramatic art. The first Roman tragedy we know about was performed in 240 BCE. The earliest Roman tragedies fell into two categories: the *fabulae togatae* ('toga-wearing' plays), which were based on older Greek tragedies; and the *fabulae praetextae* ('tunic-wearing' plays), which were new plays with plots based on Roman history. The only *praetexta* that survives is the *Octavia*, a play included in the manuscripts of Seneca's tragedies but believed by most scholars to have been written by a later imitator. In the generation or two before Seneca's time writing tragedy became a fashionable activity: Julius Caesar is said to have written a tragedy in his youth; Ovid wrote a *Medea* which was much admired by contemporaries. So while it is a pity that no other Roman tragedy survives complete, we need to remember that it did exist, and that Athenian tragedy was by no means Seneca's only literary model.

We are certain that he also made extensive use of non-dramatic poetic models. Seneca often adapts and alludes to the work of poets from the time of the first emperor, Augustus—especially Virgil, Horace, and Ovid. His allusions to these poets are not mere plagiarism or pastiche; he often creates an extra layer of meaning by referring back to Roman poetry of the past. For example, Juno at the beginning of *Hercules Furens* expresses her outrage at Hercules' success in coming back from Hades, and comments ironically that now 'coming back is easy' (49). There is a clear reference here to a famous passage in Book 6 of Virgil's *Aeneid*, where the Sibyl warns Aeneas, before his own descent into the underworld, that:

> going down to Avernus is easy.
> All nights, all days too, dark Dis's portals lie open.
> But to recall those steps, to escape to the fresh air above you,
> There lies the challenge, the labour![15]

The allusion raises a number of important questions about the relationship of Hercules' labours to those of Aeneas, founder of the Roman race. If coming back is easy for Hercules but hard for Aeneas, that might suggest that the Greek outdoes the Roman hero. Or Hercules' lack of struggle, lack of 'labour', even over his most impressive labours, might somehow undermine his achievements. Or perhaps the Virgilian intertext functions as a reminder that Hercules takes far too rosy a vision of his own success—since the rest of the play suggests that it is much harder than he had thought to escape entirely from Hell.

Examples could be multiplied of Seneca's complex and thoughtful use of earlier Roman poetry in his tragedies—including the *Odes* of Horace in Seneca's own choral odes, and allusions to Roman elegy, as well as many references to earlier hexameter poetry (such as Virgil's *Aeneid*, *Georgics*, and *Eclogues*, Ovid's *Metamorphoses*, and Lucretius' *On the Nature of the Universe*). Seneca's dense style and dense use of allusion allow him to create some wonderful descriptive passages evoking the natural world—as in the first choral ode of *Hercules Furens* (125 ff.), which draws on Virgil, Horace, Lucretius, and others to evoke the rough but innocent life of the herdsman in the fields (144–52):

> Hard work gets up, creates anxiety,
> and opens everyone's house. The shepherd drives
> his flock out to the field, and gathers up
> fodder icy-white with frost. The calf
> whose horns have not yet sprouted from his brow
> frolics free in the open meadow;
> the empty udders of the cows grow fat.
> The cheeky little kid wobbles about,
> his legs unsteady on the soft green grass.

---

[15] Virgil, *Aeneid*, trans. Frederick Ahl, Oxford World's Classics (Oxford University Press, 2007), 132, lines 126–9.

Seneca spreads himself in the choral passages, developing rich and detailed descriptions of the sky, the sea, landscape, and far-flung places of the world.

But despite the use of non-dramatic authors as models and reference-points in Seneca's tragedies, these plays are composed with a keen awareness of the demands of dramatic form. This same ode of *Hercules Furens*, for example, uses allusions to the lyric motif of *carpe diem* (a phrase coined by Horace, in *Odes*, 1. 11), to comment specifically on the action of the play. The Chorus' generalizations about the wickedness of wealth and luxury, and the importance of living for the moment, have particular point in the context of Hercules' deliberate descent into the underworld.

The performance of Seneca's plays is a vexed question. We have no external evidence about their staging, so arguments one way or the other rely on internal evidence from the plays themselves, as well as speculation about what might have been plausible in the context of imperial Rome. In the late nineteenth and early twentieth centuries it became the scholarly orthodoxy to claim that these plays were not composed for the stage at all, but for private recitation, by a single performer. Now the pendulum of opinion has swung back the other way, and most scholars agree that they were probably written for some kind of dramatic performance, though fairly certainly not for the public theatre; they may well have been used for private performances, for the enjoyment of the emperor and his court.

## Reception

Seneca was one of the most prolific, versatile, and influential of all classical Latin writers. Arguably, no other classical writer except Virgil has had so deep, so widespread, and so long-lasting an influence on European and British literature.

During the Middle Ages and early modern periods Seneca was one of the most read and most imitated authors of antiquity. His plays had an enormous influence on European tragedy, particularly in Italy and France, and on Elizabethan and Jacobean tragedy in England. The early modern revenge tragedy—including *The Revenger's Tragedy*, Thomas Kyd's *Spanish Tragedy*, Shakespeare's *Titus Andronicus* and *Hamlet*, and John Webster's *Duchess of Malfi*—could hardly have existed without Seneca. Christopher Marlowe's dramas about men who push for ever greater power or knowledge or world domination—such as *Tamburlaine* and *Doctor Faustus*—translate the Senecan tragic plot into Renaissance terms.

Particular figures from his plays had an obvious impact on early modern literature: for instance, Seneca's Hercules—the mad hero who turns on his own loved ones—has obvious affinities with such characters as Hieronimo from Kyd's *Spanish Tragedy* and Shakespeare's *Othello*. But Seneca's style and the general mood of his works were equally influential. Thomas Nashe famously satirized the tendency of English tragedians at the time of Shakespeare to use—or plagiarize—techniques from Seneca in order to achieve a bombastic effect: 'English Seneca read by candlelight yieldes manie good sentences—"Bloud is a begger" and so forth; and if you intreate him faire in a frostie morning, he will afford you whole Hamlets, I should say handfulls, of tragical speeches.'[16] Seneca's plays were well known in this period to all schoolboys, who studied them in Latin in class, but the tragedies also reached a much broader audience through a very popular set of vernacular translations, *Seneca: His tenne tragedies*, edited by Thomas Newton (1581).

Even when British and European drama became more focused on the drawing-room than the bloodbath, and moved away from explicitly Senecan models, Seneca's tragedies continued to be closely read by all educated people. But in the nineteenth and for much of the twentieth century Senecan tragedy lost its central place in the European and Anglo-American canon. His work was dismissed as bombastic and melodramatic, crude in comparison with the work of his Athenian predecessors.

Seneca's work seems now, at last, to be back in academic vogue. 'Rhetorical' and 'didactic' are no longer dirty words. Senecan drama has suffered for too long from comparisons with Athenian tragedy; it is perhaps partly thanks to the recognition that Greek drama, too, is a messy, political, emotional, self-conscious, and unrealistic genre that Seneca's plays can begin to be appreciated again. The upsurge of interest in Seneca coincides with a recognition that the term 'Silver Latin'—which implies that the writers of Augustan Rome constitute the Golden Age of Latin—is an unfairly derogatory way to refer to the rich literature of the empire.

On one level, the current revival of interest in imperial Latin in general, and Seneca in particular, needs no explanation: an unjustly neglected and important oeuvre is beginning again to get its due.

[16] Thomas Nashe, *Preface to Robert Greene's* 'Menaphon' (1589).

But it is also striking how many of Seneca's central themes seem particularly urgent and relevant in the current political and social climate. He is a writer for uncertain and violent times, who forces us to think about the difference between compromise and hypocrisy, and about how, if at all, a person can be good, calm, or happy in a corrupt society and under constant threat of death.

Seneca's tragedies can be read as a sustained meditation on various problems of evil. Why do people—and gods—do terrible things? How much depravity are human beings capable of? What limits are there—if any—to our capacity for rage, hatred, self-promotion, lust, and violence? And what drives us to be our worst selves? These plays are the product of a sensational, frightening, and oppressive period of history; perhaps we are again ready to understand and appreciate their terrible cruelty, linguistic and psychological excesses, and their black humour.

# NOTE ON THE TEXT AND TRANSLATION

THE critical edition used for this translation is the Oxford Classical
Text, edited by Otto Zwierlein (Clarendon Press, 1986). In some cases
I have used different punctuation from Zwierlein's, and have included
lines which his edition brackets. My lineation does not always exactly
correspond to his in choral passages. In a very few cases, I have
adopted a different textual reading from that of Zwierlein.[1]

Translating Seneca into modern English, while staying faithful to
the feel of the original, is a challenge. On the most basic level, verse
drama is no longer a living form on the Anglo-American stage: modern playwrights compose in prose. But Seneca was a poet, and it
would be highly misleading to translate his carefully constructed
lines into prose.

Latin verse is entirely different from English verse, since it is a
quantitative metre—based on a pattern in the length of syllables—
rather than a stress metre, based on a pattern of stressed and
unstressed syllables. Any choice of metre in which to render a Latin
poet in English will therefore be approximate; English quantitative
metre is more or less impossible.

Most recent translators have assumed that iambic pentameter is
the only possible metre for rendering the Senecan line. The argument for pentameter is based primarily on the history of English
verse: since Shakespeare, we assume that verse drama will be in iambic pentameter. But Seneca's lines are actually longer than the
English pentameter. His metre consists of three sets of two iambic
feet, with a number of possible variations and substitutions. I have
therefore used a line which is primarily, but not exclusively, iambic,
and which varies in length from five to six, and occasionally seven,
feet. I have tried to make my English correspond, line-for-line, to
Seneca's Latin. My hope in doing this is to give a better indication
of the density of the language of these plays: Seneca crams a great
deal of thought and information into a single line.

I have not attempted to replicate Seneca's choral metres in English
except for one passage from *Medea* ('Force of flame ...'), rendered in

---

[1] *Phaedra*, line 28: adopted *Phyle* not *flius*. *Medea*, line 23: adopted *optet* not *opto*.
*Medea*, lines 659–61: text is corrupt here; in the interest of readability I have followed
the text in Hine's edition. *Troades*, line 586: I have adopted *timens* not *tumens*.

English saphhics to give an example if Seneca's rhythms; but I have varied the rhythms and line lengths in lyric passages, to give some indication of the varying verse forms. Shorter lines in my translation usually correspond to shorter lines in the original.

Seneca has a highly allusive way of writing, which assumes a fairly well-educated audience or readership. The many mythological and geographical allusions pose a particular challenge for the modern reader, who is unlikely to have the same degree of familiarity with Graeco-Roman myth that the average educated Roman spectator or reader would have had. In order to re-create the ease with which a Roman reader would have understood Seneca's terminology, I have erased or glossed some of his proper names: for instance, I have sometimes rendered 'Boreas' simply as 'the north wind'.

Capturing the tone of Senecan tragedy in modern English is also a challenge. I have aimed to make my version readable, speakable, and contemporary, but without sacrificing the essential features of Seneca's tragic diction. Seneca himself is not always readable, not always easy, and certainly not always down-to-earth. I have kept some of the colourfulness in the style, trying not to clip the wings of the most purple and bombastic passages. I have also tried to stay faithful both to Seneca's verbal fluency and to his concision. At times—as in the opening speech of *Phaedra*—Seneca creates a rhetorical effect from verbal redundancy: he does not name one place-name where twenty will do, and he builds up an atmosphere by layering the components of a list. But at other moments he specializes in putting complex thoughts into the minimum number of words. It is tempting for the translator who hopes to create readable, modern English to try to counteract both these tendencies: to cut back on the verbosity and to expand the dense witticisms. I have aimed for a lively version which will also allow Seneca something of his own weird voice, and invite new readers to have their own responses to these strange, dark plays.

I have deliberately not added stage directions to my translation, on the grounds that to do so would be to pre-empt judgement on questions of staging. But Seneca's tragedies are certainly stageable, and there have been several successful recent productions. I hope that my translation may inspire actors and directors to create new stage versions of these plays, and bring them to life for the new century.

# SELECT BIBLIOGRAPHY

### Critical Editions of Senecan Tragedies

*Agamemnon*, edited with a commentary by R. J. Tarrant (Cambridge University Press, 1976).

*Hercules furens*, edited with introduction and commentary by John G. Fitch (Cornell University Press, 1987).

*Medea*, edited with translation and commentary by H. M. Hine (Aris & Phillips, 2000).

*Medea*, edited with introduction and commentary by C. D. N. Costa (Clarendon Press, 1973).

*Octavia*, attributed to Seneca, edited with translation, introduction, and commentary by A. J. Boyle (Oxford University Press, 2008).

*Phaedra*, edited by Michael Coffy and Ronald Mayer (Cambridge University Press, 1990).

*Phoenissae*, introduction and commentary by Marica Frank (Brill, 1995).

*Troades*, edited with translation, introduction, and commentary by A. J. Boyle (Oxford University Press, 1994).

*Seneca's 'Troades': A Literary Introduction*, edited with translation, introduction, and commentary by Elaine Fantham (Princeton University Press, 1982).

*Thyestes*, edited with introduction and commentary by R. J. Tarrant (Scholars Press, 1985).

*Seneca's Tragedies*, edited and translated by John Fitch, Loeb Classical Library, 2 vols. (Harvard University Press, 2002).

### History and Cultural Contexts

Braund, Susanna Morton, and Christopher Gill (eds.), *The Passions in Roman Thought and Literature* (Cambridge University Press, 1997).

Claassen, Jo-Marie, *Displaced Persons: The Literature of Exile from Cicero to Boethius* (University of Wisconsin Press, 1999).

Eden, P. T. (ed. and trans.), *'Apocolocyntosis'—Seneca* (Cambridge University Press, 1984).

Elsner, Jasl, and Jamie Masters, *Reflections of Nero: Culture, History and Representation* (North Carolina University Press, 1994).

Garzetti, Albino, trans. J. R. Foster, *From Tiberius to the Antonines: A History of the Roman Empire, AD 14–192* (Methuen, 1974).

Fairweather, Janet, *Seneca the Elder* (Cambridge University Press, 1981).

Graves, Robert, *I, Claudius* (Penguin, 1978).

Griffin, M., *Seneca: A Philosopher in Politics* (Oxford University Press, 1976).

—— *Nero: The End of a Dynasty* (Yale University Press, 1985).

Hutchinson, G. O., *Latin Literature from Seneca to Juvenal: A Critical Study* (Clarendon Press, 1993).

Massey, Michael (ed. and trans.), *Society in Imperial Rome: Selections from Juvenal, Petronius, Martial, Tacitus, Seneca, and Pliny* (Cambridge University Press, 1982).

Sørensen, Villy, *Seneca the Humanist at the Court of Nero* (Chicago University Press, 1976).

### Stoicism

Brennan, Tad, *Stoic Life: Emotions, Duties and Fate* (Clarendon Press, 2005).

Epictetus, ed. and trans. Christopher Gill, *The Discourses of Epictetus* (Dent, 1995).

Inwood, B., and Lloyd P. Gerson (trans.), *The Stoics Reader: Selected Writings and Testimonia* (Hackett, 2008).

Inwood, B., *Reading Seneca: Stoic Philosophy at Rome* (Oxford University Press, 2005).

Long, A. A., *Stoic Studies* (California University Press, 1996).

Marcus Aurelius (trans. Martin Hammond), *Discourses* (Penguin, 2006).

Reydams-Schils, Gretchen, *The Roman Stoics: Self, Responsibility and Affection* (Chicago University Press, 2005).

Rosenmeyer, Thomas G., *Senecan Drama and Stoic Cosmology* (California University Press, 1989).

Sellars, John, *Stoicism* (California University Press, 2006).

Seneca, trans. Robin Campbell, *Letters from a Stoic* (Penguin, 1969).

### Tragedy, Drama, Rhetoric

Beacham, Richard, *The Roman Theatre and its Audience* (Harvard University Press, 1991).

Boyle, A. J., *Introduction to Roman Tragedy* (Routledge, 2006).

Bushnell, Rebecca, *Tragedy: A Short Introduction* (Blackwell, 2008).

Dominik, William (ed.), *Roman Eloquence: Rhetoric in Society and Literature* (Routledge, 1997).

—— and Jon Hall, *A Companion to Roman Rhetoric* (Blackwell, 2007).

Easterling, Pat, and Edith Hall (eds.), *Greek and Roman Actors: Aspects of an Ancient Profession* (Cambridge University Press, 2007).

Poole, Adrian, *Tragedy: A Very Short Introduction* (Oxford University Press, 2005).

McDonald, Marianne, and J. Michael Walton (eds.), *The Cambridge Companion to Greek and Roman Theatre* (Cambridge University Press, 2007).

Silk, M. S. (ed.), *Tragedy and the Tragic: Greek Theatre and Beyond* (Clarendon Press, 1996).

Taylor, David, *The Greek and Roman Stage* (Bristol Classical Press, 1999).

### Seneca's Plays and their Influence

Ahl, Frederick (trans.), *Three Tragedies—Seneca* (Cornell University Press, 1986).

Boyle, A. J., *Tragic Seneca: An Essay in the Tragic Tradition* (Routledge, 1997).

Bishop, J. David, *Seneca's Daggered Stylus: Political Code in the Tragedies* (Hain, 1985).

Braden, Gordon, *Renaissance Tragedy and the Senecan Tradition: Anger's Privilege* (Yale University Press, 1985).

Davis, Peter J., *Shifting Song: The Chorus in Seneca's Tragedies* (Olms-Weidmann, 1993).

Eliot, T. S., *Essays on Elizabethan Drama* (Harcourt, Brace, 1956).

Harrison, George W. M. (ed.), *Seneca in Performance* (Duckworth, 2000).

Helms, Lorraine Rae, *Seneca by Candlelight and Other Stories of Renaissance Drama* (University of Pennsylvania Press, 1997).

Henry, Denis and Elisabeth, *The Mask of Power: Seneca's Tragedies and Imperial Rome* (Aris & Phillips, 1985).

Littlewood, C. A. J., *Self-representation and Illusion in Senecan Tragedy* (Oxford University Press, 2004).

Miola, Robert, *Shakespeare and Classical Tragedy: The Influence of Seneca* (Clarendon Press, 1992).

Motto, Anna Lydia, and John R. Clark, *Senecan Tragedy* (Hakkert, 1988).

Pratt, Norman T., *Seneca's Drama* (North Carolina University Press, 1983).

Segal, Charles, *Language and Desire in Seneca's 'Phaedra'* (Princeton University Press, 1986).

Share, Don (ed.), *Seneca in English* (Penguin, 1998).

Schiesaro, Alessandro, *The Passions in Play: 'Thyestes' and the Dynamics of Senecan Drama* (Cambridge University Press, 2003).

Sutton, Dana, *Seneca on the Stage* (Brill, 1986).

### Further Reading in Oxford World's Classics

Euripides, *Heracles and Other Plays*, trans. Robin Waterfield.
—— *Trojan Women and Other Plays*, trans. James Morwood.
—— *Medea and Other Plays*, trans. James Morwood.
Lucan, *Civil War*, trans. Susan H. Braund.
Petronius, *The Satyricon*, trans. P. G. Walsh.
Seneca, *Dialogues and Essays*, trans. John Davie.

Shakespeare, William, *Titus Andronicus*, ed. Eugene M. Wraith.
Sophocles, *Antigone, Oedipus the King, Electra*, trans. H. D. F. Kitto.
Suetonius, *Lives of the Caesars*, trans. Catharine Edwards.
Tacitus, *The Annals: The Reigns of Claudius, Tiberius and Nero*, trans. J. C. Yardley.
Webster, John, *The Duchess of Malfi and Other Plays*, ed. René Weis.

# CHRONOLOGY

| | |
|---|---|
| 44 BCE | Assassination of Julius Caesar. |
| 31 BCE | Battle of Actium, victory of Octavian (Augustus) over Antony; end of the Republic. |
| 31 BCE–14 CE | Principate of Augustus. |
| ?1 BCE–4 CE | Birth of Seneca. |
| 37 CE | Death of the emperor Tiberius, accession of Caligula. |
| 39/40 CE | Probable date of composition of *Consolation to Marcia*. |
| 41 CE | Murder of Caligula; Claudius becomes emperor. Claudius exiles Seneca to Corsica, on the charge of adultery with one of Caligula's sisters. During his exile Seneca writes at least two of his prose treatises: the *Consolation to Polybius* and the *Consolation to Helvia*. |
| 49 CE | Seneca recalled to Rome by Claudius, through the intercession of Nero's mother Agrippina. |
| 50 CE | Claudius adopts Nero as his son, making him heir to the throne. Seneca becomes Nero's tutor. |
| 54 CE | Death of Claudius, accession of Nero as emperor. Seneca composes the *Apocolocyntosis* (*The Pumpkinification of Claudius*), a satirical account of the late emperor's deification. |
| 55 CE | Nero has his rival and stepbrother Britannicus poisoned. |
| 55–62 CE | Seneca composes the *De Clementia* (*On Mercy*), to Nero; the *De Vita Beata* (*On the Happy Life*); and the *De Beneficiis* (*On Benefits*). |
| 59 CE | Nero murders his mother Agrippina. |
| 62 CE | Burrus, the praetorian prefect and Nero's other close advisor, dies. Seneca asks Nero for leave to retire. Nero refuses, but Seneca's political role is much reduced after this date. Seneca writes the *Epistles to Lucilius* and the *Natural Questions*. |
| 64 CE | Seneca officially retires, and returns his fortune to Nero. |
| 65 CE | Nero denounces Seneca as a traitor, accusing him of involvement in the Pisonian Conspiracy. Seneca is forced to kill himself. |

# MYTHOLOGICAL FAMILY TREES

m. = marriage     i. = illegitimate relationship

## THE HOUSE OF THEBES

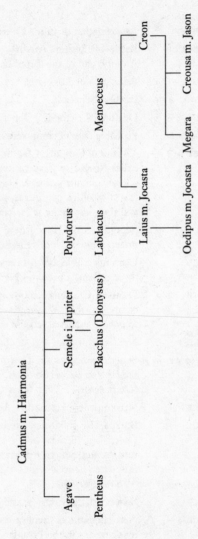

# THE HOUSE OF ATREUS

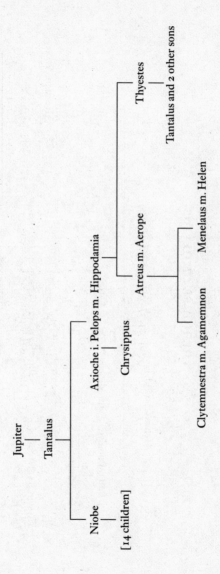

# THE HOUSE OF HELIOS

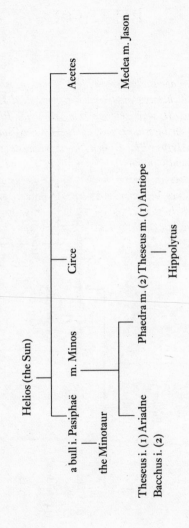

Helios (the Sun)

```
                    ┌──────────────┬──────────────┐
              Pasiphaë          Circe           Aeetes
              m. Minos                            │
                 │                            Medea m. Jason
    a bull i. Pasiphaë
         │
    the Minotaur

    ┌──────────────────┬──────────────────┐
Ariadne              Phaedra m. (2) Theseus m. (1) Antiope
Theseus i. (1)                              │
Bacchus i. (2)                         Hippolytus
```

# PHAEDRA

*As the play opens, Theseus, king of Troezen, is down in the underworld, helping his friend Pirithous steal Hades' wife, Persephone. It soon emerges that his wife, Phaedra, has developed an incestuous passion for Theseus' son, her stepson, Hippolytus. But Hippolytus is a chaste young man, interested only in hunting animals in the wild. Seneca's Phaedra goes through a number of stages as she grapples with her desire, and finally, under the influence of the Nurse, testifies falsely that Hippolytus tried to rape her. The truth emerges too late, and the family is destroyed.*

# DRAMATIS PERSONAE

THESEUS, king of Athens
HIPPOLYTUS, his son, by an Amazon woman
PHAEDRA, Theseus' wife, Hippolytus' stepmother
NURSE
MESSENGER
CHORUS

# ACT ONE

HIPPOLYTUS  Come and surround the shades of the forests,
come over the topmost peaks of the mountain of Cecrops,
run swiftly, run everywhere, come and explore
in the places beneath the rocky Parnethus,
where in the Thriasian dales* the river
beats, running through them with swift-flowing current.
Climb up the hills, always white with the snow,
of Riphaeus.*
This way, this way, some of you, to the grove,
thickly plaited with alders, where meadows spread open,        10
which Zephyr* softens with dewy breezes,
and summons the flowers of spring;
when softly the stream of Ilisos glides
through poor little farmlands,
touching the barren sands with its skimpy stream.
And you, go where Marathon opens the ravines,
on the left path,
where the new mother ewes, with small groups of friends,
look for their food in the night time.
You, where the harsh Acharneus yields        20
to the warm south winds, and softens its icy cold.
Another should tread the crags of sweet Hymettus,
another the level plains of Aphnidae.
That region has lain untapped for a long time—
round the bay where Sunion pushes back the shore
of the curving sea.
If anyone is moved by the glory of forests,
Phyle calls him.
Here lives the one that the farmers fear,
the boar, now marked with many a wound.        30
Now you, let loose the leashes of the hounds who can stay silent.
But still keep the reins on the spirited Molossians
and let the aggressive Cretans strain
against sturdy collars which rub at their necks,
and carefully restrain the Spartan dogs*—

for their breed is courageous and lusts for the hunt—
with a tighter knot.
The time will come when the hollow rocks ring with their barking.
Now low to the ground let them sniff at the winds
with their knowing noses, and seek out the lairs                    40
with muzzles pressed down, while the light is uncertain,
while the dew of the earth retains the traces of feet passing by.
Let one man hasten to carry fine ropes
loaded round his neck;
another to bring the smooth hunting-nets.
Let a line decked out with bright red feathers
trick the beasts, terrify them, trap them.
You, hurl the air-borne weapons;
you, use both hands at once, left and right,
directing all your strength to the broad piece of iron;             50
you, lie in ambush, then drive the beasts headlong
with a yell;
you, when the victory comes, slice into their bellies
with a curved knife.
Come to your friend, O masculine goddess,* Artemis
for whose kingdom lie open the secret parts of earth,
whose unerring arrows pierce through the animals
as they drink the icy waters of Araxes
and those which are playing on the frozen Histrus.
Your hand hunts down the Gaetulian lion,                            60
your hand hunts down the Cretan deer;
now with a lighter touch you shoot the swift-footed does.
The stripy tigers turn their chests to face you,
the shaggy bisons give you their backs,
and the wild oxen with their long horns.
Every beast which feeds in the lonely lands,
known in the wealthy woods to the Arab
and all which the indigent Garamantian knows,
*Likes to* or the nomad Sarmataean on the empty plains,
*hunt ... we* or hidden on the ridges of the wild Pyranees,         70
*get it.* or hidden in Hyrcanian glades,
all, Diana, all are afraid of your bow.
If a follower is favoured by your power as he comes
into the forest,

the nets will hold fast the animals he captures,
his ropes are unbroken by the kicks of their feet,
his bag will groan heavy with his spoils.
Then the hounds will be red at the muzzle with all the blood,
and the crowd of peasants head back to their cottages
in triumphal procession.                                    80
Come, Goddess, show me your favour!—The barking dogs
deliver the sign: I am called to the woods.
This way, this way, I shall go
where the path makes a long journey short.

PHAEDRA Great Crete, you dominate the huge expanse of ocean:
over your every shore there are numberless ships
keeping to the sea, where Nereus cuts a path
for the prows of boats to pass, even as far as Assyria:
Why do you force me to spend my life in tears and pain,
given as hostage to household gods I hate, and married    90
to an enemy? See, my husband has run away. He is gone.
Theseus shows his bride his usual faithfulness.* abandons his wives
What a hero! Off he goes, through the misty lake from which
there is no return. He goes as the soldier of a shameless suitor
to steal from his throne the stolen wife of the king of Hell.
He goes as the friend of mad desire. He was not restrained,
     not he,
by fear or shame. His quest is for rape, and forbidden sex,
Hippolytus' father seeks this, in Acheron's lowest depths.
But another deeper source of trouble lies on my sad heart.
I cannot rest at night, no deep sleep comforts me           100
and takes away my cares. My suffering eats and grows fat,
it burns within me, like the blast which gushes out    woman distracted
from Etna's depths. I cannot tend the loom of Pallas,* ← from work
and the wool slips down between my very hands.* ← by love
I have no wish to go to the temple with votive gifts,
nor to dance at the altars, in the Attic women's band,
when they whirl the torches, witnessing the silent rites,*
nor to approach with modest prayers and holy ritual
Athena the goddess* who was chosen as guardian for the land.
No: what I like is to rouse wild beasts, and chase them,
     and hunt them down,                                    110
and to hurl stiff javelins from my soft white hand.

Where are you going, my soul? Mad thing, why yearn for the
forest?

*mother gave birth to minotaur*

I recognize the fateful trouble of my poor mother.*
For us, my mother and me, <u>love means sin in the woods.</u>
Mother, do you pity me? Unspeakable evil
seized you, and rashly you fell in love with the savage leader
of a wild herd: he was fierce, would not submit to the yoke,
adulterous, too, and commander of a group that was still
    untamed.
But he loved you a little. Poor me! What god can help me,
What Daedalus can help assuage the flames of my love?*            120
Even if that man returned, with all his power,
who once shut up our terrible monster* in a dark home,
he could not provide any help for our present plight.
Through us, resentful Venus is taking revenge on the race
of the Sun, whom she detests* for the chains which bound her
    Mars
and herself. For that act of shame she heaps the whole Phoeban
    family
with things unspeakable. The women of Crete can never
enjoy an easy love. They always have monstrous affairs.

NURSE  You are Theseus' wife, and gloriously descended from
    Jupiter:
banish at once these unspeakable thoughts from your heart:
    keep it chaste.                                               130
Extinguish the flames, do not let yourself indulge
in this terrible hope: if you resist from the start,
and drive out love, victory is certain; it was ever thus.
If one feeds the evil with sweet caresses and flattering words,
submits to the yoke, it becomes too late to resist.
Kings and queens—I know it well—are cruel,
cannot hear the truth or turn, puffed up with pride.
Whatever will be, whatever fortune sends, I bear it:
because the old are near to freedom, they are brave.
There are two ways to be good. First: want the right
    things, no straying.                                         140
The second is knowing and setting a limit to one's sins.
Poor woman, what are you doing? Why make worse the
    shame of your house,

even[outdoing your mother?]Sinners are worse than monsters.
Monsters are caused by fate, but sin by character.
If you think that you can sin in safety, free from fear
because your husband cannot see the upper world,
you are wrong. Imagine Theseus engulfed in the depths of Lethe,
imagine that the eternal Styx bears him away;
then what about your father,* who subdues the seas,
whose realms spread wide, who governs a hundred nations?      150
Will he let so great a crime lie hidden, do you think?
Parents are perceptive. But still, let us imagine
that by our cunning we can hide so great a crime:
then what about your grandfather,* pouring his light
on the whole world? What of him who shakes the universe,
makes tremble the flashing fire of Etna, with his fiery hand,
the father of the gods?* Do you think it is really possible,
to hide in the midst of omniscient ancestors?
But even if the holy powers favour you, and hide
your wicked sexual acts, and if adultery                      160
is guaranteed the safety that great crimes never get—
what of your instant punishments: bad conscience and fear,
and a guilty heart which always fears itself?
Women may sin unpunished, but never get off scot-free.
I beg you, restrain the unholy flames of your passion,
and this crime which no barbarian land has ever committed:
not even the Getae who wander nomadic on the plains,
nor the unfriendly Taurians, or far-dispersed Scythians:
send in exile from your mind this dreadful act, and keep it
      chaste,
remember your mother, and fear unusual bedfellows.           170
Do you intend to have both father and son in your bed,
and let your tainted womb take an incestuous child?
Do it! Overturn Nature with the fires of infamy!
Why are there not more monsters? Why is your brother's* palace
      empty?                      *minotaur*
Will Nature hear of unprecedented marvels in the world,
will she suspend her laws for every passion
from a Cretan woman?

PHAEDRA                      I know the things you say
      are true: but my lust forces me to follow

the worse decision. My mind knows, but it wanders,
yearning for wise advice, and tries in vain to return.                    180
As when a sailor propels an overloaded boat
against the current, but his effort fails, he yields,
and the ship is swept away by the gushing water.
What can reason do? Passion, passion rules.
One tyrant god* has mastered all my heart.
The winged boy knows no limits, his power spreads over the earth.
He sets light even to Jupiter with the flames which no one can
     master.
The sturdy Warmonger has felt those terrible torches,
and the Blacksmith god who made the triple thunderbolt,
the one who stirs the forge of ever-burning Etna,                         190
even he grows hot with such a little fire.
Even Phoebus himself,* who aims his missiles on a string,
is pierced by an arrow fired from a keener marksman,
the boy who flits light but falls heavy on sky and earth alike.
NURSE  The fiction that love is a god was created by base lust,
yielding to degradation. To give more licence to sin,
the false name of god was given to burning desire.
You think that Venus sends her son to wander
through all the world, and flying through the sky,
launch savage weapons from his delicate hands,                            200
and though he is the youngest, he has all this power from the gods?
These are silly myths, fantasies of a madman,
who invented Venus' son, the god of sex, and his bow.
A person who delights in too much fortune,
who has too much already, always wants new things.
Then comes the dangerous companion of great riches,
called Desire. A normal dinner gives no pleasure now,
nor ordinary, wholesome furnishings, plain cups.
Why does this pestilence choose fancy, pretentious houses,
and not creep so often into moderate hearths?                             210
Why does a holy Venus live under lowly roofs,
and the average sort of people keep their emotions sane,
and practise self-restraint, while, on the other hand,
the rich and powerful rulers want more than one should have?
Those who have too much power want no limits to their power.
You are the steward of a mighty throne. Think what befits you.

Show fear and reverence to your husband's sceptre. He will be
  back.

PHAEDRA I think the rule of love has the greatest power in me.
  I do not fear his return. No one has ever come back
  to touch the upper world, after once being drowned in the dark, 220
  after going to the house which is quiet with eternal night.

NURSE Do not put your trust in Dis.* Let him shut up his kingdom,
  let the Stygian* dog watch at the terrible gates;
  Theseus alone can find forbidden paths.

PHAEDRA Perhaps even he will be lenient towards my love.

NURSE He was unforgiving even to his chaste former wife:*
  Barbarian Antiope has felt his savage hand.
  But imagine that your angry husband can be swayed;
  who will persuade the inflexible heart of this boy of yours?
  He hates even the name of women, he flees them,                230
  he is hard, he says he will live out his youth as a bachelor,
  he avoids marriage and sex. You know what these Amazons
    are like.

PHAEDRA He is the one I want to follow, even crawling over the
    ridges
  of a snowy hilltop, and leaping over the hard rocks with my feet,
  through the deep glades and through mountains.
      This is what I want.

NURSE What if he refuses to give himself to your caresses,
  if he will not exchange his chastity for sex?
  Will he lay down his hatred for you, when perhaps it is
    hatred of you
  that makes him hate all women?

PHAEDRA                            Can prayers not win him round?

NURSE He is wild.

PHAEDRA          But love has conquered even wild beasts.*   240

NURSE He will run.

PHAEDRA          If he runs even through the seas, I will follow.

NURSE Remember your father.

PHAEDRA                       I do. But I also remember my mother.

NURSE He shuns all womankind.

PHAEDRA                         So I need fear no rival.

NURSE Your husband will return.

PHAEDRA                           Pirithous' companion?*

NURSE  Your father will also come.

PHAEDRA                              Fine; he indulged Ariadne.*

NURSE  I beg you on my knees, by my hair which is white
    with age,
  by my heart worn out with worry, by the breasts which were
    dear to you,*
  stop your passion, I beg you, and Phaedra, help yourself.
  The desire to be well is part of what makes us well.

PHAEDRA  My noble heart has not yet lost all its restraint.        250
  Nurse, I will obey. The love that will not be governed
  must be conquered. Honour, I will not let you be tainted.
  This is the only solution, the only escape from the evil:
  I will follow my husband, preventing infamy by death.

NURSE  No, Mistress! Moderate the urges of your untamed heart,
  control your impulses. Even this, I think, shows you worthy
  of life, that you deem yourself deserving only death.

PHAEDRA  My mind is set on death. The only question is how.
  Shall I end my life with a rope, or fall on a sword,
  or hurl myself down headlong from the citadel of Pallas?     260

NURSE  Would I in my old age allow you to fall headlong
  and die? Stop this crazy idea, give up your plan.
  No one can easily come back to life again.

PHAEDRA  No reason can stop one from dying at will,
  when death is decided, when death is one's due.
  So let me arm myself, let my hand avenge my chastity.

NURSE  Mistress, only comfort for my tired old age,
  if such violent passion nestles in your heart,
  scorn reputation, which is never kind to truth—
  she treats the less deserving better than the good.           270
  Let us test his harsh, resistant heart.
  It is up to me to approach this wild young boy,
  this cruel young man, and change his barbarous mind.

CHORUS  Goddess, Venus, child of the savage ocean,
  you are named as Mother by Cupid—twice born.*
  Cupid has two sources of destruction:
  fire and arrows, lustful and terrible boy-child,
  smiling, too! How truly he aims his darts!
  Passion slips inside our very bones,
  laying waste our veins with hidden fire.                      280

Wounds from Love's bow seem on the surface nothing:
they suck deep within at the secret marrow.
Never will there be peace from that boy's raids:
he is always busy firing his streams of arrows
through the whole wide world: from the home of sunrise,
on to Sun's last goal, the Hesperides.*
Places lying under the burning Crab's sign,
icy places under Arcadian Ursa,
where the nomads roam unimpeded always,
everywhere knows love. For the young, he rouses                    290
raging flames; old men who are tired and weary
feel again that heat which they thought extinguished.
Fire of love strikes virgins before they know it;
Love commands the gods to abandon heaven,
making earth their home, in disguise, for love's sake.
    Phoebus drove Thessalian flocks, commanded
only sheep; he set aside his plectrum;
blowing shepherd's pipes he called the cattle home.*
Often he, great ruler of clouds and heaven,
clothed himself in shapes of inferior beings.*                     300
Now he is a bird* and he flaps his white wings,
cries with voice more sweet than the swan when dying.
Now a young bull,* lustful, he scowls with dark brows,
lets the girls play piggyback, lowers haunches,
then through brand-new realms, through his brother's ocean,
moving fast, hoofs rowing like pliant ship's oars,
breast against sea's current, he tames the ocean,
pirate god, he fears and protects his booty.
The shining goddess* of the darkened world
abandons night and hands her shining horses                        310
over to her brother; his driving style is different.
Now the two-horsed carriage of night is shaken,
taught to turn more sharply, a shorter orbit,
nor can night-time keep to its proper period,
day returns too late, and the dawn comes slowly,
while the wheels shake, weighted with heavier driver.
Hercules, Alcmena's son, has set aside his quiver,*
and the fearful skin of the mighty lion,
and holds his fingers out to be fitted with jewels;

lets the women neaten his shaggy long locks,                    320
ties his legs cross-gartered with golden laces,
dainty yellow slippers adorn his large feet.
Hands which used to carry his mighty cudgel
now were weaving thread with a flying spindle.
Persia and the fertile land of Lydia saw on the rich sand
the hide of the savage lion, flung aside.
The shoulders which used to lift the royal dome
of the vaulting sky
are dressed now in a delicate frock of Tyrian weave.
Holy the fire—the wounded believe it—                    330
and all too powerful.
Out where the earth is ringed by the salty deep
and where the bright stars make their journey through
        heaven itself,
Here that unsparing boy is the master
whose arrows can pierce through the lowermost waves
to the dark blue shoal of the Nereides,
nor can the ocean extinguish the flame.
Winged birds too feel the fires of love.
When excited by the prickings of Venus, and headstrong,
the bullock will fight for the whole of the herd.                    340
If they fear for their wives then even the deer—
cowering creatures—initiate battle
and with lowing they signal the passion
aroused in them.
Then the wild boar sharpens his damaging tusks,
frothing all over his face;
then the forests are groaning with animal noises.
The Phoenician lions shake their necks
aroused by love.
Love-struck stripy tigers terrify the dusky Indians.                    350
The monster of the violent sea, too, falls in love,
and even elephants. Nature
takes revenge on them all, and nothing is safe,
and hatred is dead, when love gives commands;
old resentments yield to the fires of love.
What more can I say? Love conquers
even the fiercest creatures: stepmothers.

# ACT TWO

CHORUS  Nurse, tell us what you know; where is the queen?
Have the raging fires of her passion somewhat abated?
NURSE  There is no hope that such great suffering can be
soothed,                                                    360
nor is there any end to the flames of madness.
She is scorched with a silent blast of heat; despite restraint,
although she tries to hide it, her face betrays her heart.
Fire bursts out from her eyes, her wounded cheeks
acknowledge the spark of love. She is pleased with nothing, listless;
now and then pain seizes her in spasms.
Sometimes her feet give way, she faints, seems dead,
her neck flops down, her head can scarcely stay upright,
sometimes she gets up from bed, forgets to sleep,
complains the whole night long. She wants to be picked up    370
then laid down again, she wants her hair undone,
now wants it braided again; she cannot bear herself,
she keeps changing her clothes. She has no interest
in food or health. She wanders, feet unsteady,
her strength has begun to go. Her vitality is lost,
gone is that ruddy glow from her bright face.
Anxiety roams across her body, she trembles as she walks,
the delicate beauty of her body is gone.
The eyes which used to bear the marks of Diana's torch
have lost the glow which suits her father's race.         380
Tears fall over her face, her cheeks are always wet,
dewy with weeping, just as on Taurus' slopes
the warm rain falls on snow and makes it melt.
But see, the gates of the palace are opening wide:
here she is, lying back on her gilded couch;
she is dressed just as usual, and gives no sign of madness.
PHAEDRA  Maids, remove this quilt, woven with gold and purple,
take from me all scarlet Tyrian dye,
all silk* from distant China, plucked from trees.
Let a simple belt cinch in my narrow waist.              390
I will wear no necklace, nor will snowy pearls

dangle from my ears, the gift of the Indian sea;
I want no Assyrian perfume sprinkled on my hair.
Let loose my hair to pour down over my neck
and over the tops of my shoulders, let it be blown about
following the swift winds. With my left hand I will hold a quiver,
with my right I will brandish a Thessalian spear.
Stern Hippolytus' mother looked exactly like this.
As one who leaves behind the shores of the cold Black Sea
and tramples the earth of Attica, driving her troops,                    400
a woman from Tanais or Maotia,* with her hair in a knot,
loose but for a single tie. She protects her torso with a shield,
in the shape of a moon. Like this will I ride to the woods.
CHORUS* Cease your complaints; resentment does not comfort
         the wretched.
Pray for the favour of the countryside goddess, the Virgin.*
NURSE* Queen of the forest glades, the only one who dwells
  in the mountains, the only one who is worshipped there as a
         goddess,
  turn your grim threats to a better set of omens.
O Goddess, potent in the woods and groves,
bright heavenly body and glory of the night,                             410
whose realm shines when the other one is dark,
Triple-formed Hecate,* come! Come to bless our endeavour.
Subdue the stubborn mind of moody Hippolytus;
let him listen kindly; make gentle his savage heart;
let him learn to love, let him feel a reciprocal passion.
Change his mind; though stern, resistant, wild,
let him come under Venus' rule. Use all your strength on him;
then may you travel on a bright-faced moon,
with clear white horns through cloudless skies,
and may no charms of Thessaly have power                                 420
to drag your chariot down from the night sky,*
and may no shepherd* boast because of you.
Come to your call, give blessings to our prayers now, Goddess:
Here he is, I see him now, praying to his favourite cult statue,
and he comes alone—why hesitate? Fate has granted
an opportune time and place. I must use all my art.
Am I nervous? Yes: the wickedness I plan
will take a lot of courage. But reverence for monarchs

means abandoning justice; expel honour from your heart;
shame is no good servant of royal power.                                        430
HIPPOLYTUS  Faithful old nurse, you are too old and weak to walk:
why have you hobbled so far? Why does your face look so sad
and worried? Is something wrong? I hope my father is safe,
and Phaedra is safe, and their pair of sons are doing well?
NURSE  Dismiss your fears: the kingdom and country prosper:
the household is blooming, we rejoice in our good luck.
But you, Hippolytus, should yield to happiness.
You are the one who worries me and makes me anxious.
You treat yourself too hard, your own worst enemy.
When the fates are against you, unhappiness can be forgiven.     440
But if you make yourself wretched of your own accord,
self-tormentor, you deserve to lose
the goods you failed to use. Remember, you are young,
and free your mind! Go out to late-night parties,
wave the torch, get drunk, let Bacchus* take your cares away,
enjoy your youth; its time is fleeting, soon gone.
The hearts of the young are light, they are blessed with the
        pleasures of Venus.*
So let yourself be joyful. Why do you sleep alone?
No more adolescent moping. Now is the time
to hurry up and join the race. These years                                      450
are the best of your life; do not let them melt away.
God's rules* tell what is proper at each stage of life.
Old men's faces should frown; happiness suits the young.
Why discipline yourself, why murder your true self?
The farmer profits most from the field whose crop grows free
in its tender youth, rejoicing* in rich corn.
The tree whose towering top is tallest of all the grove
is the one which no grudging hand has hacked or pruned.
The virtuous mind attracts its proper praise
if vigorous liberty has fed its noble soul.                                     460
Will you remain a savage wood-man, ignorant of life,
spending your youth in gloom, despising sex?
Do you believe this is duty, that men should endure
all hardships, taming horses for the track
and waging savage wars with bloody Mars?*
The great lord of the universe was provident and took care,

seeing the thieving fingers of Fate greedy for spoils,
always to repair each theft with new creation.
Come, just try to imagine human life without Venus,
who restocks and restores the losses of our race:                    470
the world would lie in squalor, its air rank,
the sea would soon be stagnant, empty, without fish,
the sky would have no birds, the woods no wild beasts;
only the winds would rattle through the open air.
How many ways to die already lurk to seize*
the race of mortals! The sea, weapons, tricks.
You think these things are not your fate? But now we seek
dark Styx* of our own accord. Imagine what will happen
if no young people have children: those you see now will be
obliterated all at once, in a single generation.                     480
Go on then, follow nature* as your guide to life.
Get out to the city more often, join in with the crowds.

HIPPOLYTUS  There is no other life so free, so clean of sin,
so respectful of the ways of old,
as that which leaves the city walls, to be happy in the woods.
Anger, lust, and greed do not set fire to the heart
of the innocent man whose home is on the mountain tops.
The winds of the faithless mob leave him unswayed,
unmoved by their perverted hate and brittle love.
He is no slave to established power, wants none for himself.    490
He does not pursue the futile goals of fame or fleeting wealth.
He is free from hope and free from fear. Black, biting envy
does not pursue him with mean grasping jaws.
He does not know the wicked crimes whose seeds are sown
in cities. He does not tremble, guilty, at each sound,
or twist his words in fear. He has no wish to be rich,
live in a thousand-columned house, and have his roof inlaid
with thick gold leaf. No altar drips for him with gore,
piously drenched; nor, adorned with sacrificial fruits,
do a hundred snow-white oxen bend their necks for him.          500
Instead, he is master of the countryside. Through the open air
he wanders in innocence. He lays his cunning snares
only for animals, and when he is tired from work
he bathes himself in melted snow from the Ilissus.*
Sometimes he chooses a place by the flowing river Alpheus;*

sometimes he walks in thickets of the dense and dark wood grove
where the pure water of icy Lerna glimmers,*
shaded from sunlight. Here, the shrill twittering birds
complain, while the branches tremble, struck by the gentle winds,
and the old beech trees. He loves to lie on the banks          510
by meandering brooks, or take a little nap
resting his head on the grass, where a waterfall
gushes down, or where freshwater streams
murmur sweetly by the new-grown flowers.
All he needs to eat is fruit shaken from the trees,
while berries picked from shrubs can easily supply
his simple meals. His whole desire is to be far away
from regal pomp. Drinking from golden cups, the proud
consume anxiety; what joy to taste fresh water
from naked hands! A deeper, surer sleep                          520
holds the man who stretches out on a hard mattress—in safety.
The wicked look for sin in secret, with lights out;
in fearfulness they hide inside a house
of a hundred rooms. Better, live in the light,
let heaven be your witness. This, indeed, I think,
is the way they lived of old, the demigods,
poured forth by the first great age of man.* They had no blind
desire for gold;* no boundary stones were set in the land
as legal markers of territory to divide the people.
As yet no trusting ships had pierced the ocean's deep;*          530
each man remained by familiar waters; no great ramparts
surrounded the outskirts of cities, nor thick ranks of towers.
No soldiers yet held savage weapons in their hands;
nor did the cunning catapult break through closed doors
with heavy stones; the earth was free from any master,
not yet enslaved to bear the teams of ploughing oxen.
The reverent people asked for nothing from the fields;
earth bore its crops for free. Woodlands produced their wealth
naturally, and shady caves provided natural homes.

    The pact was violated by the wicked lust for money,         540
precipitous anger, and all the desires which seize
on minds inflamed. The thirst for power came upon them,
bloody; the stronger preyed upon the weak, and Might
became their Right. Then first they began to make war

with fists, unarmed; then rocks and branches torn from trees
became their weapons. They had no wooden javelins,
fitted with slender iron tips, nor did they wear
long-swords at their sides, they had no helmets, trimmed
with glittering bright crests. Bitterness made their weapons.
War-loving Mars discovered new inventions,                          550
death in a thousand shapes. From that time forward
every land was stained with blood, and all the seas were red.
Then crime walked through every household without check;
there were examples of every kind of wicked deed.
Brother killed brother, parents died at their children's hands,
the husband lies dead, killed by his own wife's sword,
and wicked mothers slaughtered their own young;
I will not talk of stepmothers—beasts are more kind.
   But Woman is the root of all evil. Full of her wicked schemes,
she lays siege* to men's minds. How many cities have burned   560
because of their adulteries! How many wars they have caused,
how many kingdoms overturned, how many enslaved!
Forget the rest, remember only Aegeus' wife,
Medea*—proof enough that women are the devil.
NURSE  Why should you blame all women for the crimes of a few?
HIPPOLYTUS  I hate them all, I curse them, I shun them,
      I reject them.
Be it reason, nature, or passion* which inspires me,
my pleasure is to hate them. Water and fire will mix,
the tricksy quicksands of Syrtis will offer a friendly welcome
to wandering ships, and from her farthest shore                     570
Hesperian Tethys* will raise the shining dawn in the west,
and wolves will turn with gentle faces to the deer,
before I will yield and welcome any woman.
NURSE  The bridle of Love often curbs a stubborn heart, and
      changes
hatred to something else. Think of your mother, and her people
the Amazons;* wild things, they submitted to the yoke of Venus;*
you are the proof of that,* their one surviving son.
HIPPOLYTUS  My only comfort for my mother's death
is that I am now permitted to hate all living women.
NURSE  How like a rock he is, so hard, immovable:                   580
as a rock resists the waves and dashes far away

the waters which assail it, so he rejects my words.

But here is Phaedra, running, rushing, resistant to all delay.
What will happen? Where will her crazy passion turn?
Oh! Now suddenly she has fallen down on the ground
her body lifeless, her face pale as a corpse.
Lift up her head! Come on, say something! Quick!
Look, child, it is your own Hippolytus who holds you.

PHAEDRA  Who brings me back to suffering, and lays again the
    weights
of longing on my heart? How gladly I would die.                    590

HIPPOLYTUS  Why do you not welcome the gift of light restored?

PHAEDRA  Be brave, my soul, attempt it: do what you have to do.
Speak boldly and firmly. Diffident requests
invite refusal. The greatest part of my crime
is done already. It is too late for shame.
I have fallen in a terrible sort of love. If I press forward,
perhaps I can hide my sin under the marriage torch.
Success sometimes makes wickedness look good.
So on, my soul, begin!—Listen a moment, please;
I have something private to say. If your friends are around,
    let them go.                                       600

HIPPOLYTUS  No, the whole place is deserted; no one sees.

PHAEDRA  But when I start to speak, my mouth refuses the words.
A great urge pushes me to talk, a greater, to be silent.
Act as my witness, gods, I do not desire
what I desire.*

HIPPOLYTUS  Do you have something you cannot say, but want to?

PHAEDRA  Small worries speak but great ones hold their tongues.

HIPPOLYTUS  Mother, please tell me what your trouble is.

PHAEDRA  'Mother'! that heavy title means too much.
A lowlier name would suit my feelings better;                      610
Hippolytus call me 'sister', or 'hand-maiden'—
yes, call me your slave, I will serve you in every way.
I would not be ashamed, if you bid me go through snow-drifts,
to scale the frozen ridges of Mount Pindus.
And if you bade me walk through fire and enemy ranks in war
I would bare my breast to meet the naked swords.
Take up the sceptre entrusted to you, accept me as your servant:
it is right for you to give orders, and me to obey.

It is not women's job to govern cities.
You, who are strong in the first flower of youth,                    620
should rule the people by your father's right.
Hold and protect me in your arms, your servant and your
      suppliant;
pity a widow!

HIPPOLYTUS   May almighty god
prevent this omen! My father will soon be safe home.

PHAEDRA   The master of the silent Styx, that dungeon realm,
grants others no escape to the upper world.
Will he grant the favour to the man who stole his wife?*
Not unless maybe even Hades smiles on love.

HIPPOLYTUS   The gods are just; they will return him home again.
But while god leaves our prayers unanswered, I                      630
shall act with dutiful love towards my brothers;
I will make sure that you should not feel widowed:
I will myself act as my father to you.

PHAEDRA   Deceptive love! How lovers trust their hopes!
Perhaps I have not said enough—I will beseech him.
   Have mercy, listen to my prayer, from a frightened heart.
I want to speak, and yet I feel ashamed.

HIPPOLYTUS                              What is your trouble?

PHAEDRA   My pain is a surprising one for a stepmother.

HIPPOLYTUS   You are talking in a strange, ambiguous way.
Explain it clearly.

PHAEDRA            A kind of heat—or, love—                          640
burns up my mad heart. It rages like wildfire
in my marrow, through my veins. It scorches,
buried in my belly, secretly running through me,
as a quick flame runs over timbered roofs.

HIPPOLYTUS   Surely this is your conjugal passion for Theseus.

PHAEDRA   Hippolytus, you are right: I am in love with Theseus,
as he used to look when he was young,
when the first tufts of beard marked his cheeks,
when he saw the hidden home of the monstrous Minotaur,
and wound the long thread on the twisting path.*                    650
How fine he looked! He wore a garland round his hair.
His face was gentle, shining bright with dignity.
He had firm muscles on his soft young arms.

His face was like your goddess, Diana, or my Apollo,*
or rather, it was like yours. He looked like you when he
        conquered
even his enemy's heart.* He held his head high, just like you.
You are even better-looking, your beauty is unstudied.
All your father lives again in you, but mixed with your mother,
that wild woman, who gives you an equal share of beauty.
You have Scythian fierceness in a Grecian face.                    660
If you had crossed the sea to Crete with him,
my sister would have spun her thread for you.
Sister, wherever in the heavenly vault* you shine,
I call upon your help; my cause is just like yours!
One family has conquered both us sisters:
the father won you, me the son. Look, I beseech you,
begging you at your knees—a royal princess,
I am untainted, pure, untouched by stain, and chaste:
only for you I changed. I have stooped to prayer, and I know
this day will end my pain, or end my life.                         670
Have mercy on me. I love you.
HIPPOLYTUS                       Great ruler of gods!*
Are you so slow to hear and see the works of sin?
Oh, when will your fierce hand send down a thunderbolt?
Why is the air so calm? Let the sky be rolled together,
and rush to ruin, let black clouds bury day,
and let the stars turn back their course and run aslant
on twisted orbits! O Sun, brightest of stars,
do you not see your grandchild's wickedness?
Drown day in night and run to hide in shadows!
O king of gods and men, why are you slow to act,               680
why is your torch not burning up the world?
Thunder upon me, pierce me, let swift fire burn me up,
now! I am evil, I deserve to die: I was attractive
to my stepmother.—So, am I good for adultery?
Did I seem easy fodder to fulfil your fantasies,
the only man for such a crime? Is this restraint's reward?
No woman in the world can match your wickedness!
You have dared an evil worse than your mother's,* mother
of the monster. You are worse. She only polluted
herself with her own foul lust; she did not talk about it;       690

only the birth of the two-formed creature revealed her crime.
The child confessed to the mother's sin by its scary face.
It was a hybrid monster baby. You are child of the very same
    womb.
O how lucky, triple-blessed by fate, are those
who are destroyed and killed and given up to death
by hatred and betrayal. Father, I envy you.
This stepmother is a worse evil, by far, than the Colchian.*
PHAEDRA  Yes, I also see the patterns in our history.
We want what we should run from. But I cannot control myself.
I would follow you through fire and raging seas,                    700
over rocks, through rivers, which a rushing flood has seized,
wherever you may go, I am swept there, mad with love.
Proud boy, I beg you again, I kneel before you.
HIPPOLYTUS  Take your dirty, unchaste hands away from my
    clean body.
Do not touch me. What is this? Again she is trying to embrace me?
Let me draw my sword, she will get the punishment she deserves.
Look now! I have grabbed her hair with my left hand, pulled back
her filthy head. No sacrificial blood shed at this altar
has been spilt more justly, Diana of the crossbow.*
PHAEDRA  Hippolytus, now you have answered my dearest wish:  710
you have restored my sanity. This is better than I hoped for,
that I should die at your hands, and keep my purity.
HIPPOLYTUS  Go, stay alive, rather than get your wish! And this
tainted sword, I have thrown it away from me. My body is
    pure.—
What great river Tanais can wash me clean, or what Maeotis*
with its barbarous waves rushing down to the Pontic Sea?
Not even Neptune, father to the whole Ocean,
could wash away so great a sin.* O woods, O beasts!
NURSE  Her guilt is out. Why slow to act, my soul?
We will flip the crime around, accuse him                           720
of adultery: crime must be hidden by crime.
When you are afraid, the safest way is straight ahead.
Whether we initiated crime or suffered it,
what witness could know, when guilt is hidden?
    Help! Help! Come, Athenian women, faithful servants,
bring help! Hippolytus—the rapist! He is assaulting us!

He is insistent, he threatens us with fear of death!
He terrifies a modest woman with his sword! Oh! Now he is
    suddenly gone!
He left his sword in his great fearful rush to get away.
I will keep it as a proof of what he did. My poor mistress!    730
First look after her. But let her hair stay all bedraggled and torn,
just as it is—these are the marks which prove this dreadful
    crime.
Hurry, go to the city! Mistress, now wake up!
Why do you hurt yourself, not meet our eyes?
Impurity is caused by attitude, not fate.

CHORUS  Gone! She runs like a storm turned crazy
    faster than clouds massed up by the wind,
    faster her feet than a ravening flame
    of a comet whipped up by the winds, as it trails
    a tail of fire.    740
    Ancient history gasps with wonder
    comparing the beauty of former days with yours.
    Your loveliness shines as much more brightly
    as the full moon glows with light,
    her fires united, horns touched in a circle,
    as the goddess Diana rides on her rushing chariot,
    face aglow as she swoops through the night,
    while the lesser stars can show themselves no more.
    So when the shadows first grow long,
    the messenger of night, fresh from his bath    750
    of darkness, comes as Hesperus, and as night fades
    as Lucifer again.*
    And you, Bacchus, bringing your thyrsus* from India,
    though you are young forever, your hair forever uncut,
    and can scare your tigers with your ivy rod,
    your horned head* covered in a fez,
    you cannot beat Hippolytus, with his tangly hair.
    There is proof that you should not get too vain of your looks:
    a story well known to the world,
    that Phaedra's sister loved somebody more than Bacchus.*    760
    Beauty is a questionable gift for mortals,
    a temporary blessing, which lasts a little while,
    then swiftly slips away on running feet.

Briefer than meadows, lovely in the spring,
which the blast of summer's heat will lay to waste
when the noon-time of the solstice burns,
and night runs on a shorter track.
Lilies droop, their leaves are faded,
lovely roses bow their heads,
when the colour that shone in their delicate cheeks          770
is gone in an instant. Every single day
steals a part of beauty's loveliness.
Beauty is a fleeting thing; what wise man trusts
in a breakable blessing? While you have it, use it.
Silently time sneaks up on you, each hour
gone is followed by a worse one.
Why do you go to the wilderness? Beauty
is no safer in places without paths. They will circle around you
in a secluded glade, when noon is high,
those bad girls, the lustful water-nymphs,                   780
who have a habit of catching pretty boys* in fountains.
And hot with desire the nymphs of the wood
will pounce upon you as you sleep;
so will Pan, who lurks in the mountains.
Or the moon, the younger sister of the stars of Arcady,
looking down on you from her starry cycle,
will no longer have the power to steer her bright white horses.
See, just now she blushed, though no dark cloud
passed over her shining face.
We were worried at the goddess' trouble,                     790
thinking her dragged to earth by Thessalian spells,
and we dinned on our cymbals;* but she was concerned with you,
you were the reason she took so long, for while she watched you
the goddess of night suspended her speedy journey.
If the cold were more gentle as it bites his face,
and if the sun touched it less often,
it would shine brighter than Parian marble.
His rough face is so beautifully masculine!
How lovely and mature, his heavy frown!
You could compare his glistening shoulders with Apollo;      800
the god's long hair pours down his back,
as covering and decoration, never braided up;

Hippolytus, your hair is shorter, shaggier,
but it suits you. Warlike and fearsome gods
are no match for you in your strength
and as for the size of your body—enormous!
Though still a young man you are Hercules' height,
and your chest is wider than Mars, god of war.
If you chose to ride on the back of a horn-hoofed horse,
even Spartan Cyllarus,* your hands                              810
would guide the reins more skilfully than Castor.
Should you stretch the sling out in the tips of your fingers,
and fire the dart with all your strength,
the Cretans, masters of the javelin,
could not shoot the slim spear so far.
Or if you wish to scatter arrows to the sky
as the Parthians do, not one will come to earth
without a bird: plunged in the still-warm belly,
your shots will bring back plunder from the middle of the clouds.
    Seldom has beauty come to men unpunished.             820
Just look at history. May a kindlier god
pass you over, keeping you safe, and may your famous looks
shift to the shapelessness of bent old age.


# ACT THREE

CHORUS  This woman is hysterical; what mad thing will she dare?
    She plans a horrible crime against an innocent youth.
    What wickedness! She tears her hair, she ruins all her braids,
    she wets her cheeks, hoping to be believed:
    she uses all her feminine wiles for the trick.
      But who is this, whose looks have dignity
    worthy of a king, whose head is held up high?            830
    He would look just like Theseus, Pittheus' child,
    except his cheeks are white, his face is drawn,
    his hair sticks out in matted, dirty tufts.
    Oh! It is him, it is Theseus. He has come back to the world.
THESEUS  At last I have escaped from the land of eternal night
    the world which shadows the ghosts in their giant jail.
    My eyes can scarcely bear the day they longed for.

When four times Eleusis had received Triptolemus' gift*
and four times the scale had weighed out day to match the
    night,*
double trouble came to me, an unfamiliar fate,     840
as I straddled the sufferings of life and death.
One part of life remained to me when I was dead:
I felt my sufferings. Hercules was the reason:
after he grabbed the Dog and brought him back from Hell,
he brought me also to the upper air.
But I was not the man I used to be: so tired,
my old strength gone, I staggered. Oh, how hard
to seek the distant sky from the bottom depths of Hell,
at once escaping death and following Hercules.
    What sound of lamentation do I hear?     850
Somebody tell me. Tears, sorrow and grief?
Is the doorway of my home a place of mourning?
It makes sense: this welcome suits a guest from Hades.

NURSE Phaedra is fixated on the thought of suicide!
    I try with tears to stop her, but no, she is bent on death.

THESEUS But what is her motive? Why die when her husband
    is back?

NURSE That is the very reason she wants an early death.

THESEUS Your puzzling words must hide some mystery.
    Reveal the truth! What is she upset about?

NURSE She will tell nobody. She hides her sorrow:     860
    determined to take her secret with her to the grave.
    So hurry, hurry, please! Now is the time for speed.

THESEUS Unlatch the doors and open up the palace!
    O wife, companion of my marriage bed, is this the way
    you welcome the man you longed for, now you finally see his face?
    Will you not set down your sword, and give me back
    my life? Now tell me, what made you seek death?

PHAEDRA Theseus, you are a generous man. I beg you, by your
    sceptre,
    by your children and descendants, by your own return
    and by the ashes of my own dead body,     870
    let me die.

THESEUS     But why must you do this?

PHAEDRA If the reason is spoken, my death will be in vain.

THESEUS  Nobody will hear it except me.

PHAEDRA  A chaste wife fears only her husband's ears.

THESEUS  Speak! Trust me; your secret will be safe in my heart.

PHAEDRA  If you want to keep a secret, never share it.

THESEUS  You do not even have a means to die.

PHAEDRA  One who wants to die can never lack the means.

THESEUS  What is the crime for which you must pay by death?

PHAEDRA  My life.

THESEUS              But do my tears mean nothing to you?          880

PHAEDRA  The perfect death is dying mourned by loved ones.

THESEUS  She refuses to talk.—Time to tie up the old nurse
and whip her; she will soon reveal the secret.
Chain her up! A beating will draw out
what her mind hides.

PHAEDRA              Stop! I will tell you myself.

THESEUS  Why are you still looking sad and turning away your face,
why are you holding up your dress to hide your tears?

PHAEDRA  O maker of celestial gods, I call upon you,
and upon you, the shining orb of heavenly light;
our family depends upon your daily dawning.          890
I resisted his pleas, my heart did not yield
to physical threats; but my body put up with the violence.
My blood will wash away this taint to purity.

THESEUS  Who, I beg you, was the man who has ruined our good
name?

PHAEDRA  The one you would least expect.

THESEUS                                I am waiting to hear
who it was.

PHAEDRA  This sword will tell you. Frightened by the noise,
fearful that people would crowd to help, the rapist left it behind.

THESEUS  What do I see? Oh no! What horror is this?
The gleam of the ivory hilt is marked with the royal crest
of my forebears, the proud mark of the Athenian family.          900
But he—where did he go?

PHAEDRA                      The servants here saw him
scared and running away as fast as he could.

THESEUS  By sacred Duty, by the Lord of the sky,
and by the Ruler of the second lot,* the sea,
where did this stain upon our house come from?

Can he have come from Greece? Or from a barbarian land,
Scythia or Colchis? Our family is regressing,
tainted blood reverts to its ancestry.
That madness is typical of the warrior race:
first despising sex, then whoring out                                    910
that long-preserved virginity. What a family,
never subdued by a better country's laws!
Even animals avoid the taint of incest,
and an unconscious shame preserves the rules of mating.

Where is his arrogance now, his lying face,
his shabby clothes, in that old-fashioned style,
his gloomy ways, his pompous moodiness?
How life deceives us! You hid your real feelings,
you put a pretty face on your base thoughts;
shame hid your shamelessness, coolness hid your daring,              920
duty hid your wickedness. False men profess their truth,
soft sybarites act tough. You lived in the woods,
like an animal, untouched, chaste, innocent:
were you keeping yourself for me? Did you want
to use my bed to first become a man? What wickedness!
Now I am grateful to the powers above
that I struck my Antiope* and killed her.
I did not go down to the caves of Styx and leave
your mother to you. Run far away in exile,
run all through the world; you can go to the ends of the earth     930
where the land gives way to the worlds of endless sea,
and to the land which is upside-down under our feet;
you can cross the terrible realms of the towering Pole,
to the world hidden deep and distant in the north,
you can stand above the storms and snowy drifts
and as you leave the icy North Wind's threats
raging behind you, you will pay for your crimes.
I will pursue you in your exile everywhere you hide;
I will trace out the distant places, break all locks,
reveal your secret dens all over the world; no place
      can stop me.                                                          940
You know where I have been. Where I cannot shoot weapons
I will shoot prayers: my ocean father* promised
he would fulfil three wishes for me: this he swore

by the inviolable river Styx.

    Go on, Lord of the Ocean, grant the bitter gift!
May Hippolytus not see another shining day,
may my son go down to the ghosts who hate his father.
Now, Father, give your son this ghastly gift:
I never would have used the power of this last wish,
unless oppressed by such extreme disaster.        950
In the depths of Tartarus and awful Dis,
and amid all the threatenings of Hell,
I did not make a wish; now keep your promise:
Father, why do you hesitate? Why are the waves still calm?
Now let the winds bring forth black clouds,
knit up the night, rip out the stars and sky,
pour forth the ocean, call out all the Mer-Folk,
swell up your seas and summon the deepest waves.

CHORUS  Nature, great mother of the gods,
and you, Lord of the sky with all its fires,        960
who seize the stars whirled swiftly round the world,
and guide the revolutions of the planets,
turning the poles on the earth's quick hinge,
why do you take this care to bring the seasons,
shaking out the deep sky's everlasting changes,
so that now the white, cold frosts
make bare the trees,
and now the shadows return to the groves,
and now Leo the lion, mane blazing with heat,
bakes Ceres' wheat with his blast,        970
and then the year makes moderate its strength?
How can you be so powerful, controlling
the weights of the mighty world
as they trace out their orbits,
measuring them with so much care,
and yet neglect mankind, abandon us?
How can you forget to bless us
or even to do us harm?
Fortune rules chaotically over human life,
she scatters her gifts without looking, preferring the worse.    980
Wicked desires win, good people lose,
deceit is king in the lofty palace.

The people give power to corrupt politicians,
they cultivate people they hate.
Self-discipline and goodness win no prizes.
Poverty afflicts the faithful husband,
while crime helps lecherous cheats to gain control.
Chastity is useless, a false idol.

# ACT FOUR

CHORUS  But why is this messenger rushing towards us,
 and why is his face so sad and wet with tears?                    990
MESSENGER  Curse my cruel fate! How hard to be a slave!
 Why do you summon me to bring bad news?
THESEUS  Do not be frightened to tell me of death and destruction.
 Speak boldly: my heart is ready for any pain.
MESSENGER  My tongue is hesitant to cause you grief.
THESEUS  Speak! Our house is already shaken: what is it now?
MESSENGER  Hippolytus—I can hardly bear it—he is dead.
THESEUS  I knew my son was dead. He died some time ago.
 Now the rapist is dead as well. How did he die?
MESSENGER  When he stormed out of the city in his rage,        1000
 running as far and as fast as his feet could go,
 he went up to the ridge-way and quickly he yoked his horses.
 They clattered their hoofs but he strapped their tame heads in
   the bridle.
 He muttered to himself, and cursed his native land.
 Often he called to his father to come and help him,
 as he loosened the reins and fiercely shook them.
 Then all of a sudden the depths of the ocean resounded,
 the noise rang up to the sky. No wind blew on the water,
 no part of the silent sky had caused the sound;
 a tempest of its own had roused the quiet sea.            1010
 Auster is not so fierce as it ruffles the Sicilian sea;
 when Corus takes control of the Ionian bay
 it does not swell so wildly, though waves shake the rocks,
 and the white foam scatters on the top of Leucate.*
 A massive tsunami wave rose up from the sea
 and swollen with the monster, the water dashed on the shore.

No ships were to be wrecked by this disaster:
it threatened the land. The vast, heavy mass of water
rolled towards shore, weighted down in its swollen belly
by something strange. What land will show the stars          1020
a brand new face? Will the Cyclades add a new island?
The water rushed over the rocks which are sacred to Asclepius,*
and over the crags of Sciron,* famous for his crimes,
and hid the promontory of land* hemmed in by double sea.
As we stood aghast at the flood, see, all of a sudden
the sea gave a roar, and the cliffs all around were singing;
the peak of the wave was dripping with the ocean spray,
it foamed and drooled out water, back and forth it gushed,
as if through the waves of the ocean a giant whale
were diving, blasting water from his spout.                  1030
The wall of water was shattered and collapsed,
as a terrifying creature was washed to the shore; the sea
tried to escape the monster by rushing to land,
but bellowing aloud, the creature followed the water.
It was a bull. How huge he was! His bulk
loomed high as he lifted his blue back from the water;
a green mane flowed from his gigantic head;
his ears were hairy, his eyes flashed multicoloured;
he was the type of animal the sea-born king would own,
lord of a savage herd. At times his eyes                    1040
spurt fire, at other times they shine blue light;
his sturdy back was ridged with muscle and his nostrils
flared as he huffed and puffed great draughts of air;
green mosses stuck to his underside and dewlap,
while his vast flanks were covered with red seaweed.
Finally the monster gathers his huge rear from the water,
dragging his vast and scaly folds of flesh,
like the Leviathan of the distant seas
that shatters and engulfs swift-sailing ships.

    The earth was shaking, all the frightened flocks          1050
ran away over the fields, and the herdsmen failed
to follow their own cattle. All the beasts
fled from the forests, and every hunter shuddered,
chilled by fear. Only Hippolytus was unafraid;
he reined in his terrified horses, giving them comfort

by speaking to them in the voice they knew so well.
There is a path cut deep in the hills, winding
steeply to Argos running near the coast;
here the massive monster lurked and prepared his assault.
He paws the ground and gathers his strength, as a warm-up  1060
for his rage; then he leaps headlong, starts to gallop,
hardly touching the ground with his hoofs as he flies,
until he stops in front of the trembling horses, and scowls.
Your son jumps up to meet him, wild and fierce,
his face impassive as he cries aloud:
'This horrible illusion cannot break my spirit!
My father's job is conquering wild bulls.'*
    But all at once the horses disobey him—
they gallop away and pull the chariot off the path,
guided only by their frenzied fear, which leads them          1070
off in all directions careering across the rocks.
But as a helmsman keeps fast hold of his ship
to stop it tipping as the waves swell higher,
using his skill to cheat the ocean—so Hippolytus
steers his speeding chariot: now he pulls at the reins,
to tighten the bit on the horses' mouths; now he urges them on
with a whirl of the lash. But the monster is his shadow,
at times keeping pace, then moving out of his way
to meet him head-on. Terror surrounds the horses.
Now they can run no further: the bristly monster              1080
lowers his horns and charges them full-on.
Then the horses are stricken with total panic, their hooves
        clattering,
as they fight to break free from their master's control and
        shake off the yoke,
then rearing up, they throw his body to the ground.
    He fell down flat on his face, and was tangled up
in the strong ropes of the harness; the more he struggled
the more he bound the net around himself.
The horses realized what had happened, and feeling their chariot
lightened by lack of a master, they followed their fear and ran.
Just as when heaven's horses felt their burden changed:       1090
resentful that a false Sun got the power of day—

Phaethon* who could not keep the path—they threw him from
   the sky.
Hippolytus bloodied the countryside: his shattered skull
bounced down the rocks, and thorns tore off his hair;
his beautiful face was ruined by the hard, stone ground.
His unlucky loveliness was lost in all these wounds.
The chariot wheels rolled over his still-twitching limbs.
At last a charred branch from a tree-trunk pierced him
right in the middle of his groin, and held him fast.
The horses pause a little way away from their gored master,   1100
attached to his wounded body; then all at once they break,
making an end of their owner and delay. The thickets cut
the half-dead corpse, and thorns with their sharp brambles;
parts of the body were stuck to every tree.

   The servants of the dead man wandered through the fields,
where Hippolytus left tracks of blood,
dragged and dismembered over such a distance.
The dogs keened as they sniffed for their master's scent.
However hard the mourners tried, they could not
recover all the bits of body. Does beauty come to this?   1110
A man who used to share his father's royal power,
his noble heir apparent, shining like the stars,
is now a set of scattered body-parts, picked up
for the funeral pyre.

THESEUS                If only we could escape
   the link of nature, chaining parents to their blood!
   We follow nature even against our will.
   I wanted to kill him for his crimes, but now I mourn his loss.
MESSENGER  One cannot sincerely weep over getting what one
      wanted.
THESEUS  Yes, one can. I think the pinnacle of misfortune
   is to be forced by chance to want things one should loathe.   1120
MESSENGER  Well, but if you hate him, why are you crying?
THESEUS  Because I killed him, not because I lost him.
CHORUS  How many chances turn the wheels of human life!
   Fortune keeps her temper with the lowly,
   the blows of heaven are weaker on the weak:
   peace and obscurity keep simple people safe,
   and those who live in hovels live to a ripe old age.

High roofs must bear the buffets of the winds:
struck by the east wind, struck by the southerly,
struck by Boreas threatening from the north                              1130
and stormy Corus from the west.
Thunderbolts rarely strike
in rainy valleys:
deep-rumbling Jupiter's weapons shake
the mighty Caucasus and the Trojan woods
sacred to the Mother Goddess.* Jupiter is afraid
for heaven and attacks those that lie near it.
The low-slung cottages of peasants
are never shaken so roughly.
His thunder strikes at kings.                                            1140
Time flies on fickle wings,
mobile Fortune makes no promises
to anyone.
This man, who had returned to see the light of the world,
and shining day, as he left death's door behind,
is sad and mournful now at his return,
and finds the welcome of his native land
feels worse than Hell itself.

  Athena, worshipped by the Athenian race,
your Theseus has escaped the marshy Styx;                                1150
he sees the heavens and the upper world.
Chaste goddess, you owe nothing to your greedy uncle:
the books are balanced* for the infernal king.

# ACT FIVE

CHORUS  What is that sound of weeping from the palace?
— What crazy thing is Phaedra up to with a sword?
THESEUS  Have you gone mad with grief? What are you doing?
  What is the meaning of this sword, this screaming?
  Why are you beating your breast for the corpse of a man you
      hate?
PHAEDRA  Me, me, O cruel master of the ocean,
  attack me, and to me send all your sea-dark monsters:                  1160
  the creature hidden deepest in the buried ocean womb,

the monster folded in the deepest waves
from the most distant waters of the world.
Cruel Theseus, when you come home, you always
bring disaster.* Your father and your son
have paid for your returning with their lives.
You always destroy your home, in love or hatred for your
    wives.*
    Hippolytus, can I look at your face in this condition?
Did I make you look this way? What savage Sinis
or Procrustes tore your limbs, or what fierce Cretan bull,*    1170
half-man, his head that of a horned ox, bellowing loud
to fill the empty spaces of the Labyrinth?
Ah, where is your beauty gone, your lovely eyes
which were my stars? Can you really be lying there dead?
Just for a little while, be here, and listen to me!
I will not say inappropriate things. I swear by this hand,
I will avenge your death, I will stab my wicked heart,
I will set Phaedra free of life and guilt together.
And I will follow you blindly through the waves
through the lakes of Tartarus, the Styx, and the fiery river.*    1180
I want to do right by the dead:* I have torn my hair
and cut off a lock as a gift for you: here, take it.
You and I were not allowed to link our lives together;
but we can join our deaths. Phaedra, if you are chaste,
die for your husband. If unchaste, for your love. Can I return
to a marriage bed polluted by such crime? The ultimate sin:
to take my holy pleasure on sheets washed by revenge.
No: only death can cure such evil love,
only death can give me back my wounded honour.
Death, I run to you; forgive me, and embrace me.    1190
    Listen, Athens, and listen, Theseus—father
worse than a murderous stepmother: my story was all false.
My crazy heart drank in the cruel plot;
I lied. You have punished your son for a fiction;
an innocent young man lies dead on the charge of rape.
Truly, you were chaste and pure. Have your real character back.
This righteous sword will pierce my own bad heart.
My blood is shed as an offering for this virtuous dead man.
THESEUS  His stepmother teaches me what a parent ought to do

when robbed of his own child: hide myself down in Hell.          1200
Pale gates of Avernus and Chasms of Taenarus,*
waters of Lethe, beloved by the wretched, and stagnant
          Cocytus,*
now seize this sinner and drown me in eternal misery.
Come now, all you monsters of the sea, come vast ocean,
come all strange creatures hidden in the folds of Proteus,*
and hurl me into the deepest sea. My crime was too successful.
Father,* you have always been too quick to help my anger.
I do not deserve an easy death, when my son's was so horribly
          strange:
I scattered his fragments over the fields. While I was so stern
to punish a fabricated crime, I committed a real one.          1210
I have filled the stars and seas and underworld ghosts with
          my sin;
all three kingdoms* know me; there is no more space.
     Did I come back for this? Did the path to the sky lie open,
so that I could experience these two violent deaths,
and so, bereft of both my wife and child,
I might heap both their corpses on a single pyre?
Hercules, this black light was your gift to me;
give it back to Hades, and restore to me
the death you stole.—But I am too wicked; no point
in asking for that death I left behind.          1220
I caused a cruel, unprecedented murder.
Now I must ask just punishment for myself.
Should a pine tree be bent to the ground, then catapult back
my body, ripped apart on separate branches?*
Or should I hurl myself headlong from the Scironian rocks?
I have seen worse: the pain of criminals
encircled by the liquid flame of Phlegethon.
I know what punishment I will get, and where.*
Sinners, give way to me: let the heavy rock
weigh down my neck and weary hands—the rock          1230
which Sisyphus has been pushing since ancient times.
Let the water mock me as it flows just past my lips.
Let the savage vulture leave Tityos and fly
over to my liver, ever-regrown for fresh pain.
And you, father of my own dear Pirithous,

rest: let the wheel which never stops its turning
whirl round and round my limbs instead of yours.*
Gape open, Earth, and take me, terrible Chaos,
take me: this is a better way for me to visit Hell:
I go to find my son. Do not worry, King of the Dead:          1240
my motives are pure. Take me into your eternal home;
I will not leave again.—The gods do not listen to my prayer.
But if I were asking for help in a crime, how kind they
    would be!
CHORUS Theseus, there is infinite time for tears.
Now bury your son with all due rites, and quickly,
hiding his mangled, torn, and scattered limbs.
THESEUS Here, bring here the remains of his dear corpse,
that mass of body-parts, heaped up all anyhow.
Is this Hippolytus? I recognize my crime:
I killed you. And I spread my sin around:                    1250
when I was plotting my son's death, I called
my father. Well, now I enjoy the blessing of a father.
My years are broken already; it is hard to bear this loss.
Poor man, pick up these limbs, all that remains of your son,
hug them and hold them tight to your sad heart.

    Father, learn to rearrange these parts of a mangled body,
and put back in their place the pieces that have strayed.
This is the place for his strong right arm, and here
we must put his left hand, so skilled at guiding the reins;
I recognize the marks of his left side. So much              1260
still missing, that I cannot even wet with tears!
Hands, stop trembling! Be steady for your sad work;
eyes, dry up your flow of tears down my cheeks,
just while I count the parts of my son's body,
and build his corpse. What can this be, so ugly,
disgusting, pierced all over with multiple wounds?
I do not know what part it is, but I know it belongs to you;
Put it here: not where it belongs, but where a space is empty.
Is this your face, which used to shine with starry fire,
your spirited, piercing gaze? Has your beauty come to this?  1270
O terrible fate, O cruelly-helpful gods!
Is this the answer to a father's prayer, a son's return?
    Here are the final gifts your father gives you.

You will need multiple burials... Meanwhile, burn these parts.
    Open the house: it stinks of death. Let all the land
of Attica ring loud with piercing funeral cries.
You, make ready the flame for the royal pyre,
and you, go out and seek the missing parts of the body
scattered in the country. And as for that woman—bury her,
and may the heavy earth crush down her wicked head.          1280

# OEDIPUS

*Oedipus was the son of Laius and Jocasta, king and queen of Thebes. Since Laius had heard from an oracle that his son would kill him, he gave the baby to his shepherd, to expose on Mount Cithaeron. But the shepherd instead gave the baby to a herdsman working for King Polybus of Corinth. Oedipus was raised as the son of Polybus and his wife, Merope. But the oracle of Apollo at Delphi foretold that Oedipus would marry his mother and kill his father. So Oedipus ran away from Corinth. On his travels he met an old man—Laius. He got into an argument with him and killed him. He reached Thebes, and managed to solve the riddle of the Sphinx—a female monster who was oppressing the country. She asked, 'What walks on four legs in the morning, two at noon, and three in the evening?' Oedipus answered, correctly: 'Man.' As a reward for saving the country Oedipus was given in marriage to the widowed Jocasta, and ruled as king in Thebes for many years; the couple had two sons and two daughters. But then a plague was sent to oppress the city. Oedipus sends his wife's brother, Creon, to find out what he can do to save Thebes.*

# DRAMATIS PERSONAE

OEDIPUS, king of Thebes
JOCASTA, his wife
CREON, Jocasta's brother
TIRESIAS, a blind prophet
MANTO, Tiresias' daughter
OLD CORINTHIAN MAN
PHORBAS, a herdsman
MESSENGER
CHORUS

# ACT ONE

OEDIPUS  Now night has been driven to exile, the hesitant Sun
  reappears,
and gloomy brightness dawns from beneath a murky cloud.
With melancholy light, with flames of grief,
day looks out on these homes, wasted by greedy plague,
revealing all the devastation night has made.
  Do you think being king is fun? What a fraud, this so-called
    good!
What terrible suffering lies beneath your smile!
Just as the breezes always buffet the highest crags,
and cliffs whose rocks jut out over the vast ocean
are beaten by the waves even when the sea is calm:                    10
so high power is vulnerable to Fortune.
  How happy I was to be free from my father Polybus' throne!
An exile, released from anxiety, wandering without fear,
I happened on a kingdom. May gods and heaven bear witness!
I am afraid of unspeakable things: my father's death
at my own hands. The oracle warned me of this,
and says I will commit another, even greater crime.
Is any sin more terrible than killing one's own father?
As a loyal son, I blush to speak about my fate.
Phoebus threatens me with a parent's bed, a terrible marriage,   20
an indecent, incestuous, wicked union for a child.
Fear of this oracle exiled me from my father's kingdom,
for this reason I ran away from home and my household gods.
Doubting myself, I wanted to keep the laws
which Nature ordained. When your fears are great and terrible
you start to shudder even at things you think impossible.
I am afraid of everything, I do not trust myself.
Here, now, at every minute, the fates are plotting against me.
Why should I think that horrible curse on the race of Cadmus,*
whose dreadful carnage spread through all our family,              30
would pity me alone? What pain did they keep me alive for?
Among the rubble of the city and all these deaths, which demand
a constant flow of fresh tears, among the piles of corpses,

I stand untouched. I! The man condemned by Apollo!—
Would you have expected a healthy kingdom in reward
for your enormous guilt? I have made the heavens hurt us.

    No delicate breeze brings comfort with icy breath of wind
to the hearts which pant on the flames. No tender Zephyrs blow,
Titan the Sun increases the heat of the sweltering Dog
and presses down on the back of the Nemean Lion.                    40
Water abandons the rivers, colours desert the plants,
Dirce runs dry, Ismenos is barely a trickle,
the waves can hardly reach the naked, thirsty shores.
Apollo's sister* slips in shadows from the sky,
the gloomy world grows grey, new clouds are forming.
No star shines bright on calm and peaceful nights;
a black and heavy fog lies down upon the world.
The face of Hell obscures the highest homes and castles
of those who live in the sky. Ceres denies us a harvest.
Yellow and ripe, she sways as the spears of corn grow tall,          50
but each stalk is dry, the crop is barren, it dies.
Destruction visits everywhere, nowhere is safe.
Both men and women die, of every age.
This deadly pestilence unites young men and old,
sons join their fathers, burnt by a single torch.
There are no mourners left alive to weep or grieve.
Indeed, the overwhelming scale of this disaster
itself has dried our eyes. When things are at their worst,
there are no tears. See, a father, sick himself,
carries his son to the pyre. A mother, mad with loss,               60
brings one child, then fetches another, all for the very same pyre.
In the midst of grief another grief arises:
at funerals, the mourners drop down dead around the corpse.
Loved-ones' bodies are burnt on the pyres of strangers.
Fire is even stolen. The hopeless have no shame.
Bones are not honoured with burial in separate tombs:
burning is enough. How many are lost in the ashes?
There is no space for graves, the woods have no more fuel.
No prayers or medicine can comfort those infected;
doctors are dying too, the sickness takes the cure.                 70

    I lie down prostrate at the altar, stretching my hands
in prayer for early death. I want to die before

my country's ruin—not be the last man standing,
my death the very last in my own kingdom.
Gods, you are too cruel! Fate is too harsh!
Death is so easily come-by, but to me alone
of all the populace, it is denied. So then, reject
the kingdom which your deathly hand infected.
Leave these tears, these deaths, these plagues in the sky,
which you, unlucky stranger, brought with you. Escape,          80
quick! Even go back to your parents.

JOCASTA                              How does it help, husband,
to make our suffering heavier by complaining?
It is, I think, the job of kings to bear calamities.
The more unsure things are, the more your power slips,
the firmer you must fix your sturdy feet.
Running away from Fortune is not manly.

OEDIPUS  I have no fear of being called a coward.
I am a man, I know no fainting fears.
If all war's deadly force, with naked blades
was bearing down upon me, I would boldly                        90
fight back—even against the savage Giants.
Nor did I run from those dark, riddling words
woven by the Sphinx. Though the ground was scattered
white with bones, I faced the creature's bloody jaws.
Up on her rock she spread her wings, prepared
to seize her prey, and lashed her tail, like a lion,
savage and threatening. But I asked her: 'What is your riddle?'
Then came a terrible shriek from above;
she gnashed her teeth, and with impatient claws
she tore at the rocks, eager to eat my entrails.                100
But I solved the knotted words of fate, her twisted trick,
I answered that wild winged one's awful puzzle.

    It is too late to pray for death! Why want it now?
I could have died back then. But now I have
the gift of kingship, payment for the Sphinx.
She is the one whose monstrous dust confronts us.
I killed her but she rises up, polluting
Thebes all over again. This is our only hope:
Apollo may provide some chance of safety.

CHORUS  Noble line of Cadmus, you are dying,                    110

and all the city too. Look now, the land
is empty of inhabitants, poor Thebes.
Bacchus, death has harvested your friends,
troops that you led from far-off India;
they dared to ride over the eastern plains,
and fix their flags at the horizon of the world.
They saw the Arabs and their fertile groves
of cinnamon; they saw the Parthians,
fearful tricksters, firing arrows as they fly.*
They marched across the shores of the Indian Ocean,     120
where Phoebus brings forth dawn and opens day:
his flame approaches and makes dark the skin
of the naked natives.

 Sons of an unconquered race, we now lie dying.
A swift and savage fate has levelled us.
At every moment more march on to Death.
A long, grieving procession makes its way
to bury the dead, while other mourners halt:
even seven gates* cannot let through
the mass of those who want to reach the tombs.     130
Ruin weighs on ruin, death is joined
closely to death.

 Infection first took hold of the shambling sheep;
the rich grass could not help the woolly flocks.
A priest stands by the neck of a sturdy bull;
as his skilful hands get ready for the stroke,
the animal, horns glittering with gold,
sinks to the ground. They hack at him with an axe,
to open the creature's massive throat.
No blood comes out; black gore     140
is gushing from the wound, which taints the sword,
and pours to the ground. The galloping horse
grows slow in the middle of a race, and fails its jockey,
falling on the track, as its flanks collapse.

 The cattle hunker down, abandoned in the fields.
The herd is dying and the bull grows weak.
The master cannot help the few still left alive;
he dies amid his plague-sick animals.
The deer have now no fear of ravening wolves;

the onslaught of the raging lion is gone;                           150
the shaggy bears have now no wildness left;
the slinky snake has lost its power to harm:
its poison shrivels up, and parched, it dies.

    The wood has lost its lovely trailing hair
which poured the shadows on the shady hills.
The countryside has lost its mossy green,
the vines no longer curl, their branches full
of their own grape-crop.
Everything is sharing in our suffering.
The gates of deepest Hell have broken open,             160
out burst the sister Furies, waving fire,
Phlegethon has overflowed its banks,
the flood of Styx flows to Sidonia.
Black Death reveals its greedy gaping mouth,
unfurling all its terrible dark wings.
The hale old ferryman,* who rows the hoards,
in a roomy boat across the swollen river
can scarcely lift his arms to raise the pole,
too tired with the constant punting,
always bringing new throngs.                                          170
Indeed, they say the Dog* burst through his chains
of hellish iron, and wandered up
into the human world; the earth rumbled;
they say that ghosts were walking through the woods,
larger than lifesize; and the Theban trees
twice shook the snow from their leaves.
Twice the stream of Dirce welled with blood;
the hounds of Amphion howled
in the silent night.

    Oh terrible new form of death, much worse        180
than death itself!

    Numbness binds the languid limbs,
sick faces flush.
A rash of tiny spots covers the skin,
and liquid flame burns up the citadel
of the body's core.

    The cheeks are swollen with blood,
the eyes are stark, the ears are ringing,

the nostrils flare and black blood drops from them,
bursting the bloated veins. Often                                    190
their bowels begin to groan and whine;
and Holy Fire* begins to eat their limbs.
Now in their weariness they clutch cold stones.
If their watchman dies and sets them free, they rush outside
to gulp back fresh spring water. Now all of them flop down
flat on their faces in front of the altars,
and pray to die. This single wish alone
the gods provide. The people throng to the shrines,
not hoping that the gods may be appeased
with gifts from us,                                                  200
but wanting to glut even their heavenly hunger.


# ACT TWO

CHORUS  Who is this hurrying towards the palace?
    Is Creon, noble and heroic, here,
    or does my sick soul take falsehood for truth?
    No, it is Creon, the answer to all our prayers.
OEDIPUS  I shudder, fearful where the fates may turn,
    my trembling heart is toppling with two fears:
    where happiness is doubtful, mixed with pain,
    the mind feels fear although it longs to know.
        Brother-in-law, if you bring any help                       210
    for all our weariness, come tell us what it is!
CREON  The answer lies under a doubtful fate.
OEDIPUS  Giving uncertain help to the wretched is giving none.
CREON  The custom is for the oracle at Delphi
    to hide its secrets in enigmas.
OEDIPUS                              Tell the puzzle!
    I, Oedipus, am the expert at solving tricky riddles.
CREON  The god tells us to banish the killer of the king,
    and to avenge the death of murdered Laius.
    Only then will day run brightly through the sky,
    giving pure, fresh, healthy gusts of air.                       220
OEDIPUS  And who was the killer of the famous king?
    Tell us who Phoebus named, so we may punish him.

CREON  Things horrible to hear and see—may I speak safely!
My body is besieged by numbness, blood runs cold.
I entered the holy precinct of Apollo, like a pilgrim,
and praying to the god, reverently raised my hands.
The double peak of snowy Mount Parnassus roared;
the laurel tree of Phoebus quivered, moved its leaves,
and all at once, the holy Castalian spring stood still.
Then the priestess began to shake her bristling hair:          230
she let Phoebus take her. As she moved to the cave,
an inhuman sound burst from her with a crash:

'Gentle stars will come again to Thebes,
if you, the Stranger, Exile, Guest, depart.
Polluted with a royal murder, Apollo knew you as a baby.
You will have short enjoyment of your wicked murder:
You will bring war with you and leave it to your sons.
You have returned—disgusting!—to your mother's womb.'

OEDIPUS  I will now prepare to do, on heaven's orders,
what ought to have been done to honour the dead king's ashes,   240
to ward off treachery against the holy throne.
Kings are the ones who need to care for kings.
Nobody protects a dead man whose life commanded fear.
CREON  Our care for the dead was set aside by a greater fear.
OEDIPUS  Can any fear prevent a man from duty?
CREON  Yes! The Sphinx, and the threats of her terrible riddle.
OEDIPUS  Well now, at heaven's command, we must make
               amends.—
Whichever god looks down on our kingdom and smiles:
you, who regulate the revolutions of the sky,
and you,* O greatest glory of the unclouded sky,              250
ruling the Zodiac in your changing chariot's course,
whose speedy wheel rolls round the dawdling years,
and you, his sister, always ready to meet your brother,
Diana, wanderer of the night; and you, lord of the winds,
driving your dark-blue horses over the depths of the sea;
and you who make new homes in darkness, without light;
come here! May the man who murdered old King Laius
find no quiet home, no household gods' protection;
may he be exiled and find no sanctuary.

May his marriage shame him and his children shock him.          260
May he even kill his father by his own hand,
and do—what could be worse?—the dreadful thing
I ran from. There will be no pardon. I swear it,
by this kingdom that welcomed me Guest-King,
and by the land I left and by the household gods,
and by you, Father Neptune, whose soft waves
wash against the Isthmus of my native land;
and you come now as witness to my words,
Apollo, inspiration to the truthful oracle;
so may my father live to comfortable old age,          270
ending his days by natural means on his high throne;
and may Merope know no bed but that of Polybus;
so, I swear, the guilty one will not escape my hands.

     But tell me, where was the awful crime committed?
Was it in public on the battlefield? Or was he ambushed?
CREON   He was going to the leafy groves of holy Castalia.
The road he trod was overgrown with thorns,
till he came to a three-fork crossroad, branching to the plain.
One path cuts through Phocis, country loved by Bacchus,
where Mount Parnassus rises high, abandoning the fields          280
to seek the sky, in a gentle slope up to twin peaks.
Another path leads off to Sisyphus' double seas;*
the third, a curving road, winds round to the Olenian fields,
touching the wandering waters till it crosses
the icy waters of the river Elis.
As he approached, believing himself safe,
a band of robbers pounced with swords, in secret.

     But right on time, here comes Tiresias,
roused up by Phoebus' oracle. He staggers on slow legs,
and Manto comes with him, leading the blind man.          290
OEDIPUS   Holy man, the nearest human to Apollo,
explain the oracle! Tell us what fate wants.
TIRESIAS   Great-hearted Oedipus, you should not wonder
that my tongue hesitates to speak, wants to delay.
Much of the truth lies hidden to the blind.
But I will follow where my country calls, and god.
Let us dig out the fates; if my old blood
were fresh and hot, I would let the god possess me.*

Instead, cut open a snow-white bull on the altars,
and a heifer whose neck has never borne a yoke.                    300
Daughter, guide your blind and lightless father,
tell me what the prophetic rite reveals.

MANTO  A perfect victim stands at the holy altars.

TIRESIAS  Call upon the gods with reverent voices,
heap the altars with incense, gift of the East.

MANTO  Now I have heaped up incense on the holy hearth of the
gods.

TIRESIAS  What about the flame? Is it feasting yet?

MANTO  It suddenly flashed with light but then died down.

TIRESIAS  Was the flame bright and shiny, did it stand
raising itself clear and pure up tall to the sky,                  310
unfolding its very tip up into the air?
Or did it creep out sideways, unsure where to go,
and sink down in confusion, drowned in smoke?

MANTO  The flame kept changing, it was not just one way.
As when Iris* brings the rain and twines
multiple colours into herself: she curves right over
the arch of the sky and her colourful bow foretells the storm.
So you could hardly tell the colour of the flame:
it hovered, mixing dark blue with yellow spots,
then turned blood-red again, and finally to black.                 320
But look, the fire fights back, divides in two,
the embers of the holy rite are arguing and split.
Father, I shudder as I look at it! The gift
of wine we poured there changes now to blood,
and thick smoke circles round the head of the king.
Even denser fog descends upon his face;
the light is dirty, hidden in thick cloud.
Tell us, father: what does it mean?

TIRESIAS                              What can I say?
My mind is so astounded, in an uproar.
What can I say? These are mysterious horrors;                      330
usually the gods reveal their anger plainly.
What is it that they want to have revealed,
but also do not want to show? Why do they hide their rage?
The gods themselves are somehow feeling shame. Quick, here,
scatter the salted meal* on the cattle's necks.

Do they submit to it with calm expressions?

MANTO  The bull tossed high his head, and shuddering,
    he was terrified to face the rising dawn:
    trembling he shrank away from the rays of the sun.

TIRESIAS  Did they fall down to the earth at a single blow?    340

MANTO  The heifer threw herself upon the knife,
    and died with just one blow. But the bull, struck twice,
    lumbered this way and that, dazed and confused,
    until he was worn out, had no resistance left.

TIRESIAS  Did the blood spurt out quickly from a narrow cut,
    or was it slower, gushing from deep wounds?

MANTO  The heifer's blood flowed out through the pathway in her
      breast,
    like a river. But the bull, though badly wounded,
    was stained with little blood. It flowed perversely,
    out in a rush through his mouth and through his eyes.    350

TIRESIAS  Such unlucky signs should make us fear.
    But tell me now the sure-fire marks of the entrails.

MANTO  Father, what is this? The entrails do not quiver
    just gently, as they usually do; no, my whole hand
    is shaken when I touch them. New blood jumps from the veins.
    The heart is weak and sick and lies deep down,
    the veins are dark. A large part of the entrails is not here,
    the rotten liver oozes with black gall,
    and—always a bad omen for a monarch—
    look, there are two heads, equally bulbous.    360
    Only a delicate membrane covers both these heads,
    there is no hiding-place for these dark secrets.
    The bad side* rises up, sturdy and strong,
    with seven veins; but a sideways path cuts through,
    stopping any of these veins from turning back.
    Anatomy is altered, nothing is in its place,
    everything is wrong; on the right, the lungs
    can hold no air, for they are clogged with blood.
    The left side has no heart; the stomach does not stretch
    its soft folds out over the winding bowels.    370
    Nature is perverted. The womb does not follow the rules.
    Let us dissect and see why the entrails seem so stiff.
    What horror is this? A virgin heifer pregnant!

But the foetus is in the wrong place, filling its mother
somewhere it ought not to be. It moans and twitches,
shaking its spindly body in stiff spasms.
Dark blood stains the innards of the beast.
The mangled body-parts attempt to move,
the hollow body rises up and lowers its horns
to threaten the priests. My hands cannot hold the spleen.      380
You hear that rumbling sound? It is not from the catttle.
No frightened animal is lowing here.
The altar fires are lowing, the hearth is terrified.

OEDIPUS  What do all these awful portents mean?
Reveal it! I am not afraid to drink the truth.
The worst disasters make people feel calm.

TIRESIAS  You will look back with envy at your present troubles.

OEDIPUS  Just tell me what the gods want me to know:
whose hands are tainted by the old king's murder?

TIRESIAS  Neither the birds who plunge in the depths of the sky   390
on their light wings, nor the entrails torn from living bellies
can tell the name. We must try another method.
We must call up the king himself from Erebus,*
the land of eternal night, to point out his own killer.
Earth must be unlocked, we must implore
the pitiless power of Dis, we must drag out
the people of infernal Styx. Who will you send
to go on this quest? As king, you must not see the ghosts.

OEDIPUS  Creon, as my second-in-command,
the task is yours.                                                400

TIRESIAS           While we unloose the latches of deep Hell,
let people sing their hymns in praise of Bacchus.

CHORUS  Bind up your flowing hair with nodding ivy,
carry the thyrsis in your soft white arms.
    Glory of the shining day,
    come receive the prayers we offer,
    we raise our hands to greet you;
come to famous Thebes, your city,
Bacchus. Turn your girlish face to bless us,
shake the clouds from the starlight of your eyes,
expel the threatening scowls of Hell                              410
and greedy fate.

It suits you well to wear spring flowers in your hair,
to bind your head up in a Tyrian turban,
or put a wreath of ivy mixed with olive
on your gentle brow.
Let your hair tumble anyhow,
then tie it back again in a ponytail;
as when you feared the anger of your stepmother,
and grew yourself false limbs,
pretending to be a blonde-haired teenage girl,*                    420
with a yellow sash around your dress.
Later in life as well, you like soft dresses,
falling in loose folds with a long train.
All the vast territory of the East
saw you sitting on your golden chariot,
wearing a trailing robe, driving your lions,
from the Ganges to the snowy ice
of Araxes.
Old Silenus follows with you on his peasant donkey,
wearing ivy on his bulging head;                                   430
your sexy priests perform the hidden mysteries.
The troop of Bassarids accompany you,
beating the ground in their Edonian dance,
and now they come to Mount Pangaeus, now
the peak of Thracian Pindus. Here comes a Maenad,
a shocking figure among the Theban matrons,
companion to Ogygian Bacchus,
hips tied up with holy fawn-skins,
waving a slender thyrsus in her hand.
Now even the mothers' hearts are shaken by you,              440
they let their hair fall loose; but after mangling Pentheus,*
the Maenads find their bodies freed from madness,
and are surprised to see what they have done.
Ino,* foster-mother of glorious Bacchus,
rules the sea, surrounded by the dancing Nereids.
A stranger boy has come to rule the waves of the deep:
cousin to Bacchus, the well-known god Palaemon.*
Once, dear boy, a group of barbarian pirates*
captured you, and Neptune calmed the swelling seas;
he changed the dark-blue ocean into grass.                       450

The plane-tree sprouted green with springtime leaves,
and a whole grove of laurel, dear to Phoebus;
the chattering birds were singing in the trees.
The oars were caught in the tendrils of the ivy,
the masthead got entwined with all the vines.
On the prow a Trojan lion roared,
a tiger from the Ganges crouches at the stern.
Then the frightened pirates swim off in the sea,
and as they plunge, their bodies change their shape;
first the robbers' arms are falling off,                           460
their chests nudge up and join on to their bellies,
a little tiny hand hangs from one side,
as with curved backs they sink into the waves,
cutting through the sea with crescent tails;
now they pursue the fleeing sails
as rounded dolphins.
The wealthy stream of Lydian Pactolus
carried you with the gold of its burning banks;
the Massagetan who drinks milk mixed with blood
gave up his conquered bow, abandoned shooting;          470
Bacchus is recognized in the lands of Lycurgus with his axe.
The wild country of the Zalaces,
the nomads who suffer the blast of Boreas,
know Bacchus' power,
and the nations washed by the cold stream
of the Maeotis,
and the Amazons under the Arcadian stars,
the double plough.
He has mastered the scattered Gelonians,
seized the arms of those rough girls,                            480
the hordes of Thermodontia have bowed their heads before him:
abandoning at last their little arrows
they turn to Maenads.
Holy Cithaeron flowed with blood
and Pentheus dead.
The daughters of Proetus* fled to the woods and Argos
worshipped Bacchus, even in front of his stepmother.

   Naxos surrounded by the Aegean
handed over the girl,* abandoned

by her husband. She was compensated      490
with a better one.
Wine flowed out
from dry pumice rock;
chattering streams cut through the grass,
the earth drank deeply the sweet juice,
white streams of snowy milk
and Lesbian wine mixed with fragrant thyme.
The new bride* is led right up to heaven;
Phoebus sings the hymn, hair pouring over his shoulders,
while twin Cupids shake the torches;      500
Jupiter puts down his fiery bolt
and hates the thunder,* when Bacchus is coming.

     As long as the bright stars run through the ancient years,
as long as Ocean keeps the world surrounded by his waves,
as long as Moon grows full and gathers her lost fires,
as long as Lucifer predicts the early dawn,
as long as the high Bears stay far from the deep blue sea,
so long we will worship the beautiful face of Bacchus.


# ACT THREE


OEDIPUS   Although your face looks marked by tears,
     tell us whose life must pay to satisfy the gods.      510
CREON   You order me to say what my fear bids me hide.
OEDIPUS   If all the ruin of Thebes is not enough,
     at least the fall of your royal family should persuade you.
CREON   You will long not to know what you try too hard to find.
OEDIPUS   Ignorance is no cure for suffering.
     Would you hide evidence that could help the public?
CREON   If the cure is bad, better to be sick.
OEDIPUS   Tell us what you heard, or I will break you,
     and you will learn what violence an angry king can do.
CREON   Kings hate to hear the things they order spoken.      520
OEDIPUS   I will send you to Hell! One small life pays for all—
     unless you tell the secrets from the holy rites.
CREON   I wish I could keep quiet. Can one hope
     for freedom from a king?

OEDIPUS                    Often silent freedom
  hurts kings and kingdoms even more than speech.
CREON  Where silence is forbidden, what freedom can there be?
OEDIPUS  If you are silent when ordered to speak, you are a traitor.
CREON  You forced me speak, so listen calmly, please.
OEDIPUS  Did anyone ever get punished for speaking under orders?
CREON  Far from the city there is a grove, shaded with
        holm-oaks,                                                       530
  next to the moist ground by Dirce's spring.
  A cypress tree lifts up its head above the lofty wood,
  binding the other trees with its constant foliage.
  An ancient oak tree stretches out gnarled branches,
  rotten with neglect. Devouring age has torn
  the side of its trunk away; the root is ripped apart;
  the falling tree is propped against another.
  Laurel with its bitter berries, slender lime,
  Paphian myrtle, alder trees which rush
  through the vast ocean;* and pine, whose smooth trunk          540
  rises high to meet the sun, and can withstand the winds.
  In the very middle stands a mighty tree,
  shadowing over the smaller trees, defending
  the whole grove together with its enormous girth.
  Under it overflows a stream that knows no light,
  stiff and frozen with perpetual cold;
  a muddy swamp surrounds the stagnant pool.
    When the old priest began to enter here,
  at once the place provided him with night.
  The ditch was dug, and fire from funeral pyres                 550
  was thrown on top. Tiresias was wearing
  his funeral outfit, as he waved his leaves.
  The old man came in dirty, shabby clothes,
  his mourning cloak poured down to cover his feet,
  and deadly yew wreathed round his whitened hair.
  Black-fleeced sheep and black heifers were dragged
  backwards to the fire. The flames devoured them,
  and their living hearts were shaking as they burnt.
  He cried out to the dead, and you, Lord of the Dead,
  and you, the Guardian of the Lake of Lethe.*                   560
  Reciting the magic spell, his mouth possessed, he sang

all charms to please the flitting ghosts, or force them.
He pours blood on the hearth, and burns whole bodies
of animals, and soaks the ditch with blood.
He pours on top a stream of snow-white milk,
and also pours in wine with his left hand,
and chants again, and looking at the earth
he calls the spirits with a deeper, wilder voice.
    The hounds of Hecate are barking loud; three times
        the valley
rumbles in grief, and earth, struck from below,          570
is shaken. 'Now they hear me!' cried the priest.
'My prayers are answered; the black gulf is broken,
there is a path for the dead to the upper air.'
The whole forest shrank back, its leaves now stood on end,
the oaks were cracked, and all the grove was struck
with terror. Earth drew back and groaned within.
Either Hell was upset to feel its hidden depths
plumbed, or it was Earth herself, who burst her links,
with a moan, to give a way up out of there for the dead.
Or else the three-headed dog, Cerberus, in a rage,    580
shook himself and clattered his heavy chains.
    All of a sudden the earth gaped open; a chasm
split, enormous. I saw with my own eyes the stagnant lakes,
the spirits, the pale-faced gods, and that true night.
My blood ran cold, it froze still in my veins.
Out jumped a wild, ferocious troop, and stopped
full-armed before us, all the snaky sons,
the soldier brothers born from the dragon's teeth.*
Then the fierce Fury screamed, and blind, mad Passion,
Terror, and all together, the secret children    590
of eternal darkness: Grief, tearing her hair,
Sickness, hardly holding up his weary head;
Old Age burdened with itself, and looming Fear,
and Plague, greedy to eat the Theban people.
Our hearts sank. Even the girl, who knew
her father's art and ritual, was aghast.
Her father, bold in blindness, bravely summoned
the bloodless folk of cruel King Dis. At once
like clouds they fly and rob the clear skies of their air.

More numerous than the falling leaves of Eryx,                600
or all the flowers of Hybla in the spring,
when the dense swarm weaves round them in a ball;
or all the crashing waves of the Ionian Sea;
or all the birds who migrate from the winter
in icy Thrace, cut through the sky and swap
the Arctic snows for the warm Egyptian Nile—
more than all these were the ghosts the prophet's magic called.
The trembling spirits were eager to seek out
hiding places in the shady wood. The first to rise
up from the ground was Zethus, his right hand holding         610
the horn of a wild bull; and Amphion,* whose left hand
holds the sweet-voiced conch that leads the rocks.
Niobe, rejoined at last to her dear children,
carries her head high up with pride, and counts
her ghosts.* Here comes a much worse mother, Agave,
still crazy.* With her comes that group of women
who tore the king apart; and mangled Pentheus
follows the maenads, still furiously threatening them.
    The priest keeps calling to a single ghost; at last,
embarrassed, he lifts his head, keeping his distance,         620
and tries to hide himself; the priest redoubles
his Stygian prayers, until his face is out
into the open—Laius! I shudder to tell it.
He looked terrible, his whole body covered with blood,
his matted dirty hair covered up his eyes.
His voice was desperate: 'Savage house of Cadmus,
always happy with your family's blood,
shake the thyrsus, tear your children up
with hands possessed. The greatest crime in Thebes
is mother-love. Land of my fathers, you are ruined           630
not by the anger of gods but by your crimes.
The plague wind did not blast you, your destruction
was not from lack of rain to cause a drought;
it was a blood-stained king, who took the throne
as a reward for murder, and—abomination!—
seized his father's bed. Horrible child! But the mother
is even worse, her cursed womb pregnant again.
He pushed into the place from which he came, and got

cursed children by his mother, doing what
even the wild beasts shun—he fathered his own brothers.        640
He is a tangled web of evil, a monster worse than the Sphinx.
It is you, you, who hold the bloodied sceptre!
I, your father unavenged, seek you and your whole city,
and I bring with me the Fury, bridesmaid of your marriage,
whipping her lash. I will overturn your house,
polluted by wicked sex and wicked murder.

    So you must drive the king in exile from this land
immediately; curse upon him! Let him go anywhere.
Just let him leave. The country will grow green
and flower again, the air will be made clean                   650
and healthy, beauty will return to all the trees.
Ruin, Destruction, Death, Pain, Grief, and Rottenness
are fit companions for him, let them go with him.
He himself will want to run away
to leave my kingdom, but I will hang weights
upon his feet to keep him here; he will wander, lost,
testing the ground before him with an old man's stick.
You make him lose the earth and I will make him lose the sky.'

OEDIPUS  Cold shuddering shakes my body and my bones.
I am accused of having done all that I feared to do.          660
But Merope is still married to her husband! Proof
that this cannot be true. And Polybus' life
proves my innocence. Both parents can bear witness
I did not do these crimes. What room for guilt can there be?
Thebes was in mourning for Laius before I even came,
before I set my foot on Boeotian soil.
Is the priest lying? Is some god against us?
Now! You! I have got the cunning conspirators:
Tiresias invented it, using the gods
as cover for his trick. He promised my throne to you.       670

CREON  Why would I want to drive my sister out?
Even if holy loyalty to family
did not restrain me to my proper station,
I would be too scared of fortune itself,
which always brings anxiety. I only wish you too
could safely put this weight aside, not let it hurt
as you leave it behind. A humbler place is safer.

OEDIPUS  Are you advising me to resign the cares of state
   of my own free will?

CREON             I would advise that plan
   to one who had a choice whether to stay or go.         680
   You have no choice now. You must bear your lot.

OEDIPUS  The surest way for those who want to rule
   is praising moderation, talking of peace and quiet.
   Restless people often pretend to be calm.

CREON  Does my long loyalty mean nothing to you?

OEDIPUS  Loyalty gives traitors opportunity.

CREON  Freed from the burdens of kingship, I enjoy
   the benefits of royalty, my home throngs with visitors,
   and every day that dawns from night, I get
   plenty of presents from my royal kin.           690
   Rich clothes, and luxurious gourmet food,
   and safety—I can give these to my friends.
   What could I think missing from such happiness?

OEDIPUS  The thing you do not have. Luck knows no limits.

CREON  Will you condemn me without hearing me?

OEDIPUS  Did you provide a defence speech for my life?
   Did Tiresias hear my case? No! But you think
   I am guilty. You set the example. I follow.

CREON  What if I am innocent?

OEDIPUS               Kings usually fear
   possibilities as much as truth.

CREON              Those with false fears     700
   deserve real ones.

OEDIPUS        When guilty men go free
   they feel resentful. No more doubts for me.

CREON  The perfect way to hatred.

OEDIPUS              A man who shrinks from hatred
   does not know how to rule. Kingdoms stay safe through fear.

CREON  The rule of tyrants and of savages
   depends on mutual fear. But fear comes back to haunt you.

OEDIPUS  Shut up this guilty man in a stone dungeon.
   I will myself return to the royal palace.

CHORUS  You were not the start of all this trouble.
   The curse which haunts the House of Labdacus     710
   is nothing new; the anger of the gods

against you started long ago. Cadmus came from Sidon*
took refuge in Castalian woods, and Dirce's waters*
washed clean the Tyrians,* and they settled there.
The mighty hero, tired from searching all the world
to find his sister,* raped by Jupiter,
frightened, rested here beneath our tree,
and prayed to that same god* who stole the girl.
An oracle* from Phoebus told him: 'Follow the wandering cow,
who never bends beneath the wagon yoke,                                720
or pulls the plough.' His journey ended here.
He named our land, 'Oxonia', Boeotia,*
after that cow—an inauspicious name.

  From that time on, this country keeps producing
more and more monstrous prodigies. A dragon
springs from the earth, his mighty body reaching
from the low ground to up above the pines,
snaking his body round an aged oak.
He lifted up his sky-dark head beyond
the tall Chaonian treetops,* while he lay                                730
still resting most of his body on the ground.*
Then the land got pregnant and gave birth
to terrible children: troops in battle-gear.
The signal sounded as the horn was blown,
the curved bronze trumpet gave a piercing shriek.
The newborn men had never learned to speak;
the battle-cry was the first thing they said.
Armies of brothers line in the battlefield,
the sons you would expect from dragon's teeth,
born to live out a lifetime in a day;                                740
they rose when Lucifer* was risen, and
died when the Hesperides were not yet up.
The traveller, Cadmus, shudders at these omens,
watching in terror as they fight it out,
until those wild young men at last are dead.
Their mother earth sees them returned to her,
back to the womb from which they just emerged.
May we escape from dreadful civil war!
Hercules' city, Thebes, is well aware,
how brothers fight with brothers.                                        750

And what about what happened to the hunter,*
Cadmus's grandson, when his brow was wreathed
with fresh new sprouts—the antlers of a stag—
and when the hounds ran after their own master?
Headlong he fled the forests and the hills,
swift Actaeon. He moves more nimbly now,
rushing over rocks and through ravines.
Even a feather moving in the wind
can startle him. He runs from his own nets.
Eventually he comes to a still pool,                                760
and in the water sees the antlers, sees
the face of the wild animal. It was the very pool
where that cruelly-modest goddess* washed.

# ACT FOUR

OEDIPUS  My mind turns over worries, finds new things to fear.
  The gods of sky and underworld declare
  that I am Laius' murderer. But my own heart
  protests its innocence, and says I better know myself.
  My memory retraces the faint path of the past.
  Yes, the man died—he blocked my way—my stick struck him.
  He went to Hades. He was a proud old man              770
  and I was young—he had tried to run me down.
  It was far from Thebes, in Phocis, where the road divides into three.
    My darling, can you please resolve my doubts?
  How old was Laius when he died? Was he
  a vigorous young man, or was he old?
JOCASTA  He was in middle-age, more old than young.
OEDIPUS  And did he take a lot of servants with him?
JOCASTA  Most of them got lost. Only a few
  faithful ones still followed by his chariot.
OEDIPUS  Did any of them die beside their king?              780
JOCASTA  A single loyal servant died with him.
OEDIPUS  I know who did it. The number and the place
  all fit. But when was this?
JOCASTA                          Ten harvest-times ago.
CORINTHIAN OLD MAN  The men of Corinth call you to inherit

your father's royal throne: Polybus is dead.

OEDIPUS   How cruel Fate attacks me on all sides!

Well, come then, tell me how my father died.

OLD MAN   The old man passed away in gentle sleep.

OEDIPUS   My father is dead and no one murdered him.

Proof! I now can hold clean hands to heaven,                     790

I need not be afraid of my own actions.

But wait—the worst part of the oracle remains.

OLD MAN   Your father's royal power keeps you immune.

OEDIPUS   I will inherit my father's throne—but I still fear my
mother.

OLD MAN   Why should you be afraid of a parent, who only wants
you home again?

OEDIPUS               My duty as a son makes me run from her.

OLD MAN   You abandon her now she is widowed?

OEDIPUS                                         That is what I am
scared of.

OLD MAN   Tell me what fear lies buried in your mind.

I am used to keeping royal secrets hidden.

OEDIPUS   I shudder at marriage to Mother, foretold by Delphi.  800

OLD MAN   That is no reason for fear! You need not worry:

Merope was not really your true mother.

OEDIPUS   Why would she raise a child that was not hers?

OLD MAN   Royal lines need heirs to keep them safe.

OEDIPUS   Tell me, how did you hear their family secret?

OLD MAN   I gave you as a baby to your mother.

OEDIPUS   You gave me to her, but who gave me to you?

OLD MAN   A shepherd on Cithaeron's snowy ridge.

OEDIPUS   How did you happen to be in that place?

OLD MAN   I used to tend my long-horned sheep up there.      810

OEDIPUS   Now for the proof. How is my body marked?

OLD MAN   Your feet were scarred by being pierced with iron.

You got your name from your swollen, damaged feet.*

OEDIPUS   Who gave my body to you as a gift?

OLD MAN   He was chief shepherd of the royal flock.

He had many shepherds under him.

OEDIPUS   Tell me his name.

OLD MAN                          I cannot. Old folks' minds

get tired and the memory grows dull.

OEDIPUS  Well, could you recognize him if you saw him?

OLD MAN  Perhaps I could. Frequently, even now,                    820
a trivial detail calls old memories back.

OEDIPUS  Let shepherds bring their whole flock to the altars.
Servants! Go, hurry up and fetch the man
who is in charge of all the royal herd.

JOCASTA*  No! The truth was hidden—on purpose or by chance;
in either case, let ancient secrets stay concealed forever.
Truth often harms the one who digs it up.

OEDIPUS  What is there to be scared of? What could be
worse than this?

JOCASTA  You need to understand, this quest is something big:
the country's health and that of the royal house             830
are in the balance. Stop, do not go on:
you need not make the moves; fate will reveal itself.

OEDIPUS  In times of happiness, no point in shaking things up.
But in a time of crisis, the safest thing is change.

JOCASTA  Do you want a grander father than a king?
Be careful not to find one you regret.

OEDIPUS  I need certainty, even if I regret
the family I find.—Look, here is Phorbas, the old shepherd man
who used to have control of the royal sheep.
Old man, do you remember his name or face?             840

OLD MAN  His face smiles to my mind… I am not sure.
His appearance seems familiar, but I do not know.

OEDIPUS  Did you serve Laius, when he was the king,
driving his rich flocks under Mount Cithaeron?

PHORBAS  Yes, Mount Cithaeron always had good grazing.
In summertime our flocks fed in those meadows.

OLD MAN  Do you know me?

PHORBAS                              My memory hesitates.

OEDIPUS  Did you once give a baby to this man?
Speak! Do you hesitate? Why are you pale?
Why search about for words? Truth hates delay.             850

PHORBAS  These things are hidden by long lapse of time.

OEDIPUS  Speak! Or let torture force you to the truth.

PHORBAS  I gave the child to him, a useless gift:
that baby could not live to enjoy the light.

OLD MAN  Hush! He is alive and will, I hope, live long.

OEDIPUS  Why do you say that baby must have died?

PHORBAS  An iron pin had been driven through his feet
    to bind his legs up, and the wound was swollen;
    foul pus infected the child's little body.

OEDIPUS  What more do you want? Now fate is drawing near—  860
    Who was the baby?

PHORBAS                Loyalty forbids—

OEDIPUS  Servants! Bring fire. Burning will change his mind.

PHORBAS  Is truth discovered by the path of blood?
    Master, have mercy.

OEDIPUS                If you think me cruel
    and violent, the cure is near at hand:
    tell me the truth. Who was the baby? Who were
    its parents?

PHORBAS      The mother of the child was your own wife.

OEDIPUS  Gape open, earth! Lord of the Underworld,
    master of shadows, seize and return me to lowest Hell,
    reverse my birth and let me be unborn.                870
    Thebans! Heap stones on my accursed head,
    slaughter me; let fathers, sons, and wives,
    and brothers take up arms against me,
    let this sick people take fire-brands from funeral pyres,
    and hurl the flames at me. The guilt of my times is mine:
    I wander hateful to the gods, a blasphemy.
    The day I first breathed unformed infant breath,
    already I deserved to die. Now, match your sins,
    dare an achievement worthy of your crimes.
    Go on, make haste into the royal house:                880
    congratulate your mother on her children!

CHORUS  If I had the power
    to shape Fate to my will,
    I would let the gentle breezes
    guide my sails, and my yardarms
    would never shudder under whirlwind blasts.
    May soft and gentle winds
    guide my fearless boat,
    never turn it from its course.
    May life carry me on                                890
    down the middle path.

Frightened of the Cretan king
the mad boy* sought the stars,
trusting new technology
competing with real birds
and hoping to control
wings all too false.
He robbed the sea of its name.
But the clever old man
Daedalus, kept a middle course,                           900
and stopped in the middle of the clouds,
waiting for his winged child
(as a bird flees from the threat
of the hawk, then gathers together
her brood, scattered by fear)
until the boy, in the sea,
waved his drowning arms
tangled by the ropes of his bold flight.
All excess hangs
in doubt.                                                 910

# ACT FIVE

CHORUS  But what is this? The gates are creaking;
  look, a servant of the king
  is beating his head in mourning.
  Tell us the news you bring.
MESSENGER  When Oedipus understood the words of fate
  and realized his awful heritage, he cursed himself:
  'Guilty!' he cried, and thinking of death, he rushed
  into his hated home, fast as he could.
  Just as the Libyan lion rages in the fields,
  shaking its yellow mane and threatening;            920
  his face is dark with anger, his eyes wild,
  he roars and groans, cold sweat runs over his body,
  he froths at the mouth and hurls out threats,
  and his enormous buried pain spills out.
  He was full of wild imaginings and plans
  to fit his fate. 'Why put off punishment?

Bring swords and drive them through my guilty heart,
or burn me with hot fire, stone me to death.
Is there a tigress or a bird of prey
to tear my chest apart? Cithaeron, you contain                    930
such wickedness already: set against me
beasts from the forest or bloodthirsty hounds—
or send again Agave. My soul, why fear death?
Only death can save me from my guilt.'
    He set his tainted hand upon the hilt
and drew his sword. 'But no! Can you absolve
such evil with so short a punishment,
a single blow? Death can pay for your father—
But your mother? What about the children,
disgustingly conceived? How can you atone                         940
for your country, mourning and ruined by your crimes?
You cannot be redeemed! In Oedipus alone
the laws of Nature are perverted, even birth
is strange. Then let my punishment be novel too.
May I live and die, and live and die,
constantly reborn, to feel again
new punishments. Use your head, poor fool:
suffer for many years unprecedented pain.
Have a long death. I must think of a way
to wander, distant from the dead and from the living.           950
I want to die, but must not meet my father.
Why do I hesitate?' Look now, a sudden stream
gushes down his face, his cheeks are wet with tears.
'But is it enough to weep? Do my eyes pour
only this thin liquid? Drive them from their homes,
to follow their own tears. Are you satisfied yet,
gods of marriage? Gouge them from their sockets!'
He raged, his cheeks showed a ferocious fire,
his eyes could scarcely stay inside his head;
his face was wild and full of feeling, angry, savage,           960
as if he had gone mad. He lets out a terrible scream,
and plunges his hands at his face. But his goggling eyes
pop out, trying to meet his thrust of their own accord.
They want to meet the source of their destruction.
Greedily his nails dig into his eyeballs,

ripping and tearing out the jelly from the roots.
His hands stay stuck in the empty spaces, glued there,
and buried deep inside, he scrabbles with his nails
at the deep empty caverns where his eyes once were.
He rages more and more, too much, achieving nothing.    970
      There is no danger now of light; he lifts his head,
scanning the vault of heaven with empty sockets,
testing his new night. Fragments still hang
from his clumsily excavated eyes. He rips them off,
and cries in triumph to the gods: 'Now spare my homeland,
I implore you! Now I have done right, I have accepted
my proper punishment. I found at last a night
appropriate for my marriage.' A horrible dripping
covers his mangled face, bloody with ripped veins.
CHORUS  Fate is driving us: give in to fate.    980
No amount of worrying can change
the threads of fate's fixed spindle.
All that human beings suffer,
all we do, comes from on high.
The decrees determined by the spindle
of Lachesis* will never be reversed.
The path of everything is always fixed,
our first day tells our last.
Even God cannot turn back
the things which rush by in the web of cause.    990
No prayer can change the swift-revolving pattern
fixed for each life. Many people find
fear itself can harm; while they fear fate,
they find themselves encountering their fate.

# EPILOGUE*

CHORUS  Listen! The gates! He struggles to approach,
blind and with no guide to help him walk,
on his dark way.
OEDIPUS  Good! It is done. I have paid my debt to my father.
I am happy with the darkness. What god blesses me,
pouring this dark cloud upon my head?    1000

Who forgave my sins? I escaped day's knowing eyes.
Father-killer, you owe nothing to your hands.
The light ran from you. This face suits Oedipus.

CHORUS  Look, Jocasta skitters out, leaping and wild,
a madwoman, like Agave, frenzied mother,
who grabbed her own son's head, but then at last
realized what she had done. Seeing poor Oedipus
she hesitates: she wants him and she fears him.
Shame gives way to grief, but her words get stuck.

JOCASTA  What can I call you? 'Son'? No? But you are my son.        1010
Ashamed? Talk to me, son! No? Why do you turn away
hiding your empty eyes?

OEDIPUS                    Who wants to spoil my darkness?
Who gives back my eyes? It is my mother's voice.
My work is wasted. Such monsters as we are
must never meet again. Let the seas divide us,
and lands far distant, and if under here
there hangs another earth, with other stars
and another, exiled sun—let one of us go there.

JOCASTA  It is the fault of fate; fate cannot make one guilty.

OEDIPUS  Do not speak to me, I will not listen.        1020
I beg you, by the remnants of my body,
by the unlucky children of my blood,
by all the good and evil names we share.

JOCASTA  Why are you numb, my soul? And why resist
sharing his punishment? You ruined woman,
through you all human laws are muddled and confused.
Die by the sword, release your wicked life.
Even if the father of the gods, shaking the world,
should hurl his curving thunderbolts at me,
I could never pay for all my sins.        1030
Evil mother! I want death. I need to find
a way to die.—Come, use your hands to help
your mother, if you killed your father; this is your last job.
    No, I ought to grab his sword; my husband died
by this same blade.—Why not call him the right name?
He is my father-in-law. Should I use this weapon
to pierce my heart, or push it deep into my naked throat?
Where should I strike? How can I not know? Of course!

Strike my all-too-fertile womb, which bore a husband-child.

CHORUS  She falls down dead. She died by her own hand,                    1040
the sword is driven out by so much blood.

OEDIPUS  Prophet, guardian, god of truth, *j'accuse*.
I only owed the fates my father's death;
now I am a double parent-killer, worse than I feared:
I killed my mother. She died for my crime.
Apollo, you lied! My sins outdid my fate.

Totter along your darkened path, and use
your hands to feel the way for your faltering feet,
the trembling kings of your nocturnal life.
Hurry! though your footsteps slip, go, rush away!                         1050
But stop! Be careful, do not fall upon your mother.

People weary with disease, heavy with plague,
half-dead already, look, I am leaving you.
Lift up your heads. Now gentler skies are yours,
after I go. Those who are dying, whose lives
are wandering below, may now breathe in
the breath of life. Go on now, help the dying;
I take the deadly plague away with me.
Harmful Fate and dreadful spasms of Disease,
Black Plague, Wasting and Ravening Pain,                                  1060
come with me! Come! I am glad to have such guides.

# MEDEA

*Pelias seized control of the throne of Thessaly, which rightly belonged to Jason. He told Jason that he would only give up the throne if he could bring back to Greece the Golden Fleece from the barbarian land of Colchis. Jason assembled a group of all the strongest and most talented men of Greece to sail on the first-ever international sea voyage, in a ship called the Argo, to steal the fleece, which hung from a tree in a sacred grove and was guarded by a dragon. Only the young princess Medea, who had magical powers, could help Jason. The king of Colchis, Medea's father Aeetes (son of the Sun), set Jason three tasks before he could win the fleece: to yoke a fire-breathing team of cattle and use them to plough a field; to sow a field with dragon's teeth, which would sprout up as armed warriors; and to lull the dragon to sleep. Medea helped Jason achieve all the tasks and take the fleece home. As they escaped in the Argo Aeetes tried to pursue them; Medea distracted him by killing her brother Aspyrtus and throwing his limbs one by one behind the ship.*

*As Seneca's play opens, Jason and Medea have been married for many years and have children. Jason is preparing to divorce Medea and marry a new wife.*

# DRAMATIS PERSONAE

**MEDEA**
**NURSE**
**CREON**
**JASON**
**MESSENGER**
**CHORUS**

# ACT ONE

MEDEA O gods of marriage! Juno, childbirth goddess,
and you, Athena, who taught Tiphys how
to harness the first ship* that would subdue the waves,
and Neptune, cruel master of the ocean deep,
and Titan,* portioning the world's bright day,
and you, whose moonlight sees all secret rites,
Hecate triple-formed*—all gods Jason invoked
when he swore to me; and gods who better suit
Medea's prayers: Chaos of endless night,
kingdoms that hate the gods of heaven, blaspheming powers,    10
master of the melancholy realm, and queen*—
abducted, but he kept his word to you.* Now let me curse:
Come to me now, O vengeful Furies, punishers of sinners,
wild in your hair with serpents running free,
holding black torches in your bloody hands,
come to me, scowling as you did of old
when you stood round my marriage bed.* Kill his new wife,
kill her father, and all the royal family.
What is worse than death? What can I ask for Jason?
That he may live!—in poverty and fear.    20
Let him wander through strange towns, in exile,
hated and homeless, an infamous guest, begging a bed.
Let him want me as wife, and want—the worst I could pray for—
children who resemble both their parents.
Now it is born, my vengeance is delivered:
I mothered it.—But why this weaving of words,
this pointless whining? Will I not attack my enemies?
I will hurl the torches from their hands, the light from heaven.
O Sun, my grandfather,* do you see this? Are you still there?
Do you still ride your chariot, as usual, through the sky,    30
and not turn back towards the east, trace back the day?
Give me the power to ride my father's horses through the air,
Grandfather, give me the reins, and let me guide
with flaming harnesses the fiery team.
Let Corinth, whose twin shores now block the gulf,

burn up in flames and join two seas in one.
Just one more thing: I have to take the torch
to the marriage room myself; after the prayers,
I will be the one to kill the victims on the altar.
Find out a path to vengeance even in the entrails,                40
my soul, if you are still alive, if you retain
any of your old strength. Away with feminine fears,
dress up your mind like your own cruel home.*
All the horrors witnessed back at home by the Black Sea,
Corinth will see now. Evils to make
heaven and earth both shudder equally
are what my mind revolves: wounding, murder, death
creeping through the limbs. But all this is too slight;
I did those as a girl. Let weightier rage swell up:
now I have given birth, my crimes ought to increase.            50
Take on the armour of anger, prepare for destruction
possessed by fury. The tale of your divorce
must match your marriage. How should you leave your man?
The same way that you married him. Enough delay.
A family formed by crime must be broken by more crime.

CHORUS  Come to the royal wedding, all you gods,
lords of the sky, lords of the sea, and bless them,
while the people stand in respectful silence.
First a white bull must hold high his neck
for sacrifice to the royal Thunderer.*                         60
Then a snowy cow that never felt the yoke
should satisfy Juno with her death; and give
the goddess who restrains the bloody hands of Mars,*
who brings to warring peoples peace
and holds rich plenty in her horn,
give her a soft lamb and melt her heart.
And you, who bless all legal weddings,*
dispel the night and bring them luck,
come here with slow and drunken steps
a wreath of roses on your head.                                70
And you the messenger of double times,*
star whose return seems always slow to lovers:
mothers long for you, as do their daughters,
wanting your shining rays to shine for them right away.

This girl's beauty far surpasses
all the brides of Athens,
and the women who exercise
like boys, by the mountains of Taygetus,
by the city without a wall,*
and Boeotian women, and those washed                    80
by holy Alpheus.*
If he wants to be judged by looks,
the commander, Aeson's son,*
would win against the child of thunder,*
whose chariot tigers draw,
and the shaker of the tripods,
the fearsome virgin's brother.*
Castor will yield to him,
with Pollux, better boxer.*

   Just so, just so, O gods, who live in heaven, I pray,    90
his woman may outshine all other wives,
and he by far surpass all other men.
When this girl takes up her place in the women's dance,
her beauty, hers alone outshines them all:
just as the beauty of the stars is lost at sunrise,
and the thick flocks of the Pleiades lie hid
when Phoebe* binds with borrowed light
her solid orb with circling horns;
as snow-white colour blushes, dyed
with scarlet; like the shining light                     100
the dew-wet shepherd sees at dawn.
Jason, you used to tremble as you held an untamed wife,
reluctant as you held her body close;
now torn away from your barbarian marriage,
lucky man, take hold of this Corinthian girl.
Your in-laws—unlike last time—give consent.
Young men, now play around, and slander whomever you like;
sing your songs in choruses and rounds.
Abusing masters is, for once, allowed.*

   Hymen, noble and bright, son of Bacchus with his thyrsus,  110
the time is at hand to set light to the torch made of finely split
        pinewood.
Shake out with your languorous fingers prescribed ceremonial fire.

Pour forth festive abuse in sharp-tongued verses;
let the crowd be free with their jokes. But a woman who marries
    a stranger,
running away from her homeland—let her go to the silent shadows.


# ACT TWO

MEDEA  I am done for. Wedding music struck my ears.
Such cruelty! Even I can scarce believe it.
Could Jason do this, with my father gone,
my land and kingdom lost? Abandon me, alone in a foreign land,
unfeeling man! Did he scorn my achievements,                    120
when he has seen how sin can conquer flames and sea?
Does he believe my evil powers so lost?
What should I do? Madness is driving me
in all directions. How can I be avenged?
If only he, too, had a brother! But—he has a wife.
Stab her in the heart. But can this answer my pain?
If any cities, Greek or barbarous,
know of a crime your hands have not yet done,
now is the time for it. Your past crimes urge you,
and let them all return.—The golden glory of the kingdom      130
stolen,* and the wicked girl's young playmate
ripped by the sword,* his murder forced upon his father's sight,
his body scattered on the sea, and old Pelias'
limbs cooked up in a bronze pot.* How much blood
I have shed by murder! When I did this
I was not even angry; I was driven by painful love.

    But what could Jason do? Another's rule and power
forces him to this.—He should have bared his breast
to meet his sword.—Ah, no, find better words,
my raging grief! If he can, let him live, still mine,          140
just as he used to be. If not—still let him live,
remember me, and spare the life which once I gave him.
Creon is to blame. His untamed lust for power
is breaking up my marriage, tearing a mother
away from her children, ripping a close-knit trust.
Let him be hunted down, may he alone

pay as he deserves. I will heap deep ashes on his house.
The dangerous curving coast of Malea*
will see the black crest driven by the flames.

NURSE  Silence, I beg you! Hide your grievances                    150
in a secret bitterness. If one can bear deep wounds
with patient, quiet endurance and a mellow heart,
one can get payback: hidden anger hurts;
the hate you speak of will not be revenged.

MEDEA  Light is the grief which can accept advice,
and mask itself; great troubles do not hide.
I want confrontation.

NURSE                    Stop this crazy passion!
Mistress, even silence scarcely saves you.

MEDEA  Fortune fears the brave and crushes cowards.

NURSE: Try valour at a time when valour has its place.        160

MEDEA  It is never inappropriate to be brave.

NURSE  No hope reveals a way out from our troubles.

MEDEA  The one who knows no hope knows no despair.

NURSE  Your friends from Colchis, and your husband's faith
Are gone; nothing survives of all your wealth.

MEDEA  Medea still survives. Here you behold
the sea, the earth, sword, flame, the gods, and thunder.

NURSE  But fear the king!

MEDEA                    My father was a king.

NURSE  You fear no arms?

MEDEA                    Not even earth-born soldiers.*

NURSE  You will die.

MEDEA            I want to.

NURSE                    Run away!

MEDEA                                Enough of running.    170

NURSE  Medea—

MEDEA        I will be.

NURSE                You are a mother!

MEDEA                                By you-know-who.

NURSE  Hurry, escape!

MEDEA              I will, but first, revenge.

NURSE  Vengeance will follow.

MEDEA                        I may slow it down.

NURSE  Hold back your words, madwoman, stop your threats,

bridle your heart; it is best to suit the times.

MEDEA  Fortune can take my wealth away, but not my spirit.
But who is this, making the doorway creak?
It is Creon himself, puffed up with his power in Greece.

CREON  Medea, poisonous child of Colchian Aeetes,
have you not yet got yourself away from my kingdom?—          180
She is up to something; I know her cunning, her history.
Whom will she pity, whom will she leave safe?
I had intended to eliminate this infection once and for all,
to put her to the sword; my son-in-law begged mercy.
Life is granted her, now let her free from fear
my country. Go in safety.—Wild thing! She wants to attack me;
she threatens me, comes nearer, wants to talk.
Stop her, you guards, keep her away, no touching;
tell her to be quiet. Time she learnt to submit
to royal power. Go quickly on your way!          190
This monster has been here too long; take it away!

MEDEA  What charge is there against me, punished by exile?

CREON  An innocent woman asks why she is expelled!

MEDEA  If you are judging, seek the truth. If ruling, give your orders.

CREON  You must submit to power, just or unjust.

MEDEA  Kingdoms which act unjustly never last.

CREON  Go complain in Colchis.

MEDEA                                    I am going. But the man
who brought me here should take me home.

CREON                                         Too late; my decision
is made.

MEDEA  A man who makes a decision without listening to both sides
is unjust, even if his ruling is a fair one.          200

CREON  Did you hear Pelias before you punished him?
But speak, let your great case be given a chance.

MEDEA  How difficult it is to turn a mind from wrath
when once it is aroused! When arrogant hands once seize
power, the ruler thinks authority resides
in stubbornness. All this I learnt in my own royal home.
Though pitiless disaster overwhelms me,
though exiled, abandoned, abject, and alone,
troubled on every side, once I shone bright,
born from a glorious father, descended from the Sun.          210

Lands made wet by Phasis, gently winding through,
places seen by Scythian Pontus behind its back,
and where the seas grow sweet with marshland water,
and where the riverbanks of Thermodon enclose
the ranks of women warriors,* terrifying,
with their crescent shields—all this my father ruled.
I had high birth, good luck, and royal power;
I shone in glory; suitors sought my hand
who now are sought by me. Fortune is swift and fickle,
headlong, she snatched me from my kingdom and gave
     me to exile.                                     220
Put trust in royal power, when fickle chance
carries your treasure to the winds! The greatest wealth of kings,
a joy forever, is to help the weak,
and shelter suppliants, give them a home.
This is the only thing I brought from all my kingdom:
that it was I who saved the glorious flower of Greece,
the guardians of Achaea, sons of gods:
I am their saviour. Orpheus is my gift,
who softens stones with song and leads the woods;
Castor and Pollux, double gift, are mine,                  230
mine are the sons of Boreas, and he whose darting eyes
can see across the Pontus, Lynceus,
and all the Argonauts. Their leader—I pass by.
No thanks are due for him, no debt is owed;
I brought back all the rest for you, just him for me.
   Go on, heap all my misdeeds on my head:
I will confess: but this is my one crime:
the *Argo*'s safe return. Should that girl stay a virgin,
obey her father? Then the whole Greek land
is lost, as are its leaders, and he first—your son-in-law—     240
will die, in the flaming jaws of the savage bull.
Let Fortune press what charge she will upon me,
to have saved such heroes needs no saying sorry.
Whatever prize I won from all my crimes
is in your hands; condemn me if you wish,
but give back my sin. I am guilty, I confess it;
Creon, you knew it when I knelt and begged
for safety and protection at your hands.

I ask some little corner, a poor hovel, home for pain,
but in this land; if you drive me from the city,                    250
grant me some distant place within your kingdom.

CREON  I have provided quite sufficient proof
that I am obviously not a tyrant,
the kind to trample wretchedness with lordly foot.
I chose an exile as my son-in-law:
he was in trouble, shaking, terrified:
Acastus,* heir of Thessaly, said he should die.
His grudge was that his trembling weak old father
was murdered, and his old limbs torn apart:
his sisters were deceived by you to dare                            260
this treachery to the father that they loved.
Jason has a case, if you remove yourself;
no innocent blood pollutes him, and his hands
kept clear of the sword. He is clean,
as long as he is not tainted by your company.
You! You scheming source of every criminal act
you have a woman's wickedness; your daring
shows masculine strength, ignoring what men say.
Go, wash clean the kingdom, and take with you
your deadly drugs. Free citizens from fear;                         270
stay in some other country to bother the gods.

MEDEA  You force me to leave? Then give back my ship
or give me back my friend. Why tell me to go alone?
I did not come alone. If you fear war,
then drive us both from your kingdom. Why do you separate us?
Both are guilty. Pelias died for him, not me.
Charge him with theft, desertion, my abandoned father,
my brother torn apart, all the new crimes
which even now he teaches his new brides—did not do them.
I have done so much harm, but never for myself.                     280

CREON  You should have left by now. Why spin things out with talk?

MEDEA  I am on my way, but please, one final favour:
do not make my innocent children suffer for their mother's guilt.

CREON  Go! I will hold and cherish them like a father.

MEDEA  By the happy royal marriage bed,
its future hopes, and by the state of kings,
which fickle Fortune shakes this way and that,

I beg you grant brief respite for my exile;
I am a mother; let me kiss my children one last time.
I may be close to death.
CREON                    You want the time to plot.                    290
MEDEA  What fear of plots in such brief span of time?
CREON  No time is too short for criminals to do wrong.
MEDEA  You will not grant a poor, unhappy woman time to weep?
CREON  Although my deep-set fear fights back against your prayers,
    yes, have a single day, to ready yourself for exile.
MEDEA  It is too much, you can cut back the time;
    I too am in a hurry.
CREON                On pain of death
    you must leave the Isthmus before the light of dawn.
    Now I am summoned by the marriage rites
    and Hymen's holy day calls me to prayer.                    300
CHORUS  That man was too bold who first in a boat—
    so fragile a boat—on the treacherous waves,
    went watching his homeland receding behind him
    as he trusted his life to the changeable winds;
    his direction uncertain, he cut through the waters,
    putting his faith in the delicate wood,
    though too slender a boundary made the division
    between the alternatives, life and death.
        The constellations were still unknown,
    and the bright stars with which heaven is painted          310
    remained unused. No boat could yet
    avoid the rainy Hyades.
    The shining she-goat, Capella,
    and the Plough, which the slow old man
    both follows and controls,* and Boreas,
    and Zephyr—none of these yet
    had names.
    Tiphys had the courage to spread out his canvas sails
    to the vast ocean
    and to prescribe new laws for the winds;                    320
    now to stretch out the ropes with the round sails full,
    now to take hold of the crosswinds with foot set forward,
    now safely to set out the yards
    in the mist of the mast,

now to fasten them tight at the top
at the time when the sailor too eagerly yearns
for the full gusts of wind and above the high sail
the scarlet topsails quiver.
    Glorious were the ages our forefathers saw
when deception was far distant.                                    330
Each person lived an unambitious life, at home,
then growing old on ancestral farmland,
rich with a little, they knew no wealth
except what their native soil brought forth.
The world was once divided into strict partitions,
but those were broken by the pinewood ship,
which ordered the ocean to suffer a beating
and the sea, once inviolate, to turn into
one of our reasons to fear.
That wicked boat was given rough treatment,                        340
sailing on and on through endless terrors,
when the two mountains, gates of the deep,
driven this way and that by impetuous force
groaned with a noise which sounded like thunder
and the sea was struck and it sprinkled the stars, right up
       to the clouds.
Brave Tiphys grew pale and his slackening hand
relinquished all hold of the tiller.
Orpheus was silent, his lyre lying idle,
and even the *Argo* lost her voice.
Remember Scylla,* the Sicilian monster,                            350
bound at her belly with ravening dogs,
opening together all her wide-gaping mouths?
Who did not shudder and tremble all over
at the multiple howlings of this single threat?
What of the time when those dangerous females
brought peace to the sea, with melodious voices,
when, singing to his own Pierian lyre,
Thracian Orpheus
almost compelled the Siren to follow him—
although her habit was to trap ships with her voice?                360
What was the prize for this journey?
The Golden Fleece,

and Medea, greater evil than the sea,
a worthy cargo for the world's first boat.
Now at last the sea has yielded and obeys all laws.
Now there is no need of a ship made by Pallas' hand,
rowed back by kings, a well-renowned vessel—an *Argo*.
Any old skiff can wander the deep.
All boundaries are gone and the cities
have set up their walls in new lands:                              370
the world is a thoroughfare, nothing remains
where it was.
The Indian drinks from the chilly Araxes,
the Persians can drink from the Elbe and the Rhine.
The ages will come, in faraway years
when Ocean will set free the links of Nature
and the great earth lie open, and Tethys will open,
new worlds, and Thule* will be no longer
the end of the earth.

# ACT THREE

NURSE  Mistress, why are you rushing away from the house?     380
    Stop, suppress your anger, control yourself.
    As a Maenad staggers on uncertain feet,
    mad with the inspiration of the god,
    on the peak of snowy Pindus or Mount Nysa,
    so she runs to and fro, her movements wild,
    her face displays her crazy passion's marks.
    Her cheeks are flaming and she draws deep breaths,
    she shouts, her eyes are wet with tears, she smiles;
    she shows the signs of every kind of passion.
    Hesitant, aggressive, raging, bitter, full of grief.     390
    Where will the weight of her angry heart tip down?
    Where will this wave break? Her madness froths over.
    The crime she contemplates is complex and extreme:
    she will outdo herself; I recognize this passion.
    She intends some terrible deed, wild and unnatural.
    I see the face of Passion. Gods, prove my fear false!
MEDEA  Poor woman, do you want to know where hatred ends?

Look to love. Should I endure this royal wedding,
and fail to take revenge? Will I waste the day
I tried so hard to get, got at such cost?                              400
No, while earth lies in the centre and supports the sky,
while shining heaven in fixed circles turns,
while sands are numberless, while night brings forth
the stars, and day the sun, while the North Pole
revolves the unsinking Bears, while rivers flow to the sea—
never will my bitter rage fall short of total vengeance;
no, it will always grow. What vast wild beast,
what Scylla or Charybdis,* who drained deep
the seas, or Etna, crushing the panting Titan,*
will boil up with threats as vast as mine?                             410
No rushing river, gusty sea, or ocean wild
whipped up with wind, or force of fire helped on
by hurricanes, could stop my fixed intention,
or my rage. I will destroy and ruin everything.

    Was he afraid of Creon, and of war with Lord Acastus?
True love is afraid of nobody.
But grant that he was forced to yield and to surrender;
he surely could have come to talk for the last time
with his wife. That was exactly what this mighty hero feared...
Surely as son-in-law he could have put off the time          420
of cruel exile: I got just one day
for two children.—I do not mind that the time is brief.
It will go far. This very day I will do
a deed of which all days will speak. I will attack the gods.
I will shake the world.

NURSE                Lady, you are upset;
  yes, things are bad, but calm down!

MEDEA                    Peace can only be mine
  if I see everything ruined along with me.
    Let fall the world with me. How sweet to destroy when you die.

NURSE  See all the dangers you face if you persist.
  Attacking those in power is never safe.                          430

JASON  My luck is always bad, and fate is always cruel:
  just as bad to me, in kindness or in anger.
  How often god finds for us antidotes
  worse than the threatened pain. If I wanted to be faithful

to my wife—she had earned it—I had to forfeit my life.
If I did not want to die, I had to give up—poor me!—
fidelity. It was not fear that conquered faith
but quaking duty; she killed her parents; it was likely
the children would be next. O Holy Power, if you,
Justice, inhabit heaven, I call to you as witness:                     440
love for my children defeated me. Though she is fierce,
spirited, she will not bear the yoke,
she still, I think, cares more for her children than her marriage.
I have made up my mind to beseech her, though she is angry.
and look, now she sees me, she jumps, in a towering rage.
      She shows
how much she hates me: all her bitterness is in her face.
MEDEA  Jason, I have fled before, and now I flee again.
Exile is nothing new to me; only the cause has changed.
Once I fled for your sake. Now I leave, I go away,
because you force me to abandon your home, your hearth,
      your gods.                                                       450
You are sending me back, but to whom? Should I go to the
      people of Colchis,
my father's kingdom, and the fields which we soaked with
      the blood
of my brother? Tell me, what country should I go and seek?
What seas do you point me towards? The mouth of the Pontic
      strait,
through which I led back home that glorious band of kings,
when I followed you—adulterer!—through the Clashing Rocks?*
Or should I go to your uncle's lands *—to Iolchos, or Tempe?
All the paths I opened up for you, I closed for me.
Where are you sending me back to? You impose exile on an exile,
but grant me no place to go.—I must go. The king's son-in-law
      says so.                                                         460
I do not resist. Pile up horrible punishments on me;
I have earned them. Let the king in his anger crush this concubine,
torture me, make me bleed, weigh down my hands with chains,
shut me up in a stony jail for an unending night.
My guilt will still outweigh my punishment.—Ungrateful!
wind back your mind to the bull,* and its fiery gusts of breath,
and to all the barbarian terrors of a never-conquered race,*

the flaming herd of Aeetes in the field of armoured men, *
and the weapons of the enemy which suddenly sprang up,
when at my command the earthborn soldiers fell, in a
    mutual slaughter.         470
Remember the prize of your whole long quest, the Phrixean ram,*
and the sleepless monster,* whom I ordered to close his eyes
in mysterious sleep, and my brother,* betrayed to death,
a crime not achieved in a single criminal act, but many;
and the daughters deceived by my trickery, who dared
to chop up the limbs of that old man* who never would
    live again.
[I left my realm behind to come to someone else's.]*
By your hopes for your children, by your nice safe home,
by the monsters I defeated, by my hands,
which I wore out for you, by all our dangers past,     480
by sky and sea, witnesses of my marriage,
have pity. In your good fortune, reward me, please, I beg you.
From all that wealth the Colchian pirates win
from distant lands, the sunburnt Indians,
treasure that crams our house full up to bursting,
and we deck our trees with gold—from this wealth in my
    exile I took nothing,
except my brother's body; and I spent even that for you.
For you I gave up my kingdom, my father, my brother,
    my shame—
this was my dowry when I married you. I am leaving; give
    me back what is mine.
JASON  When Creon was against you and wanted to destroy you,  490
  my tears persuaded him to grant you exile.
MEDEA  Exile, it seems, is a gift. I thought it was punishment.
JASON  Go while you still can, run, take yourself far from here:
  the anger of kings is always dangerous.
MEDEA                    Your advice
  is given to be loyal to Creusa. You banish her hated rival.
JASON  Medea blames me for love?
MEDEA              And murder, and betrayal.
JASON  What crime, in the end, can you charge me with?
MEDEA  All I have done.
JASON         Ah, that was all I needed;

MEDEA

that your crimes would be treated as my fault.

MEDEA  They are yours, yours! If you gain from a crime, 500
    you did it. If your wife is disgraced, everyone is against her,
    you alone must protect her, you shout out her innocence.
    One who sinned for your sake should look clean to you.

JASON  A life of which one feels ashamed is an unwelcome gift.

MEDEA  One who feels ashamed of life need not cling to it.

JASON  I disagree. You need to tame your heart, too quick to anger:
    make peace with our sons.

MEDEA               They are no sons of mine!
    Will Creusa give my children brothers?

JASON  Yes, though she is a queen, to the wretched children of
    exiles.

MEDEA  May such an evil day never come to my poor boys, 510
    for that filthy bloodline to taint my glorious stock,
    the children of Phoebus joined to the sons of Sisyphus.*

JASON  Why, poor woman, are you dragging us both into ruin?
    Leave, I beg you.

MEDEA          Creon heard my supplication.

JASON  Tell me what I can do.

MEDEA             A crime for me; my turn.

JASON  Hemmed in by two kings...

MEDEA              And by worse danger:
    Medea. It is time for a face-off: let us fight,
    and let the prize be Jason.

JASON            I am tired; I give in.
    You, too, should be afraid: you have seen so many dangers.

MEDEA  I have always stood above each turn of Fortune. 520

JASON  Acastus is pursuing us.

MEDEA            Creon is the nearer enemy:
    flee both. Do not take up arms against your father-in-law
    nor stain yourself with your own kinsman's blood.
    Medea does not force you to. Be guiltless, run with me.

JASON  But what defence is there, against a double war,
    if Creon and Acastus join their arms together?

MEDEA  Add the Colchians, and Lord Aeetes too,
    with Scythians and Greeks: I will destroy them all.

JASON  I shudder at great power.

MEDEA           Be careful not to want it.

JASON  Talking too long looks suspicious; time to break off.        530
MEDEA  Now, King Jupiter, thunder your loudest across the sky,
stretch out your arm, prepare the flames of vengeance,
let the clouds be split, make tremble all the world.
Weigh your weapons in both hands, do not distinguish
between me and him: whichever of us falls
will die guilty. Your thunderbolt against us
cannot strike wrong.

JASON                          Now make your thoughts more wholesome,
and act more calmly. If anything from my in-laws' home
can comfort you in exile, now is the time to ask.

MEDEA  My heart, as you know, can despise the wealth of kings;        540
and it does. But let me have the children in my exile,
for company, so when my tears fall fast,
I may hold them in my arms. You will have new children.

JASON  Certainly, I would like to say yes to your prayers,
but fatherly devotion must say no. To endure such a thing!—
not even the king, my father-in-law, himself could make me do it.
They are my reason for living; my scorched heart finds in them
my comfort for my pain. I would rather lose my breath,
my body, or the light.

MEDEA                          —Does he love his children so much?
Good! I have him trapped: there is a place to hurt him.—        550
But of course you will allow me, as I take my leave,
to give the children my final words, and hug them for the last time?
Thank you. And this, now, is my very last request:
that if, in my distress, I have spoken out of turn,
forget about it: let your memory of me
be of my better self: let what I said in anger
be totally erased.

JASON                  I have driven those words from my mind.
I, too have a request: control the fire in your heart,
and take things easy: peace makes sorrows soft.

MEDEA  He has gone. Is that it? You go off and forget about me        560
and all that I achieved? Do you see me as finished?
I will never be finished. Come on now, summon all
your strength and skill. The reward you have won from your
        crimes
is to think nothing a crime. There is little chance of deceit:

people suspect me. So choose a point to attack
which nobody could suspect. Go on, be daring, begin
to do whatever Medea can do, and even more than that.
    You, faithful nurse, companion of my sorrow
and of my changing fortune, help with my grim plan.
I have a cloak, a gift from the house in the sky,                   570
the kingdom's glory, given to Aeetes as proof
that he was the child of the Sun. I also have a necklace
shining with plaited gold, and I tie up my hair with a band
of solid gold set off by brilliant gems.
Let my children carry these things as gifts from me to the bride,
but first, let them be smeared and daubed with deadly poison.
Let Hecate* be summoned, prepare the rites of death:
let the altars be set up, let the flames ring through the halls.
CHORUS* Force of flame, wind's turbulent buffet, javelins,
none of these come down with a force so mighty,                     580
none as fearful as when an ex-wife, rejected,
hates with hot passion.
Nor the wintry storms of the cloudy South Wind
nor when Hister* floods in a rush, torrential,
forcing bridges down, letting none be mended,
vagabond river.
Nor the Rhone's crash into the deep of ocean,
nor when snows have melted and turned to small streams,
under hot sun, when in the midst of springtime
Haemus* is melting.                                                 590
Anger goaded on is a fire in darkness,
will not be controlled, will not suffer harness,
fears not death, desires to encounter danger,
runs to the drawn sword.
Mercy, gods, I pray your forgiveness for him,
let the man live safe, though he touched the ocean.
But the deep sea's master is angry his realm
now has been conquered.
Boldly that boy* drove the eternal chariots,
never paying heed to his father's limits.                           600
Wild, he scattered fires from the pole; the same fires
took him and hold him.
No one ever suffered from taking safe paths.

Take the same way many have trod before you.
Do not wildly break up the holy, sacred
bonds of the cosmos.
Each of those who entered that daring vessel,*
seizing well-born oars from the sacred woodland—
Pelion's mountain glades* were deprived of thick shade—
each of those who pushed through the wandering clifftops,          610
measured all that period of seaborne suffering,
reached at last barbarian shores, took anchor,
stole the gold from foreigners, sure of return,
paid with awful death, having boldly broken
laws of the deep sea.
Ocean punished forcefully those who wronged it.
Tiphys* first, the man who had tamed the waters,
left his helm's control to a clueless captain,
far from home he died, in a foreign country,
lying on a foreign shore, in a pauper's tomb,                      620
he lies among dead souls unknown to him.
Aulis keeps in mind its lost king, and therefore
makes the ships stop, keeps them in harbour, stagnant,
though they resent it.
Born the child of the tuneful Muse, Orpheus*
at whose plectrum, plucking the strings in rhythm,
waterfalls stood still and the winds were silent,
at whose song birds ceased their own sweet singing, flying
swift to him; the woods were his true companions;
he lay scattered over the Thracian farmlands,                      630
while his head bobbed, rolled by the scowling Hebrus.
Styx he knew of old, and again he crossed it,
never to come back.
Hercules laid low the two sons of North Wind,*
killed the sea-god's offspring,* who always altered
how he looked, changing to shapes unnumbered.
After Hercules had brought peace to the land and ocean,
opened up the kingdoms of savage Hades,
living he lay down upon burning Oeta,
gave his body up to the cruel furnace.*                            640
Two destructive poisons* consumed the hero,
gifts of his own bride.

Death brought low Ancaeus:* the bristly wild boar
gored him. Then, bad man, Meleager* slaughtered
his uncle. His angry mother kills him
with her own hands. All, all were guilty—
no: the young boy,* snatched from the hero,
Hercules, who searched but never found him.
He died without guilt, seized in the quiet waters.
Come now, heroes, pray to the sea, beseech its                        650
dangerous fountains.
Idmon* also, though wise in the ways of fortune
lies beneath the Libyan sands: the serpent
killed him. Mopsus,* truthful to all but himself,
fell, and Thebes has lost her most faithful prophet.
Thetis' husband,* if he can tell the future,
knows he must go wandering, an exile, homeless.
Ajax,* killed by thunder and ocean, paid back
father's transgression.
Nauplius* had planned an attack on Argos;                            660
fire betrayed him, headlong he falls to deep sea.
You reversed fate, wife,* for your Pherean husband,
paid with your own life for the life of your man.
Even he who ordered the quest and booty,
'Bring me back the gold in the first of vessels!'
Pelias, boiled up in the heated cauldron,
burned, his limbs dispersed in the narrow waters.
Now enough, O Gods, of your vengeance. Jason
acted on orders.

# ACT FOUR

NURSE  My soul is terrified; it shudders. Evil is near.               670
    How great her bitterness is growing! Now it fires
    itself, and it restores the force that it had lost.
    I have often seen her in her rages, attacking the gods
    bringing down the sky. But horrors, greater horrors,
    Medea plans. She goes with feet of thunder
    out from the house to the sanctuary of death;
    there she spreads out all her treasures. Things that even she

has feared for years, she now takes out, unpacks
her whole array of evil, secrets long concealed.
With her left hand she makes ready the uncanny rites:               680
she summons the powers of destruction: scorching heat
      from the sands
of the Libyan desert, and the force of cold, which the mountains
of Taurus freeze with Arctic ice, perpetual snow.
She calls up every horror. Drawn by her magic spells
the scaly ones slip from their holes. They are here.
Here a savage serpent slithers its massive bulk,
its forked tongue darting to and fro; it looks for victims
whom it may kill. But hearing her voice, it stops,
plaits its swollen body into a heap of knots,
and piles them up in coils. Now she says: 'From the earth         690
come only minor evils, weaker weapons.
I shall search the sky for poison. Now, now the time has come
to start something grander than ordinary deceit.
Let the Dragon descend, which lies like a rushing stream,
here let him come, whose massive coils touch the Bears,*
those two wild beasts, the Great Bear and the Small,
(Greek sailors use the Great Bear, Tyrians use the Small)
and let the Serpent Holder at last release his grip,
and pour out venom. Let Python* come at my call,
who dared provoke Diana and Apollo, the twin gods.               700
And let the Hydra come; let every snake, mown down
by Hercules, return, and heal its own death wound.
And you, abandon Colchis, my always-wakeful Dragon,
come to me; you were the first serpent I charmed to sleep.'
After she had summoned every kind of snake,
she heaped together all her poison plants.
Whatever grows on trackless Eryx's rocks,*
and the mountain ridges clothed with eternal snow
of Caucasus, which is drenched in Prometheus' blood,*
and the herbs which the wealthy Arabs use to anoint their
      arrows,                                                          710
and the Medes, those fearsome archers, or the light-armed
      Parthians,
or the juices which the high-born German women gather
under a frozen sky, in their barbarian groves.

Whatever the earth produces while birds are building nests,
or when the frozen winter has already thrown aside
the beauty of the woodland, heaping up the freezing snow,
every plant whose blooming flowers bring death,
and deadly sap which lurks in twisted roots,
to bring us harm—she took them in her hands.
Some of the poisons came from Thessalian Athos;*          720
Others from great Mount Pindus; on Pangaeus' ridges,*
this plant's delicate leaves were lopped with a bloody sickle.
Some the Tigris fed, restraining his deep current;
others the Danube; some, bejewelled Hydaspes,*
running with warm waters through the desert lands,
and these by the river Baetis, which gave its own name to its
          country,*
which hits the Western Sea with a quiet plash.
Some of the plants were cut by iron, while Apollo got
          ready the day,
the stem of others is cut at the dead of night,
others cropped with a fingernail, while a charm is said.       730
She gathers the poisonous plants and squeezes the venom
of the snakes, and mixes it with birds of ill omen,
the heart of a melancholy eagle-owl, and the innards
cut from a living screech-owl. These, the great criminal
          mastermind
laid out separately. Some contain the devouring power
of fire; others hold the icy cold of bitter frost.
She added to the poisons certain words—themselves
equally dangerous. Listen! You can hear her crazy feet.
She is chanting and the world is shaking at her spell.
MEDEA I pray you, silent hordes, and ghostly gods,            740
   Chaos obscure, dark home of shady Dis,*
   caverns of ugly Death, bound by Tartarus,*
   Spirits, be free from your torments, hurry to this new wedding.
   Let stop the wheel which wrenches his body, may Ixion touch
          the ground,
   may Tantalus* freely drink the waters of Pirene.
   Only for his in-laws should punishment increase:
   let the slippery stone send Sisyphus* tumbling down the rocks.
   You too, who vainly work to fill the leaky urns,

Danaids,* gather here: this day requires your hands.
Now, summoned by my rituals, come to me, moon of the night, 750
put on your fiercest faces, scowling with all three.*

    For you I have loosened my hair and bared my foot
to sway as my people do through the secret parts of the wood.
I have called down gushing water from dry clouds,
driven the ocean to its bed; the swelling tides,
defeated, have withdrawn inside the sea.
I have confounded the law of the sky: the world has seen
both sun and stars together, and you, Bears, have touched
the forbidden sea. I have bent the course of the seasons,
the summery earth has shuddered at my spell, 760
Ceres has been compelled to see harvest in winter.
Phasis' wild waters turn to their source again,
and Hister, with its many mouths, restrains
its waters, sullen in all their separate banks.
The waves have roared, the frenzied sea rose high
without the sound of wind. The home of the ancient wood
has lost its shadows when it heard my voice.
Phoebus, abandoning day, has stopped in the middle sky,
the Hyades* are shaken by my spells and totter.
Now, Diana,* is the time to come to your own rites. 770

    For you I weave these wreaths with bloody hand,
wreaths bound up with serpents nine,

    To you I give these limbs which rebel Typhon* bore,
who shook the realms of Jove.

    Here is the blood of that treacherous ferryman,
which dying Nessus* gave.

    Here is the ash from the fading pyre of Oeta,*
which drank the poison of Hercules.

    Here you see the torch of a good sister, a wicked mother,
Althaea* the avenger. 780

    These are the feathers left in a far remote cave
by the Harpy, fleeing Zetes.*

    Add to these the wings of a wounded Stymphalian bird,*
struck by Lernaean arrows.

    Altars, you crackle: I see my tripods tremble
as the goddess gives consent.
I can see Hecate's swift chariot in the sky,

not that which she drives when her face shines full,
all through the night,
but the one that she rides with a mournful expression,          790
troubled by threats from Thessalian witches,*
picking her way through the sky with a tighter rein.
With just that pallid face, pour grim light out through the air,
frighten the people with a new source of terror,
and let the precious cymbals of bronze* ring out,
to help you, Diana.
For you we offer the holy rite
on the bloody turf,*
for you the torch is seized from the midst of a pyre,
to burn for you with fires in the night-time,                   800
for you I toss my head and twist my neck
and chant my spells,
for you I have tied up my flowing hair
in a headband like corpses wear,*
for you I shake the gloomy branch from the waters of Styx.
For you, bare-breasted, like a Maenad,*
I slash my arms with a holy knife.
My own blood drips on the altar:
hands, get used to unsheathing the blade,
and submit to shed your own dear blood.                         810
I have struck myself! The sacred fluid flows.
But if you do not like the frequent summons
of my prayers, please forgive me.
Hecate, I call so many times
for your arrows
for just one reason, always the same. Jason.
Now anoint Creusa's clothes,
and as soon as she puts them on, let a snaky flame
burn up very marrow of her bones.
Let the fire lie hid in yellow gold,                            820
in darkness. He who robbed heaven for fire,
and paid with ever-growing liver for his theft,
gave me this flame, and taught me how to hide
power by art: Prometheus.* Mulciber* gave
flames hidden in delicate sulphur,
and I got from my cousin Phaethon*

the thunder of living flame.
I have the gifts of the middle of Chimaera,*
I have the flames stolen from the scorched throats
of the bulls,*                                                                                    830
which mixed with the gall of Medusa,*
I have ordered to create a secret venom.
    Hecate, whip up my poisons,
and keep secret the seeds of flame in my gifts:
may they deceive the eyes, submit to touch,
but may the heat swim to the heart and veins,
make melt the limbs and smoke the bones
and may that newly wedded bride outdo her marriage torch
with her own smoking hair.
    My prayers succeed: she barks three times,                    840
bold Hecate, and shoots
sacred flames from her melancholy torch.
    The whole power of my rites has been achieved.
        Call here the children,
who will take my precious gift to the newly wed bride.
    Go, go my children! Though the mother who bore you
        is unlucky,
make peace with your mistress, your stepmother: give her
        these presents
and pray to her all you can. Go, and come quickly back
to your home, and let me enjoy a last embrace with you.
CHORUS  Where is this blood-stained Maenad rushing,
    headlong, seized by barbarian lust?                                   850
What crime does she plot
in her violent fury?
Her face roused up in anger
is glazed, she shakes her head
proudly, wildly;
she sets out to threaten the king.
    Who would believe her an exile?
Her cheeks flame red,
her pallor puts her blush to flight.
She keeps no colour long,                                                        860
her shape is ever-changing.
Here and there she moves her feet

as a tigress, her cubs lost,
scans the groves of the Ganges
on thunderous paws.
Medea cannot understand restraint
for anger, or for love.
Now anger and love have joined
to give her a cause: what will happen?
When will this Colchian monster                          870
leave the lands of Greece
and release from fear
the kingdom and royal family?
Now, Phoebus, speed your chariot,
let your reins lie loose,
may gentle night bury the light,
may Hesperus, night's leader,
drown this fearful day.

## ACT FIVE

MESSENGER   Now all is lost, the whole state of the kingdom is
        fallen:
    daughter and father together lie mixed with ash.          880
CHORUS   What trickery deceived them?
MESSENGER                              The usual one for kings:
    gifts.
CHORUS     What fraud could there be in those?
MESSENGER   I am astounded too, and though I know it happened,
    I find I can scarcely believe it.
CHORUS                              What was the cause of death?
MESSENGER   Devouring flame is raging through the palace,
    obeying some command. Now the whole house has fallen,
    people fear for the city.
CHORUS                     Get water, put out the flames!
MESSENGER   In this disaster, something magical:
    water feeds the flames, the more they fight the fire,
    the higher still it burns. It robs our defences.          890
NURSE   Carry yourself away, fast as you can, from the land
        of Pelops,

Medea, run away: find anywhere else to live.

MEDEA I? Would I run? Would I yield? If I had fled before
I would return for this, to watch a new type of wedding.
Why hesitate, my soul? Follow your lucky strike.
This is a tiny fraction of your triumph.
You are still in love, mad heart, if this is enough:
to see Jason unmarried. Look for new punishment,
unprecedented, and prepare yourself:
let all morality be gone, and exile shame;       900
that vengeance is too light which clean hands can perform.
Spur on your anger, rouse your weary self,
from the depths of your heart draw up your former passions
with even greater violence. Whatever I did before,
name it dutiful love. Come now! I will reveal
how trivial and ordinary they were,
those crimes I did before. With them, my bitterness
was only practising: how could my childish hands
do something truly great? Could the rage of a girl do this?
Now, I am Medea. My nature has grown with my suffering.    910
I am happy that I ripped my brother's head away,
I am glad I sliced his limbs, and glad I stripped my father
of his ancestral treasure,* I am glad I set on the daughters
to murder the old man.* Now, pain, find your new chance.
You bring to every action a hand that knows its way.
Where then, my anger, shall I point you? Fire what weapons
at that traitor? My savage heart has made a plan,
a secret one, stored deep inside, and does not dare
reveal it yet, even to itself. Fool! I went too fast.
I wish my enemy had had some children       920
by that concubine of his.—Whatever was yours by him,
Creusa was its mother. That kind of punishment
is what I want; yes, good. My great heart must do
the final wickedness. Children—once my children—
you must give yourselves as payback for your father's crimes.

     Awful! It hits my heart, my body turns to ice,
my chest is heaving. Anger has departed,
the wife in me is gone, I am all mother again.
Is this me? Could I spill my own children's blood,
flesh of my flesh? No, no, what terrible madness!       930

Let that horrible deed, that dreadful crime, be unthought of,
even by me. Poor things! What crime have they ever done?—
Jason is their father: that is their crime. And worse:
Medea is their mother. Let them die; they are not mine.
Let them die; they are mine. They did nothing wrong, they
        are blameless,
they are innocent: I admit it. So was my brother.
Why, my soul, do you waver? Why are my cheeks blotched
        with tears,
why am I led in two directions, now by anger,
now by love? My double inclination tears me apart.
As when the wild winds make their brutal wars                    940
and on both sides the seas lift up discordant waves,
and the unstable water boils: even so my heart
tosses and churns: love is chased out by rage
and rage by love. Resentment, yield to love.

    Here to me, darling children, only comfort
for this troubled house, bring yourselves here, embrace me,
fold yourselves in my arms. Let your father have you safe,
as long as your mother has you too.—But I must go in exile.
Any minute, they will be ripped from my arms,
weeping and wailing. Let their father lose their kisses,           950
their mother has already lost them. Again, my anger grows,
my hatred boils. My ancient Fury seeks
my reluctant hands again—anger, I follow your lead.
I wish as many children as proud Niobe* bore
had come from my womb, I wish I had
twice-seven sons! I was infertile for revenge:
but my two are just enough to pay for brother and father.
Look! What are they doing, this violent crowd of Furies?
Whom are they seeking, at whom are they aiming those
        flaming blows,
at whom does the hellish army aim its bloody torches?            960
The great snake hisses and twists as the whip comes down.
Whom is the head of the Furies seeking, with her
        menacing brand,
Megaera? Whose shade comes half-invisible, his limbs
scattered apart? It is my brother, he wants revenge.
We will pay it: we will all pay. Fix deep your torch in my eyes,

ravage me, burn me up, see, my whole breast is open for
    the Furies.
    Leave me, my brother, and you avenging goddesses,
and order your ghosts to go back safe to the depths of Hell.
Leave me to myself and use this hand, my brother,
which has drawn the sword: we appease your spirit now,    970
with this sacrificial victim.—What was that sudden noise?
They are taking up weapons against me, they want to kill me.
I will climb up to the topmost roof of our house
though the killing is unfinished. All of you, come with me.
And I myself will carry away with me your body.
Now do it, heart: you must not waste your courage
in secret: prove to the people the things you can do.

JASON  If any man is loyal, and mourns the princes' death,
    run, gather here, let us arrest that wicked woman
    who did the dreadful crime. Come, my brave band of warriors,    980
    bring here your weapons, push her from the top of the house.

MEDEA  Now, now I have regained my throne, my brother,
    and my father.
    The Colchians keep the treasure of the Golden Ram.
    My kingdom comes back to me, my stolen virginity returns.
    O gods, you favour me at last, O happy day,
    O wedding day! Now leave, the crime is complete:
    I am not yet revenged. Go on, while you are at it:
    Why do you hesitate now, my soul? Why are you doubtful?
    Does your powerful anger now subside? I am sorry for what
        I have done,
    I am ashamed. What, wretch, have you done? Wretch?
        Even if I regret it,    990
    I have done it. Great pleasure steals over me against my will,
    and see! now it grows. This was all I was missing,
    that Jason should be watching. I think I have so far done nothing:
    crimes committed without him were wasted.

JASON  Look, she is hovering on the outermost part of the roof.
    Somebody, bring fire, and burn her up, let her fall
    consumed by her own flames.

MEDEA                 Heap up a funeral pyre
    for your own sons, Jason, and strew the burial mound.
    your wife and father-in-law now have their proper rites:

I have buried them. This son has already met his fate;          1000
this one will die the same, but you will watch.

JASON  By all the gods, by the exile we shared,
and by our marriage bed, which I did not betray,
now spare this child. If wrong was done, I did it.
I give myself to death: slaughter this guilty man.

MEDEA  I will drive my sword into that very spot which hurts
      you most.
Now, proud man, go off and marry virgins.
Leave mothers alone.

JASON              One boy is enough for revenge.

MEDEA  If my hand had been able to find satisfaction in just one
      murder,
I should have done none. Although I shall kill two,          1010
the number is too small to satisfy my pain.
If my womb even now contains any pledge of our love,
    I, the mother,
will scrape my insides with my sword, I will bring it out
      with the blade.

JASON  So go on with the crime you began, I will beg you no longer.
But at least grant respite for my sufferings.

MEDEA  O bitter heart, enjoy slow crime, do not hurry:
this is my day: I am using the time I was given.

JASON  Hell-cat, kill me too!

MEDEA              You ask me for pity?—
Good, it is done. Rage, I had no more
to sacrifice for you. Now wipe your swollen eyes          1020
ungrateful Jason. Do you not know your wife?
This is the way I always leave a country. The way in the
      sky lies clear.
Twin serpents lower their head, their scaly necks
accept the yoke. Now, Daddy, take your children back.
But I will fly amid the winds on my chariot with wings.

JASON  Go, travel on up high through the deep expanse of
      the heavens,
prove that there are no gods wherever you go.

# TROJAN WOMEN

*The action is set in the city of Troy, in the aftermath of the ten-year war. The Greeks—led by Ulysses and Agamemnon—have used the trick of the wooden horse to break the siege, invade the city, and defeat the inhabitants. The wealth of Troy is looted; the Trojan men are dead, including the great hero Hector, killed by Achilles; the Trojan women are raped and enslaved, and will be taken home as servants and concubines by the various Greek soldiers. But before the Greek fleet can set sail, fate has decreed that two Trojan children must be killed: Astyanax, son of Hector and Andromache, must be thrown from the city walls; and Polyxena, daughter of Hecuba and Priam, the king and queen of Troy, must be given in 'marriage' to the dead Achilles, and then slaughtered. Seneca's play plots the fulfilment of these terrible predictions.*

# DRAMATIS PERSONAE

HECUBA, Queen of Troy
TALTHYBIUS, Greek herald
PYRRHUS, son of Achilles
AGAMEMNON, Greek leader
CALCHAS, Greek prophet
ANDROMACHE, wife of Hector
OLD MAN
ASTYANAX, Andromache's son
ULYSSES
HELEN
MESSENGER
CHORUS
[POLYXENA: silent part]

# ACT ONE

HECUBA  Do you believe in power? Do you rule a palace,
and are you not afraid of the fickle gods?
Are you naive enough to trust in happiness?
Then look at me, and at this city, Troy. Fortune
has never given greater proof that those who stand
proud, have no sure footing. The pillar of mighty Asia,
the glorious work of the gods, has toppled and lies on the ground.
Men came long ways to fight for Troy: from where they drink
the freezing river Tanais, which spreads to seven mouths;
and men who feel the day's first newborn light,                    10
mingling the warm Tigris with the scarlet sea,
and even the Amazons came, neighbours to Scythia,
who gallop down the shore in hordes of virgin girls.
But Troy has been cut down by the sword. Pergamum*
    crushes itself.
Look! Those beautiful high walls now lie in a heap.
Our homes are burnt. Flames circle round the palace,
thick smoke engulfs the house of our forefathers.
But the winners want their booty; fire cannot stop them.
Burning Troy is torn apart: we cannot see the sky
for the waves of smoke. As if under a dense cloud            20
this black day is dirty with the ash of Troy.
We lost, but they are hungry still, and eye
our stubborn city, slow to fall. Now at last those brutes
forgive us for the last ten years. Even they feel horror
at this ravaged city, and though they see Troy conquered
they cannot yet believe the victory possible. Looters are stealing
the treasures of Troy. The thousand ships cannot hold the plunder.
I call as witnesses my enemies—the gods,
and the ashes of my homeland, and my lord the king of Phrygia,*
buried beneath your kingdom, covered by your city,            30
and you, the hero whose death marked Troy's fall,*
and you great flocks of my dead children,
smaller ghosts: all this disaster,
all that from her crazy mouth Cassandra*

predicted would go wrong—god banned belief—
I, Hecuba, foresaw when I was pregnant, and I spoke my fear,
before Cassandra I was the first to prophesy in vain.*
It was not the cunning Ithacan hero and his friend*
whose night raid set you alight. Nor was it Sinon's lies:*
this fire is mine. O Troy, my marriage torch burnt you.                    40
But why are you weeeping for the ruins of a city destroyed?
Remember, poor old woman—ancient but alive—
more recent causes of grief: Troy's fall is old news.
I have seen a horror, the killing of a king,*
and an even greater sin, they killed him at the altars.
Clad in full armour, savage Pyrrhus, with left hand
twisted the king's hair, pulling back his head,
and plunged his dreadful sword deep in the wound.
The king accepted the hard thrust with joy.
The blade came out of the old man's throat still dry.                      50
Who would not soften and turn from cruel slaughter,
knowing the man was at the final turn of life,
the gods above were witness to the crime, the place was once
the fallen city's sanctum? Now that father of so many kings,
Priam has no tomb: deprived of a funeral pyre
while Troy is burning. But still the gods are not content.
Look! They are picking lots for Priam's daughters and son's wives.
I too will follow. See me. I am nothing but a prize of war.
This man lays claim to Hector's marriage bed,
another chooses Helenus' wife, another Antenor's.                          60
And there is somebody,* Cassandra, who wants you.
I am the prize they fear:* only I can frighten the Greeks.
Where are your tears? Are they stopping? My people, all you
        slave-women,
beat your breasts with your hands, give shrieks and wails,
a funeral for Troy. At last, let Ida ring
with tears, that place of death, home of that terrible judge.*
CHORUS  You tell us to weep. We know well how to do it.
We have been practising.
We have been in mourning for years,
ever since our Phrygian prince visited                                      70
Spartan Amyclae,* and the pine tree
holy to Cybele, cut through the ocean.

Ten times Mount Ida grew white with snow,
ten times she was stripped for our pyres,
ten crops have been cut down on the fields of Troy
by the mower's trembling hand,
while every day brings tears
serving up new reasons to cry.
Come, time to lament.
Unhappy Queen, lift up your hand.                        80
We are just ordinary girls. We will follow our queen.
When it comes to grief, we know all about it.

HECUBA  I trust you, friends who shared my downfall.
Let your hair fall free.
Let it flow sadly down your backs
dirty with the tepid dust of Troy.
Fill your hands:
this at least we can take away from our city.
All of you, stretch out your arms, and be prepared:
let down your dresses, hitch up the fabric,               90
let your bodies be naked to the belly.
What wedding can you wait for, that you bother to cover
      your breasts,
such self-respecting slaves?
Let loose your dresses, kirtle them with shawls,
set free your frenzied hands to beat and beat your breasts:
this is the perfect way for you to look. Perfect.
Now I recognize a Trojan company.
Now let the old laments return again.
Outdo the way we used to weep.
We weep for Hector.                                     100

CHORUS  We have all let loose our hair, already torn from
      so much dying.
Our hair is down, untied and free,
hot ash is sprinkled on our faces.
Our dresses fall down from our naked shoulders
bunched up to cover our thighs.
Now our naked breasts demand a beating.
Now is the time. Agony, come out in full force.
Let the beaches of Troy ring with our cries,
and let Echo, who lives in the cavernous mountains,

give more than her usual short reply,                    110
may she echo all Troy's cries of pain;
let all the ocean hear it, all the sky.
Hands, go wild:
beat my breasts as hard as you can.
The usual noise is not enough for me.
We weep for Hector.

HECUBA  My hand beats my arms for you,
for you it beats my back, already bloody,
for you my hands attack my head,
for you your mother's hands have harmed         120
your mother's breasts.
I hurt myself when you died: let the scars from those wounds
burst open and flow in a stream of plentiful blood.
You were our country's pillar, you delayed our destiny,
you were safety to the Trojans when they tired,
you were our wall, our strong support, whose back
lifted the city up for ten long years.
Troy fell when you did: Hector's day of death
was also his city's end.
Now change your lamentation.                             130
Shed your tears for Priam.
Hector has enough.

CHORUS  King of Phrygia, let us give you tears:
accept our weeping, old man, twice defeated.*
Troy's sufferings in your reign were never single.
Twice Trojan walls were battered by Greek arms,
twice the bow of Hercules* was turned on Troy.
After Hecuba's royal children died, you last of all,
their father finished the line of death. You lie on Trojan sand,
a sacrifice slaughtered to great Jupiter,                140
a headless corpse.

HECUBA  Now turn your tears to someone else.
The death of my Priam is not so sad,
Trojan women.
Say it, all of you: 'Priam was lucky.'
He went down free to the land of the dead,
he will never have to carry the Greek yoke on his neck in defeat.
He does not have to look at the sons of Atreus,

or see that trickster, Ulysses.

He is not walking as a prize in an Argive triumph,          150
his neck bowed down with trophies.

His hands, accustomed to the sceptre, are not bound
behind his back, nor will he be weighed down
with golden chains, to follow Agamemnon's chariot,
a spectacle for wide Mycenae.

CHORUS  Lucky Priam, we all agree.

When he died he took his kingdom with him.
Now he wanders safely in the shadows
of the Elysian fields, and lucky man, he looks
for Hector among the spirits of the good.          160
Lucky Priam. This is happiness:
to die in war and take away, with loss of self,
all other losses.


# ACT TWO

TALTHYBIUS  What a long delay! The Greeks are always stuck
          in a harbour,*
whether they want to go to war or go back home.

CHORUS  Tell us what is keeping the Greek fleet.

Explain what god bars the way.

TALTHYBIUS  My heart is frightened. A terrible trembling
          shakes my body.

I have seen horrors, incredible horrors, with my own eyes.

Dawn was touching the mountain tops, and day had
          conquered night,          170
when all of a sudden a bellowing roar came up from the darkness
as the earth groaned, collapsed, and gathered up all her folds.

The trees swayed their heads, the forest and sacred grove
thundered with a mighty crash all over.

An avalanche of rocks poured down Mount Ida.

Earth was not the only one to shake: even the sea
felt that its own Achilles* was at hand, the waves lay prostrate.

Then the valleys split, opening vast chasms,
the gaping of Hell gave a path to the upper world
through the broken earth. The mound of the dead was raised.          180

Out came the giant ghost of the lord of Thessaly,*
strong as when he was in training, Troy, for fighting you,
when he beat Thrace in battle, or as when
he overpowered Neptune's shining, white-haired son.*
Or when, raging with battle-lust on the front lines
he packed the rivers with corpses, and Xanthus* flowed
slow and meandering, with blood for water, blocked.
Or when he stood victorious, proud in his chariot:
holding the reins he dragged behind him Hector*—and Troy.
His angry cry filled the whole shore:                          190
'Come, come, you idlers! Get me the prizes
I earned by the work of my hands. Let loose your useless ships,
go sail my seas. Greece already paid dear
for the anger of Achilles, and will pay even more.
Let Polyxena be married to my ashes,
with Pyrrhus' hand to slaughter her, and let my tomb be wet.'
Then he sent day away, brought back deep night,
and he returned to Hell. Sinking, he closed up
the mighty chasm; earth was whole again. Still lay the sea
and calm, the wind abandoned all its threats,                  200
the peaceful ocean burbles with a gentle wave,
while a merman chorus sang a wedding song.

PYRRHUS  You merrily launched your sails to go home on the sea,
and you forgot Achilles. It was his hand alone
that made Troy fall. Once he was gone, Troy paused:
standing only while she wondered where to fall.
Even if you eagerly gave him what he asks,
it is too late. All the other leaders have already
taken prizes. What lesser reward can be given
for such a hero? Did he not deserve much,                      210
who, when he was ordered to avoid the war,* grow old
sitting out his long life, and to outdo
the years of Nestor,* stripped off his disguise,
and bared his mother's tricks, and proved himself a man by arms.
Impulsive Telephus* refused to grant
a way through his fierce and unfriendly kingdom.
This king's blood was the first to wet his novice hand,
this king who knew Achilles as harsh and gentle both.
Thebes fell and Etion,* conquered, saw

his city captured. Likewise little Lyrnesos,                       220
set on its mountain tops, was overthrown.
The homes of captured Briseis and Chryseis,*
over whom kings once fought, now lie in ruins.
and famous Tenedos, and fertile Scyros,
whose rich pasture feeds the Thracian herds,
and Lesbos, cutting through the Aegean Sea,
and Cilla,* loved by Phoebus. What of the other lands
which Caycus* washes, bringing springtime floods?
So much genocide and so much fear,
so many cities sacked, as by a tornado,                            230
would be, for anyone else, the utmost triumph.
For Achilles it was normal. That was how my father was,
he waged enormous wars just as a warm-up.
If I skip his other achievements, would not Hector
have been enough? My father won Troy,
you others just demolished it. I am happy to follow
my great father's glorious honors and his famous deeds.
Hector lay dead before his father's eyes,
Memnon* before his uncle's—grieving for him, his mother
Dawn made sunrise sad, because her face was grey.          240
Achilles was the victor but he shuddered at the lesson:
even the sons of goddesses* can die.
Then he killed the savage Amazon,* the last fear of all.
Achilles, if you judge his merits fairly, has deserved
any girl he wants, even from Mycenae or Argos.
Are you still hesitating? Do you disapprove of our customs,
all of a sudden, and think it barbaric to slaughter
Priam's daughter to the son of Peleus? But you had a daughter,*
and you slaughtered her for Helen. I am asking for the
     usual thing.
AGAMEMNON Lack of self-discipline is a young man's fault.     250
Other boys are seized by their own hot adolescence:
Pyrrhus, by his father's. In the old days, I was tolerant
to proud Achilles, with his temper and his threats.
The more power you have, the more patience you need.
Why soak the glorious tomb of a noble leader
with shocking bloodshed? First learn the crucial lesson:
there is an etiquette to victory, a limit to defeat.

Those who abuse their power never stay powerful long.
Moderate governments survive. The higher Fortune
has raised aloft the works of human hands,                    260
so much the more the wise man, feeling lucky, checks himself.
He knows how many ways things can go wrong, and fears
gods when they act too kindly. Victory itself
taught me how fast you can lose everything. Does Troy
make us proud or savage? No. We Greeks stand at the height
from which Troy fell. I admit, sometimes I was
tyrannical, too proud, out of control.
My pride is humbled by the very thing
which would have puffed up others: Fortune's smile.
Priam, you make me proud, but also frightened.              270
Can I believe that royal power is anything
but an empty, gilded name, hair fettered with false beauty?
A sudden mishap may take all away—
maybe it will not even take ten years, or a thousand ships.
Fortune is not so slow to pounce on everyone.
Listen, I will admit—forgive me, Argos—
I wanted the Trojans conquered, beaten, crushed.
I did not want the city sacked. I would have stopped it.
But there are things no harness can restrain:
anger, a burning enemy, and victory                         280
let loose upon the night. Brutality, and crimes
against humanity, were caused by bitterness
and darkness, which provokes our wildest rage,
and by the luck of the sword: when blood once wets the blade
it goes crazy craving more. Whatever survives
from ruined Troy, let it be. We have taken enough revenge,
and more than enough. Should a virgin princess die,
a gift to a tomb, and her blood wet the ashes,
should this foul murder be called 'marriage'? No.
I will not allow it. The faults of all my men return to me.     290
Allowing a crime you could stop is instigation.
PYRRHUS  So will the dead Achilles get no prize?
AGAMEMNON  He will, and everyone will sing his praises,
and countries yet unknown will learn his glorious name.
But if his ashes take delight in streams of blood,
then chop the necks of good plump Trojan cattle:

let blood be shed for which no mother weeps.
What is this custom of yours? When was a human life
offered as payment for a human ghost? Protect your father
from hatred. The ritual that you want will damn him.            300
PYRRHUS  You are so full of yourself. When things go well
you get all high and mighty, and when panic comes
you lord it over kings. Is your heart on fire,
have you suddenly fallen in love with some new flame?
Are you, yet again, the only one of us to get a prize?
With this right hand of mine, I will give Achilles a victim.
If you refuse to give her, keep her back,
I will offer a better victim—a match for Pyrrhus.
I am a prince. Too long my hand has rested
from killing kings. Priam needs a partner.                     310
AGAMEMNON                             I do not deny
that this is the greatest glory of Pyrrhus in war,
that Priam lies hacked down by a cruel sword,
a father begging for help.
PYRRHUS                    I realized, to my father,
all enemies begged mercy. But Priam came
to ask in person. You, overwhelmed with fear,
were not brave enough to ask. You made your request
via Ajax and Ulysses.* You skulked, you avoided conflict.
AGAMEMNON  So presumably it was not fear that made
your father opt out of war, forget his weapons.
When Greeks were getting killed and ships were burning,       320
he sat there picking out pretty tunes on his lute.
PYRRHUS  At that time mighty Hector had contempt for you,
but feared Achilles' songs. In the midst of such great terror,
deep peace lay on the ships of Thessaly.
AGAMEMNON  Yes. And among those same Thessalian ships,
deep peace came back again for Hector's father.
PYRRHUS  It is the mark of a high king to grant life to a king.
AGAMEMNON  Why then did your hands tear life from a king?
PYRRHUS  Mercy often means giving death, not life.
AGAMEMNON  Are you being merciful, in asking for the girl
        to be sacrificed?                                      330
PYRRHUS  It is too late for you to say that killing girls is wrong.*
AGAMEMNON  A king should put his country before his children.

PYRRHUS  No law protects prisoners of war. Punishing them is
     legal.*
AGAMEMNON  Conscience prevents the crimes that law allows.
PYRRHUS  Winners in war can do whatever they like.
AGAMEMNON  The man who may do most should be the most
     restrained.
PYRRHUS  You dare to boast of that to men who have endured
     ten years of tyranny—till Pyrrhus set them free?
AGAMEMNON  Typical Scyros arrogance!*
PYRRHUS                                   Brothers are brotherly
     there.*
AGAMEMNON  A remote little island—
PYRRHUS                                   Washed by my cousin,      340
     the sea.*
     I know the famous family of Atreus and Thyestes.
AGAMEMNON  You are the product of a virgin's secret rape.*
     When Achilles fathered you, he was not yet a man.
PYRRHUS  I am the son of that Achilles whose inheritance
     spread out through all the world of heavenly gods:
     he got the sea from Thetis, Hell from Aeacus, sky from Jove.*
AGAMEMNON  Of that Achilles now shot dead by Paris.
PYRRHUS  Of that Achilles whom gods feared to fight.*
AGAMEMNON  I could shut you up and curb your insolence
     with torture. But my sword understands                        350
     how to show mercy, even to captives. Instead, come, Calchas,
     prophet of the gods. If the Fates demand, I will pay.
          You released the chains that tied up our Greek fleet,
     and ended the wait for war; your art opened up the sky,
     you read the signs of fate in the hidden entrails,
     in the thunder, in the star which trails
     its path with a long flame; your words have always cost
     a heavy price for me.* Calchas, tell us
     what god demands, and guide us with advice.
CALCHAS  Fates grant the Greeks a way home, at the usual price:    360
     the death of a girl, to be slaughtered at the Thessalian
          leader's tomb.
     But let her wear the clothes girls wear for getting married
     in Thessaly, Ionia, or Mycenae.
     Let Pyrrhus give a new wife to his father.

That is the proper offering. But this is not the only
cause of delay to our fleet: more blood is needed,
bluer blood than yours, poor Polyxena.
The fates demand the boy. Let him fall from the highest tower:
Hector's son, Priam's grandson. Let him die.
Then let the thousand sails of our fleet fill up the ocean.          370
CHORUS  Is it true, or a myth to deceive the fearful,
    that spirits live on after bodies are buried,
    when the wife has laid her hand on the dead man's eyes,
    and his last day has blocked out the sun
    and the mournful urn contains his ashes?
    Is it pointless to give our souls to death,
    since we, poor things, still have to keep on living?
    Or do we totally die, and does no part of us
    remain, when with a fleeting gasp
    our spirit mixes with the clouds and turns to air,          380
    as the torch beneath the pyre ignites the naked flesh?
    In the lands the rising sun knows well, and the lands of the sunset,
    and places where the ocean with its dark blue waves
    ebbs twice a day, and washes with the tide,
    time will swoop like Pegasus, take everything away.
    As the Zodiac goes rushing, flying through the sky,
    fast as the lord of the stars,* making the seasons turn,
    as swift as Hecate,* queen of the moon, when she hastens
    whirling around on her slanting path,
    so all of us hurry to our appointed ends.          390
    The person who has touched the lake by which gods swear
        their oaths*
    is nowhere any more. As smoke from a hot fire
    looks dirty for a minute and then fades,
    as heavy clouds which we have glimpsed just now
    suddenly disappear with a puff of the cold North Wind,
    so flows away this breath which is our master.
    After death is nothing. Even death itself
    is nothing: just the finishing-line in the race.
    If you hunger for life, abandon hope. If you worry, let go fear.
    Hungry time and emptiness devour us.          400
    Death is a single whole: it kills our body
    and does not spare the soul. The realm of Taenarus,*

kingdom of cruel Hades, and the guard-dog
Cerberus, fierce defender of the gate,
are fictions, tall tales, empty fairy stories,
myths, as close to truth as a bad dream.
Do you want to know where you will be after death?
Where the unborn are.


# ACT THREE

ANDROMACHE  Why, sad Trojan chorus, do you tear your hair
and beat your breasts and wet your cheeks with tears?    410
Our sorrows are slight if we can weep for them.
For you, the fall of Troy only just happened;
I felt it long ago, when that brute whipped his horses
to drag away my body,* and with a groan
Achilles' wheels vibrated with the weight of Hector.
Since then I have been a ruin, and whatever happens,
I am numb to suffering, I bear it without feeling.
I would already have escaped the Greeks and joined my husband,
but this boy holds me here. He tames my spirit,
keeping me from death. He forces me still to pray,    420
even now, to the gods. He adds time to my pain.
He has taken from me sorrow's greatest prize:
fear of nothing. All chance of happiness
is gone, but horrors can still find a way.
Fear is worst of all when you have lost all hope.
OLD MAN  What are you suddenly so frightened of?
ANDROMACHE  From a bad situation a worse trouble has come:
the fate of falling Troy has not yet ended.
OLD MAN  What new disasters can god find to make?
ANDROMACHE  The fastenings of deepest Styx and its dark lairs    430
are loose; our buried enemies are coming out of Hell—
just in case we broken ones should feel safe for a moment.
Is it only Greeks who can find a way back up?
No, death is universal: the same terror
disturbs and shakes all Phrygia. But I have my own
personal horror that haunts my mind, my private nightmare.
OLD MAN  What were your dreams? You can tell me all your fears.

ANDROMACHE  The gentle night had almost passed two watches
   and the seven stars had almost turned the Plough.*
   I was troubled, could not rest, but finally peace came,                    440
   and a short sleep crept over my tired face—
   if the numbness of a panicked mind is sleep.
   When suddenly, before my eyes, stood Hector—
   not as he was when he rushed to storm the Argives,
   igniting those Greek ships* with Trojan torches,
   nor as when he was wild with battle-lust against them,
   seizing from the fake Achilles the real hero's armour.*
   He did not have that radiant face of fire;
   he looked downcast and tired, heavy with tears,
   like me, and matted hair covered his face.                                 450
   But how glad I was to see him! Then he shook his head
   and said: 'Wake up, and seize hold of our son,
   my loyal wife. Hide him; that is our only hope.
   Do not cry. Are you sad because Troy has fallen?
   If only the whole city had been flattened.* Hurry, take away
   our tiny little seedling, the last left of our house.'
   Cold shudders and fear shook me awake,
   and I was terrified as I looked all around:
   desperately seeking Hector, I forgot our child.
   The unreal shade slipped from my outstretched arms,
         he was gone.                                                         460
      O child, the certain son of a great father,
   only hope for the Trojans, and for our poor family.
   You are descended from an all-too-famous bloodline:
   you look too much like your father. My dear Hector
   had this same face. This was how he walked
   and how he held himself. His hands were strong,
   like yours; like you, he was tall; like you, he tossed his head
   shaking the scattered hair, his eyebrows frowning sternly.
   Son, you were born too late for the Trojans, too soon
         for your mother.
   Will that time ever come, the longed-for happy day                        470
   when you will be the defender and avenger of Trojan soil,
   when you will raise up fallen Pergamum, bring home
   our exiled citizens, and restore their rightful names
   to Troy and the Trojan people? But I remember my fate

too well to pray for much. This is all a prisoner asks:
let us live. Ah, if only! What place can be safe enough
for my fear to trust, where on earth can I hide you?
Our rich and powerful citadel, its walls the work of gods,
famed and envied throughout all the world,
is now deep dust. Fire has destroyed it all;                        480
from such an enormous city there is not even room
to hide a child. What secret place can I choose?
There is my darling husband's tomb, a holy place;
the enemy respect it. Priam spent great sums
to build a huge construction—in his grief, the king
spared no expense. Good idea: I will give the boy to his father.
Cold sweat drips down my body, I feel cold.
I shudder at the omens of this place of death.

OLD MAN  In safety you have choices; in danger, take your chances.

ANDROMACHE  But he cannot hide, without great fear            490
   of treachery.

OLD MAN       So let there be no witness.

ANDROMACHE  And if they come to find him?

OLD MAN                                        He died when the
      city fell.
   Many have been kept from death only by this:
   belief in their death.

ANDROMACHE            There is almost no hope.
   A great weight crushes him: his noble birth.
   What good is it to hide him if he gets taken after?

OLD MAN  Conquerors are fiercest in the first attack.

ANDROMACHE  What place is inaccessible enough
   to hide you safely? Who will help us in our terror?
   Who can shield us? Even now, Hector, watch us,          500
   protect your family as always. Help my loyal theft;
   taking him to your ashes, let him live.
   Son, go up to the tomb. Why are you pulling back?
   You reject hiding as cowardly? I recognize your breeding;
   you are ashamed to show fear. But now let go of your courage,
   abandon your old pride and take what fortune gives.
   Look at us, all the multitude surviving from the war:
   a tomb, a boy, a female prisoner. We have to yield to disaster.
   Come now, be bold enough to enter the sacred tomb

of your dead and buried father. If fate helps those in trouble,  510
you are safe; if fate refuses to let you live,
you have a tomb.
OLD MAN         He is inside, the tomb's gate covers him;
Do not let your fear bring him back out to the open;
move back here and keep yourself away.
ANDROMACHE  The nearer the danger, the lighter the fear.
But yes, if you wish, we can go somewhere else.
OLD MAN  Hush for a moment, quiet down your tears;
that damnable Greek chieftain, Ulysses, is coming.
ANDROMACHE  Crack open, Earth! And, husband, tear the land,
ripping it down to the lowest cavern, and bury                520
in the deepest gulf of Styx, the dear one I laid down.*
Ulysses is here. His demeanour and face
are hard to read. He is weaving some cunning plan in his mind.
ULYSSES  I represent a cruel lot. I ask this first:
that though the words are spoken by my mouth,
you must not think them mine. It is the voice
of all Greeks and their leaders, kept from their long-lost homes,
by Hector's son. The Fates demand to take him.
Worry and mistrust in an unreliable peace
will always trouble the Greeks, fear at our backs will always  530
force us to look back, never let us drop our swords,
while your son heartens the defeated Trojans,
your child, Andromache. So says the prophet Calchas.
And even if Calchas had not said it, even so,
Hector used to say the same. I fear even his offspring.
Seeds of good stock grow up to match their birth.
Just as a young calf, in the midst of a mighty herd,
whose first horns have not even pierced his skin,
suddenly lifts his head and neck up high
the leader of his father's folk, lord of the flock;               540
so the slender sapling from a tree axed down,
in a little while grows up as big as her mother,
casting shadows on the ground and leaves to touch the sky;
so the ashes left neglected from a mighty fire
grow strong again. Yes, sorrow is no judge
of circumstance. But if you think things over carefully,
you will forgive us: after ten winters, ten harvests,

our soldiers have grown old, fearful of war,
frightened that slaughter will begin again, and Troy
will never lie down dead. This is our big worry:                    550
Hector come again. So free us Greeks from fear.
This is the only thing that keeps the ships tied up,
this is what stops the fleet. And do not think it cruel
that I, ordered by lot, demand the son of Hector.
I would have sought Orestes.* Bear it—Agamemnon did.*

ANDROMACHE  If only, child, you were in your mother's arms,
if only I knew what you are going through,
separated from me, or even where you are.
If enemy arrows shot my ribcage full of holes,
if my hands were bound by biting chains, if cruel fire           560
engulfed my body, I would never cease
to be a mother and to love my child. Son,
where are you? What is your fate? Are you wandering, lost,
over the fields? Or has the enormous fire
that burnt our city, taken you as well? Did the cruel
conqueror play with your blood? Or did a great wild beast
pounce to bite you, and now your bones feed Ida's birds?

ULYSSES  Stop pretending. It is not easy for you
to fool Ulysses. I have beaten tricky mothers before—
even divine ones.* Your schemes are useless: drop them.        570
Where is your son?

ANDROMACHE              Where is Hector? Where are all the Trojans?
Where is Priam? You want one: I want them all.

ULYSSES  If you will not tell me willingly, force will make you.
Stupid to hide what soon you will have to show.

ANDROMACHE  Safe is the woman who can, should, wants to die.

ULYSSES  The approach of death shakes off pomposity.

ANDROMACHE  If you, Ulysses, want to force Andromache by fear,
threaten her with life, for death is my desire.

ULYSSES  Pain will compel you to tell against your will
your secret: whipping, branding, death, and torture.           580
Pain will spit out the truths hidden deep inside your heart.
Generally compulsion can do more than love.

ANDROMACHE  Bring out your fire, your terrible instruments
of wounding and of pain, bring hunger, bitter thirst,
and all types of destruction, clamp the iron

to flesh already burnt, bring dark and dirty dungeons;
all that the angry victor dares to do—from fear.
The heart of a brave mother has no room for fear.
ULYSSES  This parental love, which you stubbornly insist on,
advises Greeks to think about their children.                    590
After so long a war, after ten years,
I would not have such fear of Calchas' warnings
if my fears were for me. You make ready a war for my son.
ANDROMACHE  I have no wish, Ulysses, to give joy to the Greeks.
But I must give it. Sorrow, tell the pains which you kept down.
Be happy, sons of Atreus; and you, as usual,
can take good news to the Greeks. Hector's son is dead.
ULYSSES  What proof can you give the Greeks that this is true?
ANDROMACHE  So may the worst threats of the conquerors
come true, and may I die a timely death,                         600
gently released by fate, and buried in my land,
and let our native earth rest lightly upon Hector:
so, I swear, he is out of the sun. He lies among the dead;
given to the tomb, he has the dues of death.
ULYSSES  Since Hector's seed is gone, fate is fulfilled,
and I will be glad to take a sure peace to the Greeks.
     What are you doing, Ulysses? The Greek women trust you;
but you trust—whom? A mother?—Would a mother lie
about this, unafraid of the bad omen?
Those who have lost all other fear, fear omens.                  610
She pledges her faith by swearing this oath of hers.
If she is lying, what worse can she fear?
Now, my mind, it is time to summon up your cunning;
time for deceit and fraud, time to be all Ulysses:
truth never dies. Check out the mother.
She weeps, cries, wails; but still she keeps on pacing
and strains her ears to hear any voice that comes.
This woman is more terrified than mournful.
Time to be smart.—Normally, people comfort grieving parents;
I give you congratulations for the death of your son,            620
the son who would have been hurled to a cruel, headlong death
from a tower, the last remaining from the fallen walls.
ANDROMACHE  I am fainting, I am shaking, I collapse,
my blood is overcome by ice, it begins to freeze.

ULYSSES  She shivered. This is the subject I must pursue with her.
Fear uncovered the mother. I will redouble her fear.
Go, go, quick! Find the enemy, hidden by the tricks
of his mother, the last blight on the Greek name.
Wherever he is hiding, root him out, into the open.
Well done! Got him. Go on, hurry, drag him…                    630
—Why look round in terror? He is surely dead.

ANDROMACHE  If only I were frightened. Fear has long been normal.
The heart is slow to unlearn what it learnt long ago.

ULYSSES  He owed us a death from the walls, a purification,
advised by the priest—which he missed by dying too soon,
taken by a better destiny. So Calchas says
the ships for sailing home can be cleaned this way:
by scattering Hector's ashes on the sea,
and razing the whole tomb-mound to the ground.
Now, because the child escaped his rightful death,          640
I must lay my hands on the sacred space.

ANDROMACHE  What am I to do? Fear pulls my heart two ways:
my son's life, or my dearest husband's ash.
Which part will win? Witness, you cruel gods
and you, my real god, spirit of my husband:
what I love in my son, Hector, is only you.
Let him live, just to revive your face.—
Will the ash be flung from the tomb and hurled in the sea?
Shall I allow his bones to be drowned in the waves,
scattered upon the deep? Better let our son die.             650
But I am his mother! Can I watch him murdered
so horribly? Can I see him topple over
the high battlements?—I can do it, I will bear it, yes:
just so long as my dead Hector is not tossed about
by the conqueror's hand.—But the boy can still feel pain.
Hector is held safe somewhere by Fate.
Why do you hesitate? Decide which one to save.
Bad wife, is it not obvious? There is your Hector.
No, wrong! Both of them are Hector. This one has feelings;
maybe one day he will take revenge for his dead father.     660
Both of them have to be spared. But what can I do?
Protect, Andromache, the one whom the Greeks fear.

ULYSSES  I will obey the oracle, I will destroy the tomb.

ANDROMACHE  But you sold him to us.*

ULYSSES                                  I will drag down the grave
  from the high mound.

ANDROMACHE            I call the faithful gods
  and trustworthy Achilles: Pyrrhus, now protect
  your father's gift.

ULYSSES            Soon that pile will be spread
  over the entire field.

ANDROMACHE            Till now, Greeks did not dare
  such atrocity. You violated temples to the gods,
  even those that blessed you.* But your blood-lust
        bypassed tombs.                                      670
  With my weak hands I will fight your armoured soldiers,
  rage will give me strength. Like a fierce Amazon
  slaughtering troops of Argives, or a Bacchant
  who rushes through the woods, inspired by god,
  armed only with her thyrsus, gone insane,
  insensibly she wounds and terrifies: I too
  will fall to protect my comrade: the dust of this tomb.

ULYSSES  Are you hesitating, does a woman's wailing
  and useless passion check you? Hurry up,
  carry out your orders.

ANDROMACHE            Me, kill me first with your swords.   680
  They are pushing me aside. Oh, break through the chains of fate,
  Hector, push up the earth. Make Ulysses tame:
  you can do it, even as a ghost.—He is shaking his weapons,
  he is hurling torches! Do you see Hector, Greeks?
  Or am I the only one?

ULYSSES            I will destroy it all.

ANDROMACHE  What are you doing? You will ruin your son and
        your husband,
  mother, in a single disaster.—Perhaps you can win over
  the Greeks with pleas. The vast weight of that tomb
  will instantly crush the boy I hid inside. Poor baby,
  let him die anywhere else—not crushed by his own father,   690
  nor father smothered by son.—I come to kneel and beg you,
  Ulysses. I have never knelt to any man.
  I kneel before your feet. Have mercy on me, please!
  I am a mother, a good person; please be kind,

listen to my prayers. The higher gods have raised you,
the more you should be gentle to the fallen.
A gift to the unlucky is a gift to fate.
So may you see again your holy marriage bed,
so may Laertes still extend his years, until
he sees you back. So may your son greet you,                    700
turned out a better man than all your prayers could hope;
may he outdo his grandfather in years, father in brains.
Have pity on a mother. My child is
my only comfort in disaster.

ULYSSES                    First bring him out. Then ask.

ANDROMACHE  Come out here* from your hiding-place,
sad trick of your poor mother.
Here he is, Ulysses, the terror of a thousand ships.
Hold up your arms, lie down before his feet,
and grovel to your master.
Nothing fortune forces on us in our time of trouble                    710
is real humiliation.
Forget your royal heritage,
the old king's power, which was famed
through all the world. Forget about Hector;
behave like a prisoner, and bend your knees;
if death does not yet feel real to you,
copy your mother's tears.
Troy has already seen, in olden times,
a boy-king weeping: Priam, when he was little,
turned aside the threats of fierce Hercules.*                    720
Hercules was so savage, even wild beasts
cowered at his enormous strength;
he even broke the gateway up from Hell
and made his dark way back;
the tears of a little boy defeated him.
'Take up the reins,' he said, 'be king;
sit high on your father's throne,
take his sceptre but rule in better faith.'
That was how that victor treated prisoners.
Let Hercules teach you to be angry gently.                    730
Or do you only like Hercules' arms?
A suppliant lies at your feet, no less distinguished

than that other one. He begs for his life.
Let fortune take the throne of Troy,
wherever it will.

ULYSSES  Certainly I feel moved by a frightened mother's sorrow,
but more moved by Greek mothers, who will suffer
terribly, if that little boy grows up.

ANDROMACHE  Can this boy raise these ruins, this wreck of a city,
turned to dust? Can these hands build Troy again?          740
If this is all the hope of Troy, there is no hope.
Could anybody fear the Trojans now,
lying in ruin? Can his father inspire him?
His father was dragged in the dirt. Even that father
would have surrendered after Troy's sack: disaster
destroys dignity. If you want revenge—what worse
is left to want?—clamp a servile yoke on his royal neck.
Let the boy be a slave. Can anyone refuse a king this favour?

ULYSSES  It is not I but Calchas who refuses this request.

ANDROMACHE  Schemer, always plotting wicked tricks!          750
You did not kill a single person by brave fighting,
but by your lies and evil cleverness
you killed even Greeks.* Will you put the blame on the priest
and the guiltless gods? This crime comes from you.
You prefer fighting by night;* in the daytime by yourself
at last you are not afraid—to kill a child.

ULYSSES  The courage of Ulysses is well known to Greeks,
and all-too familiar to Trojans. There is no time
to waste on pointless speeches. The fleet is weighing anchor.

ANDROMACHE  Wait, let me have a moment more, to give          760
my son a mother's final care; just one last time
to hold him in my arms, my hungry sorrow's food.

ULYSSES  I wish I could be merciful. I cannot.
But I will give all that I can: a little time.
Fill up your heart with tears; tears lighten grief.

ANDROMACHE  My darling boy, the jewel of a fallen house,
last Trojan death, last terror to the Greeks,
your father's empty hope, madly I prayed for you:
'May you be praised in battle like your father, and achieve
your grandfather's prime.' But the gods refused my prayer.          770
Now you will never stand tall in the royal court, or wield

the Trojan sceptre, never forge laws for your people,
never bring the conquered nations under your yoke.
You will not rout and kill the Greeks, drag Pyrrhus in the dust,
you will not carry child-size weapons in your delicate hands
or boldly hunt wild beasts which scurry everywhere
throughout the forests. Nor, on the proper day,
will you perform the holy rite of Trojan Games,*
the young prince leading the swift band of troops.
Nor, at the altars, running on quick feet                     780
as the curved horn plays its exciting music,
will you honour foreign temples with an ancient dance.*
     O form of death, more terrible than death!
These walls will see something even more sad
than mighty Hector's murder.
ULYSSES                      Mother, stop crying now.
     Great sorrow does not stop of its own accord.
ANDROMACHE Ulysses, I only want a bit more time to weep.
     Let me have these few tears, let me close with my own hands
     these living eyes. Yes, you are small to die
     but you are still a source of fear. Your Troy awaits you.     790
     Go, go, walk free; go see the free Trojans.
ASTYANAX Mother, help me!
ANDROMACHE                     Why do you cling to my breast
     and grab your mother's arms? They cannot help you.
     A baby calf, when it hears the lion's roar
     huddles its trembling body against its mother;
     but that fierce lion hurls the mother away
     seizes the smaller prey in its huge jaws,
     crunches it, carries it off. So will our enemy
     carry you from my arms. Take from me, little one,
     kisses and tears and hair torn out, and full of me     800
     go meet your father. Take him, from your mother,
     a short complaint: 'If ghosts can still have feelings
     for those they cared for once, and love's fire does not die,
     how can you let Andromache become a Greek man's slave,
     cruel Hector? Are you lying there, lazy and idle?
     Achilles has come back.' Now take again my hair,
     take tears, all I have left, after my husband's funeral.
     Take kisses; you can give them to your father.

Leave your mother for her comfort only this:
the cloak that used to touch this tomb of mine,                810
and the ghosts I love. If it still hides any dust,
I will nuzzle it out with my lips.

ULYSSES                               These tears go on forever.
Seize her; she is holding up the Argive fleet.

CHORUS  Where will we poor slave women find to live?
Shady Tempe, mountains of Thessaly,
or Iolchas, mistress of the mighty ocean?
or little Gyrtone, or barren Trice,
or Mothone refreshed with little brooks?
Or a place more fitted to yield soldiers,
Phthia, or stony Trachis, best                                820
breeding ground for a strong herd,
overshadowed by Mount Oeta's woods,
source of that fatal bow, which came to ruin Troy
twice over?*
Sparsely populated Olenos,
Pleuron, enemy to the virgin goddess,
or Troezen, curving on the ocean?
Pelion, proud kingdom of Prothoos,
the third step to heaven? This was the place
where Chiron,* tutor to that boy—already fierce—        830
lay at full stretch in the cave hollowed out from the mountain,
strumming the ringing chords with his pick,
as he sharpened the boy's aggression—already intense—
by singing of war.
Will it be Carystos, home of the coloured marbles,
or Chalcis, where Euripus always rushes
to the shore of the restless sea?
Calydnae, calm whatever the weather,
or Gonoessa, where it is always windy,
or Enispe, shuddering at the North Wind,                 840
or Crete which stretches to a hundred cities?
Peparethos off the coast of Attica,
or Eleusis, proud home of the Mysteries?*
Not Salamis, land of true Ajax,
or Calydon known for its savage boar,
or the countries washed by Titaressos

as its slow waters trickle downwards?
Bessa, Scarphe, ancient Pylos,
Pharis, Jupiter's Pisa, or Elis
with its garlands of victory?                                    850
Let the cruel gusts carry us poor girls
anywhere, let them give us to any old land,
anywhere but the ones that brought destruction
to Troy and to Greece: let it not be Sparta,
let it not be Argos, or fierce Pelops' Mycenae,
little Neritos, littler Zacynthos,
or dangerous Ithaca,* whose hidden rocks deceive.
What fate awaits you, or what master,
Hecuba? Where will he lead you, as a spectacle?
Whose will be the kingdom where you die?                         860


# ACT FOUR

HELEN  Helen calls the banns for weddings fraught with tears,
deadly weddings, full of mourning, slaughter, blood.
I find myself compelled to hurt the Trojans
even after their ruin. My instructions are to report
the false marriage of Pyrrhus, and provide
the Greek clothes and accessories. My cleverness
and tricks will trip up Paris' sister. She will be fooled.
Actually I think it is better for her like this.
The best way to die is without the fear of death.
Why hesitate to do as you were told? The instigator         870
deserves the blame for a crime he forced on me.

   Trojan Princess, a kinder god begins to look at us
in our affliction. He blesses you with a happy wedding.
You could have hoped for no better match, not even
when Troy was safe, or when your father lived.
The greatest hero of the Greeks, whose lands
stretch out enormous over Thessaly,
wants your hand in holy matrimony.
All the naiads of the sea, with their queen Tethys,
and Thetis, calming goddess of the stormy waves,           880
will be your family. Peleus and Nereus

will welcome you as daughter-in-law, the gift of Pyrrhus.
Take off your dirty clothes, put on a party dress,
forget you are a captive. Brush out your tangled hair,
let expert hands arrange it beautifully.
Perhaps this lucky chance will raise you up
to an even higher throne. Many have done well by capture.

ANDROMACHE  This was the only pain we ruined Trojans lacked:
happiness. Smoke pours from flattened Pergamum.
What a time for a wedding! Would anybody dare to refuse?      890
Who would hesitate to get married, if Helen advised it?
You are an abomination, an infection, a pollution
to both our nations. Can you see these leaders' tombs,
and the bones stripped bare that lie all over the fields,
unburied, on the ground? Your wedding scattered them.
The blood of Europe and of Asia flowed for you,
while you were lazily watching your husbands at their duel,
wondering who to pick. Go on, deck out the marriage bed.
Who needs torches, or the traditional wedding brand?
Who needs fire? Troy lights up this new wedding ahead
          of time.                                                        900
Come on, Trojan women, celebrate Pyrrhus' marriage;
do it the right way—with moans and groans of grief.

HELEN  Great misery is irrational, inflexible,
and sometimes hates even the ones who share it.
But still, I can defend my own position
before a hostile judge, since I have suffered more.
Andromache may weep for Hector, Hecuba
for Priam; but my grief is secret, I alone
must weep for Paris. Is it so very hard
to be enslaved? I have borne that burden longer,                910
a captive for ten years. Is Troy sacked, the old gods gone?
Yes, it is hard, to lose your native land,
harder to fear it. At least in your great suffering,
you have each other. Both sides rage against me.
For a long time nobody knew which woman each man
          would choose.
My master dragged me away on the spot, he did not pause
for the drawing of lots. Was I the cause of war,
and of the Trojan massacre? Well, believe it,

if a Spartan ship ever came to invade your seas.
But if the Trojan rowboats stole me as a prize,                    920
and the goddess in her victory gave me to the judge,
then pity Paris. My case is to be heard
before an angry judge: the decision will be made
by Menelaus. Now, Andromache, stop crying
just for a while. Persuade her. I myself can scarcely
hold back my tears.

ANDROMACHE          It must be bad, if even Helen weeps.
But why is she crying? Tell us what tricks or crimes
the Ithacan is weaving. Is the plan to hurl the girl
from the top of Mount Ida, or to drop her from the crag
of the highest citadel? Maybe she is to be tossed              930
into the ocean, over this sheer cliff,
where the city rises over the curving bay?
Tell us what it is your lying face keeps hidden.
Any bad news is better than that Pyrrhus should be family,
son-in-law to Hecuba and Priam. Tell us, spit it out,
what punishment you plan. Spare us this at least:
deception. You see women ready for their deaths.

HELEN  I wish the priest had ordered that I, too,
should break with the sword my wasted time in the light,
or that I should accompany you, killed by the raging         940
hand of Pyrrhus, on Achilles' grave,
poor Polyxena—whom Achilles orders
as his gift, to be slaughtered on his ashes,
so he may be a bridegroom in the Elysian fields.

ANDROMACHE  See! Her great soul is glad to hear of her death.
She wants the fancy royal clothes, and lets
the hand comb through her hair. She used to think
the marriage death; now she thinks death is marriage.
But her poor mother, hearing the news, is stunned;
her mind is overwhelmed by grief, she faints. Get up,      950
poor woman, lighten your heart, make yourself strong;
how slender is the chain her life hangs on.
A tiny thing can make Hecuba happy.
She breathes and lives. Death runs from the wretched first.

HECUBA  Is Achilles still alive to hurt Trojans?
Is he still waging war? How weak Paris was!

Even Achilles' ash and tomb are thirsty for our blood.
Only lately I was surrounded by a happy brood.
I got tired with sharing all those kisses,
a mother to such a big flock. Now she is the only one left,    960
my hope, my friend, my comfort, and my rest,
she is the only child of Hecuba. Only by her
can I be still called 'Mother'. Unlucky life of mine,
slip away now at last, and spare me just this death.
Her face is wet with weeping, and all of a sudden
she burst into tears; her face is defeated.
Daughter, be happy, rejoice. How Cassandra and Andromache
would have wished for this marriage of yours.

ANDROMACHE  It is us, us us, Hecuba, whom you should weep for.
When the fleet is launched we will be scattered,
    all over the world.    970
She will stay covered up in the dear earth of our home.

HELEN  You will envy her even more when you know your future.

ANDROMACHE  Is part of my suffering still unknown to me?

HELEN  They have shaken out the urn and assigned a master
    for each captive.

ANDROMACHE  Who gets me as their concubine? Tell me!
    Who is my master?

HELEN  The boy from Scyros* won you with the first lot.

ANDROMACHE  Cassandra was lucky, her madness—and
    Phoebus, her god—
made her exempt from this lottery.

HELEN                    No, the king of kings* got her.

HECUBA  Did anybody want to have Hecuba for his own?

HELEN  You fell to the Ithacan. He does not want you. You will not
    live long.    980

HECUBA  To give a queen to a king! Whoever supervised
this unfair lottery was stupid, crazy, cruel.
We captives were assigned by an unlucky god.
The judge is a sadist, he stamps on the wretched:
he has no idea how to pick out our masters; barbarian,
he makes unfair decisions in our time of trouble.
Who would make Hector's mother sleep with Achilles' sword?
They give me to Ulysses! Now comes defeat, now comes
captivity, now I am overwhelmed by total ruin.

This master is a greater shame than slavery. Will he          990
who got Achilles' spoils* get Hector's too? That barren island
locked in by brutal waters will not hold my tomb.
Take me, take me, Ulysses. I am ready to follow my master:
my destiny will follow me. There will be no tranquil seas,
the ocean will grow wild with whirling winds. My followers
are war and fire; my sufferings, and Priam's.
Until those troubles come, this is your punishment:
I got your lot, I stole your prize from you.
But now look, here comes Pyrrhus, running fast;
his face is grim. Pyrrhus, why hesitate? Come,          1000
strike at my breast with your sword, and join together
the in-laws of Achilles. Go on! You are used to killing
        old people,
and you like my family's blood.*—Then grab her,
        drag her away,
pollute the gods with murder, even pollute the dead.
I will curse you—but how? I pray that you get
the seas you deserve for this sacrifice; and that
the whole Greek fleet, the thousand ships,
suffer the curse I will inflict upon the boat I ride.

CHORUS  How sweet for those in pain, that others also suffer!
What pleasure is the nations' loud lamenting!          1010
Grief and tears bite more gently
when misery finds company.
Pain is cruel: always, always,
pain seeks many victims,
happy not to be alone.
Nobody resists the painful fate
shared by everyone.
People will not think themselves unhappy, though they are,
if nobody is happy.
Eliminate the rich, and the landed gentry,          1020
with their estates ploughed by a hundred oxen.
Poor people will no longer feel oppressed.
All wretchedness is relative.
    How sweet for someone in the midst of ruin
to look around and see no happy face.
If your boat sets out to sea alone

and you are washed naked into the harbour,
you moan and complain of your fate.
It is easier to bear the storms of fortune
if you see a thousand other ships                        1030
drowned in the waves and the beaches
strewn with wrecked ships, while the violent wind
keeps back the swelling waves of the sea.
Phrixus grieved for the fall of Helle,*
when the ram with the golden fleece, leader of the flock
bore up brother and sister together
on his shining back, and cast him down
into the middle of the sea. They checked their tears,
Pyrrha and her husband,* when they saw
sea and only sea, the only people                        1040
left upon earth of all humanity.
When the fleet sets out from here, it will melt
our friendship, scatter our tears,
when the sailors hear the trumpet's order to set sail,
and winds and oars will speed their way
as they plunge into the ocean and the shore recedes.
What will our feelings be, poor pitiful wretches,
when all the land grows small and the sea grows big,
when even Ida's height is hard to see?
Then a boy and his mother will turn to each other,   1050
pointing to the place where Troy lies fallen,
far in the distance, and say as they point:
'There is Troy, where the smoke creeps high
into the sky in dirty clouds.'
By this signal the Trojans will recognize their home.

# ACT FIVE

MESSENGER  What cruel fate! How harsh, terrible, pitiful!
    The god of war has seen no crime more savage
    in twice-five years of war. In my tears, I hardly know
    whose suffering to begin with: yours, or yours, my lady.
HECUBA  If you weep for anybody's pain, you weep for mine.   1060
    Other people suffer singly; I suffer a mass destruction.

All death is mine. All grief is Hecuba's.

MESSENGER  The girl has been slaughtered, the boy has been
   thrown from the walls.

But both of them bore their deaths with a noble spirit.

ANDROMACHE  Tell us every detail of the double murder,
 all the abominable crime. Agony likes dragging out
 every single wound. Go on, tell us the whole story.

MESSENGER  One tall tower still survives from Troy,
 a haunt of Priam's. There he used to sit,
 to judge the war and rule his regiments,     1070
 from its high battlements. On that very tower
 he comforted his grandson in his arms,
 while Greeks ran terrified from Hector's sword and fire.
 The old man showed the child the father's fights.
 This tower, once renowned, the glory of the wall,
 is now a cruel crag, surrounded on all sides
 by soldiers and their leaders. The whole rabble
 assembled there, abandoning their ships.
 Some went up a distant hill to get a better view,
 others crowded to a high rock, on whose peak   1080
 they stretched up on their tiptoes, trying to see.
 People climbed the trees: pine, laurel, and beech:
 the whole wood quivered with suspended men.
 Some choose the edge of a sheer mountain cliff,
 while others perch on burned-out buildings, others on the rubble
 of the ruined walls, and one man—what an obscenity!—
 sits to watch—barbarian!—on Hector's tomb.

  Through this packed crowd the Ithacan strides,
 dragging along by the hand the little boy,
 grandson of Priam. The boy goes readily    1090
 towards the high walls. When he stood on the top of the tower
 he looked around him with a keen, fierce face,
 no fear in his heart. So the cub of a massive lioness
 though small and delicate, unable yet to bite,
 already growls and makes his threats,
 snapping his milk-teeth, swollen up with pride:
 just so the boy, in the grip of his enemy, showed
 a proud ferocity which moved the crowd,
 and leaders, even Ulysses. The only one

who did not weep was he for whom they wept.                    1100
While Ulysses performed the prophet's prayers,
and summoned savage gods, of his free will
the boy jumped down to Priam's kingdom.*
ANDROMACHE  Colchis* never saw such horrors, Scythian nomads
    never did such things, nor the lawless people
    who live by the Caspian Sea. Busiris* never stained
    his altars with children's blood, cruel though he was.
    Diomedes* never fed his animals
    on child-size limbs.—But who will cover your body*
    and bury it?
MESSENGER    There is no body left                              1110
    after so steep a plunge. His bones are broken,
    smashed by his fall. His weight as it crashed to the ground
    obliterated his fine face and body. No sign left
    of how he once looked like his famous father.
    His neck was snapped off as he hit the rock.
    His head cracked open and the brains burst out.
    His corpse is mangled, shapeless.
ANDROMACHE                          Still so like his father!*
MESSENGER  When the boy toppled headlong from the walls,
    Greeks wept to watch the crime they had done themselves,
    then that same crowd turned back to further wickedness,     1120
    and to Achilles' tomb. On its far side
    beat the soft waves of the river Rhoteum;
    the other side is bounded by the plain,
    where gentle slopes enclose a central space,
    like a theatre. The whole shore thronged
    with an enormous crowd. Some of them believe
    this killing can set free the fleet from calm. Others
    are happy at an enemy child mown down. But mostly,
    the fickle mob hates the crime, but watches anyway.
        Even the Trojans
    crowd to see their own death, terrified                     1130
    they watch the final scene of Troy's destruction:
    when suddenly, as at a wedding, comes a torchlit procession,
    and out comes the Maid of Honour: Helen, with her head
    bowed down by sorrow. The Trojans pray: 'May Hermione*
    suffer with a wedding like this: may hateful Helen herself,

return to her own husband in just this way.' Now horror
stuns both Greeks and Trojans. The girl looked down
modestly, but her cheeks were bright, and at the last
she was more beautiful than ever before,
just as the light of the sun is often sweeter                    1140
as it sets and the stars are taking up their places
and doubtful day is pressed by the neighbouring night.
The whole crowd was dumbfounded: indeed, people
have more respect for things about to die. Some notice her beauty,
others her youth, while some are moved to think
of Fortune's mutability. All are affected
by her courage in meeting death. She walks before Pyrrhus.
Everybody quivers with pity and wonder. As soon as she reached
the top of the mound, and the young man stood up there
high on the top of his father's tomb, the brave young girl      1150
did not step back. She stood there strong and fierce,
with a fixed frown as she turns to face the blow.
Everyone is moved to see such courage.
And look, another wonder: Pyrrhus is slow to kill.
As soon as he drove his sword deep into her body,
she died at once, and suddenly blood burst out
from the massive wound. But even in death
she did not lose her spirit. She fell down face-first, furious,
as if to burden the earth that buries Achilles.
Both sides were weeping, but the Trojans wept                    1160
fearfully, while the winners made their lament ring loud.
This was the way the sacrifice went. The spilt blood
did not pool or flow over the ground: immediately
the savage funeral mound drank all the blood.

HECUBA  Go home, go home, you Greeks; you are safe now
        to go home.
Your fleet may safely spread its sails and set to sea,
just as you wished. The boy and girl are dead.
The war is over. Where can I go to cry?
Where can this old woman vomit out the rest of her days?
Should I weep for my daughter and grandson, should
        I weep for my husband,                                   1170
or my country? For everything, or for myself? Only death
can answer my prayers. Death comes roughly to babies and virgins,

always pouncing, wild thing. I am the only one
feared and avoided by death. When swords and spears and
    torches
surrounded me, and I spent the night in search of death,
death fled from me. No enemy, no city's sack, no fire
could kill me, though I stood so near to Priam.
MESSENGER Hurry, captured women, hurry to the sea.
Already the sails are unfurling on the prow, the fleet is moving.

# HERCULES FURENS

*Juno was jealous of Hercules, who was the most powerful
and heroic illegitimate son of Jupiter. She caused him to be
enslaved by Eurystheus, king of Argos, who forced him to
perform twelve almost impossible labours. As the play opens,
Hercules is finishing the last of the twelve labours: capturing
the guard-dog of Hades, Cerberus, and bringing him back
to the upper world. Hercules' family—his wife Megara,
and his father Amphitryon—are suffering under the threats
of a tyrant, Lycus, who has killed Megara's father Creon,
and seized control of the kingdom while Hercules is away.
Hercules returns in triumph from the underworld; but madness sent by Juno turns his victory upside-down. Hercules,
in the final scene of the play, recovers his senses and has to
decide how to respond to what he has done.*

## DRAMATIS PERSONAE

JUNO, goddess, wife and sister of Jupiter
AMPHITRYON, father of Hercules
MEGARA, wife of Hercules, daughter of Creon
LYCUS, a tyrant
HERCULES
THESEUS, king of Athens, friend of Hercules
CHORUS

# ACT ONE

JUNO  I am sister of the Thunderer—only his sister.*
   I have abandoned Jupiter to all his other girls.
   Like a widow, I left the temples of high heaven;
   exiled, I gave up my place in the sky to those whores.
   I have to live on earth. Concubines live in heaven.
   High in the sky the constellation of the Bear,*
   up in the frozen north guides Argive fleets;
   over there, where springtime days grow long,
   shines the Bull* who carried Europa over the waves;
   and there is the league of the Pleiades,* who wander          10
   all through the sky, and threaten sailors and sea.
   Here is Orion,* brandishing his sword at the gods,
   and here, the stars of golden Perseus.*
   Here, the sparkling stars of Gemini,*
   and those whose birth made the wandering island stop.*
   Not only Bacchus* and his mother have achieved
   a place in heaven; my disgrace is everywhere,
   since Ariadne's crown* shines over earth.

      But these are old complaints. A single savage country,
   Thebes, is swarming with adulteresses;                        20
   how many Theban stepchildren I have!—But imagine
   Alcmena* beats me to the sky and takes my place,
   and her son, too, gets his promised star—
   the night he was conceived,* the world stopped day,
   and the sun dawned late from the eastern sea,
   ordered to keep back his bright light drowned in ocean—
   my hate will never end; my passionate heart
   will whip up everlasting anger; wild resentment
   will drive out peace and wage eternal war.

      What war? Whatever monstrous thing earth brings to birth—   30
   earth, his enemy—or sea, or air:
   terrible, strange, diseased, awful, and wild—
   all are subdued and broken. He wins!* Trouble makes him
         stronger,
   and he enjoys my rage. He turns my hate

to his own glory. When I act the tyrant queen,
I give him room to prove himself a hero,
and his father's son. All countries touched by the light
of sunrise and sunset, the two dark-painted peoples,*
all revere his dauntless courage. The whole world
tells stories of his godhead. I have no monsters left.          40
Hercules finds it easier to do what I command
than I to make the orders. He is glad to obey.
What new and savage forms of domination
could harm this tough young man? Remember, for his weapons
he wears the things he used to fear, which he laid low.
His armour is the Lion and the Hydra.* All the world
was not enough for him. He breaks Hell's gate,
defeats the king and brings his prizes back to earth.*
Coming back is easy; the laws of the dark land are broken.
With my own eyes I saw him scatter night          50
and boast of conquering Hades to his father—
Hades' brother.* Why not chain up Jove's equal,
Hell's defeated king? Why not drag him in triumph?
Why not seize power in his realm? Look, Styx* is open!
There is a broad path up from the land of the dead.
The rites of ghastly Death are now revealed.
But Hercules is power-crazy now he has burst that prison.
He triumphs over me, proudly displaying
that black dog through every Argive town.
When Cerberus is seen, day slips and Sun is scared:          60
I have seen him myself, and even I was frightened:
the three bowed necks of that defeated monster
made me fear my power. But enough of trivial complaints.
Watch out, heaven! He might seize the kingdom
up here, like the one below, usurping his father's throne.
He will not climb up gently to the stars
as Bacchus did. He wants to strew his path
with ruin, tyrant of an empty sky.
His proven strength has puffed him up. Bearing the world
has taught him he can conquer heaven. He raised          70
the massive weight of the world* without a wobble;
the universe was more stable on his neck.
His shoulders held the stars and sky in place,

and even me, pushing him down. Now he wants to come up here.
   Rage, do your worst! Stamp out his great ambitions!
Go on, tear him apart with your own hands!
Why delegate such hatred? No more monsters!
Eurystheus is tired, he need give no more orders.
Send the Titans, daring rebels against Jove,
who tried to break his power. Crack open Etna,                    80
let Sicily, which trembles as he moves,
set free the monstrous giant* from his jail.
[And let the lofty moon bring forth new monsters.]*
But he has conquered these. Do you want his match?
There is none but himself. So let him fight himself.
   Come, from the very depths of Tartarus,
Furies, scatter fire with your hair of flame,
shake your snaky torches in your savage hands.
Go on, arrogant man! Aim for the home of the gods,
despise humanity. Do you think you have already               90
escaped from the land of the dead? I will show you hell
    on earth.
I will call back Chaos, hidden in thick mist,
from far beyond the sinners' place of exile—
imprisoned in her cave beneath the mountain.
I will drag out from the very depths of Hell
all that remain there: hated Crime will come,
and savage Treachery to god and man,
lapping at his own blood; Madness, and Passion,
always armed against itself. Let all these serve my hate!
   Begin, servants of Hell, rise up and whirl            100
your burning torches. Let Megaera lead
the serpentine procession; with cruel hands
let her seize an enormous timber from the pyre.
Take your revenge for Hades' desecration!
Beat your chests, let your minds burn with fire
hotter than the furnaces of Etna.
To capture Hercules' mind, to whip him up
to desperate, passionate madness, you must first
go mad yourselves.—Juno, why so calm?
Sisters, let me be the first flung from my mind;             110
turn me upside-down and make me ready

to do what a stepmother should. So flip my wish:
now I pray: 'May he come back, and see his children safe!
And may his hands be strong.' Today, for once,
I will be glad at his heroic strength.
He beat me? Let him also beat himself.
Returned from Hell, let him desire to die.
At last I benefit from the fact Jove is his father.
I will stand and take my aim, make sure
the arrows hit their mark. I will guide his maddened hands.    120
This once, I will help Hercules in a fight.
After such evil, let his father welcome him
to heaven—with those hands!—Now time for war; day dawns,
the shining Sun climbs from his yellow bed.

CHORUS  Now the bright stars are few
and tired as they turn to set.
Defeated night tucks in her wandering fires
as light is born again.
Lucifer leads off his sparkling troops:
the icy constellation way up high,    130
Ursa Major with its seven stars,
has turned around its Plough* and summons day.
Now the Sun rides out on his blue horses,
looking out over Mount Oeta's heights.*
Now the thickets known for Pentheus' death*
are scattered with the redness of the day.
Apollo's sister* leaves; she will be back.
High up in the branches birds are crying:
the nightingale, mistress of the Thracian king,*
flaps her wings among her cheeping chicks,    140
eager to fly up to the new sun.
The flocks of different birds mixed up together
sing their various songs to greet the day.
   Hard work gets up, creates anxiety,
and opens everyone's house. The shepherd drives
his flock out to the field, and gathers up
fodder icy-white with frost. The calf
whose horns have not yet sprouted from his brow
frolics free in the open meadow;
the empty udders of the cows grow fat.    150

The cheeky little kid wobbles about,
his legs unsteady on the soft green grass.
The sailor risks his life and trusts his sails to the winds,
as the breezes fill their spreading folds.
One man perches on the craggy cliffs
preparing his hidden hooks;
anxiously he peers at the prize; his hand is steady;
the line can feel the quiver of the fish.
This is how they live: in innocence—
in peace and quiet,                                                    160
each home happy with its own small stock.
In cities, great ambitions roam around,
and so do quaking fears.
See this man—he does not sleep,
haunting the doorways of the royal palace,
resting on hard lintels. Here, another
endlessly hoards his wealth, gaping at treasure:
he is poor on top of a heap of gold.
Another man is dazed by hopes of popularity;
the fickle mob, more mutable than the waves,                            170
lifts him high, puffed up with empty air.
Another yet is set on selling off
the crazy arguments of the noisy city-square,
wickedly hiring out his anger and his words.
The lucky few, familiar with deep peace,
are always conscious of time's rapid passing,
and they keep hold of moments which will not come back.
While fate allows, live happy.
Life rushes by so fast!
The wheel of the headlong year is turned                                180
with each soon-ended day.
The brutal sisters finish their spinning,*
and never wind their threads backwards.
But the human race is borne to meet its rushing fates,
        unsure of itself;
we seek the Stygian waters of our own accord.
Hercules, you are rushing to see the grieving ghosts;
your courage is too much.
The Fates come at a fixed time.

Nobody gets to dally when they call,
nobody can postpone the written day.                          190
Summon the people, and in the urn they go.
    Love of honour leads a man
to travel the world; Reputation,
that chatterbox, may praise him through the towns;
another man rides high up on his chariot.
I would rather have a safe, secluded home,
hidden in my own native land.
Unambitious people live to white old age;
the unimpressive fortune of a tiny house
is humble but it stands on solid ground.                      200
Impetuous courage falls from a great height.


# ACT TWO

CHORUS  But here comes Megara, overwhelmed by grief,
    her hair is down. She is bringing the little ones with her,
    and Hercules' old father, hobbled with age.
AMPHITRYON  O mighty ruler of Olympus, lord of the world,
    now is the time to put an end to all our pain.
    We have suffered long enough. Every new dawn
    has brought me yet more worry. The end of one disaster
    leads straight to another. As soon as my son gets home,
    new enemies confront him. Before he even reaches           210
    his happy house, the orders come: 'Go off and fight again.'
    He has no respite, no time off, no rest—
    except while he gets his orders. Juno, his enemy,
    has tracked him from the first. He was not even safe
    as a newborn baby!* He had to conquer monsters
    before he could tell their names. Two crested snakes
    pointed their tongues at him; but he crawled towards them,
    staring straight into their fiery eyes.
    His face was calm and peaceful, even gentle,
    as they seized hold of him in their knotted coils.          220
    He squashed their swollen necks in his tiny fists—
    good practice for the Hydra. He ran to seize
    the speedy hind,* its lovely head adorned

with golden horns. The terrifying lion*
groaned as Hercules wrapped his arms to squash him.
I could go on: those awful Thracian stables,*
the king who was given as fodder to his herd;
the bristly wild boar,* whose thundering feet
jolted the woods of Arcady, the slopes of Erymanthus;
the bull* who menaced over a hundred towns.                    230
Among the distant peoples of the west,
the triple-bodied shepherd* of the shore
was killed. The prize was driven from the Occident;
cattle from Ocean grazed on Mount Cithaeron.
They told him: 'You must go to the lands of the summer sun,
deep in the countries singed by the noon-time heat.'*
He burst the mountains open. Into the gulf
he made a highway for the rushing ocean.*
Next he entered the rich woodland den,
and took the golden spoils* from the sleepless snake.          240
Do I need to mention mores? In Lerna,*
he finally used fire, won out against the monster,
and taught it how to die. And what about the birds,*
which used to cloud the day with wings? He got them down
even from the clouds. The ever-virgin queen,*
her bed untouched, could not defeat him. His hands were brave
for every glorious act, but did not shrink
from the dirty work of the Augean stable.*
   What good did all this do him? He is gone from the
      world he saved.
The earth has understood: its peacemaker                       250
has gone off-duty. They give the name of virtue
to successful crime. The good obey the bad.
Might is right, and fear stifles the law.
I have seen with my own eyes our sons
slaughtered in defence of their father's land;
and King Creon, last of Cadmus' noble line,
dead. I saw them rip his crown from him,
along with his head. Ah, who could weep enough
for Thebes? Mother of gods, what master can you fear?
From her fields and from her fertile lap                       260
an army jumped up,* newborns with drawn swords;

and Amphion,* Jove's son, built up her walls,
lifting the stones with lovely harmonies.
The father of the gods abandoned heaven
not once but often, to come visit Thebes. This city
has hosted and made gods—now and perhaps again
(if it is lawful to say so). But now a degrading yoke
presses down on Thebes. O children of Cadmus,
what depths have you sunk to? You shiver at this stranger,*
who has left his home to ruin ours.                                    270
He whose righteous hands destroyed the rule of tyrants,
who pursued all wickedness by land and sea,
is now enslaved and banished; forced to endure
what he fought against. Lycus has Hercules' city.—
But not forever! He will return to take revenge. All of a sudden
he will come out to the stars; he will find a way,
or make one. May you come safe back, I pray!
May you come as conqueror to your conquered home.

MEGARA  Husband, come up to the air! Scatter the darkness,
tear it with your hands. If there is no way back,                      280
and the path is closed, then split the world! Come back!
Let loose whatever lies hidden in realms of dark,
as long as you free yourself. Just as you stood firm,
cracking open hilltops to find the river's path,
and it gushed forth when all Mount Tempe*—boom!—
exploded and lay open—your chest bore the weight
to chop the mountain up, part here, part there;
the rushing river flowed on a new bed.
So now, come to your home, your father and your children;
burst through the limits of the universe,                              290
take them away with you. Give back all the things
stolen by greedy time through all the years.
Lead out the self-forgetful dead,* despite their fear of light.
You deserve to bring a prize far greater
than what you were told to bring.—But I am talking too big!
I do not know what the future holds, nor when
I can hold you, have you hold me, in your arms—
and tell you: 'You took so long to come home!
Did you forget about me?'—I will sacrifice
a hundred perfect cattle for you, Jove; and Ceres,*                    300

I will enact your secret rites. I will not tell—
trust me. The long torches of Eleusis will be waved.
Then I will think my brothers' lives restored,
my father alive and well and on his throne.
Or if some power too great holds you imprisoned,
I will come to you. If you can come back safe,
you must protect us all. If not, drag us down with you.—
Yes, drag us down. No god will help us. We are ruined.

AMPHITRYON  You are family and friend to me. You have
        been faithful
to great-souled Hercules' bed, and looked after the children.   310
Cheer up! Be more positive in your thinking.
He will be here soon. He has succeeded
in every labour up till now.

MEGARA                        Unhappy people
are ready to believe what they so dearly wish.

AMPHITRYON  No, they think their paranoia must come true.
Frightened people always believe the worst.

MEGARA  He is drowned and buried and submerged
under the world; how can he get back up?

AMPHITRYON  The same way he crossed over the dry beach,*
the sands that rose and fell like waves of the sea,            320
and the ocean washing over then retreating.
He left his ship behind and he got stuck
in the Syrtean shallows. The prow stayed fixed.
He crossed over the seas with just his feet.

MEGARA  Hostile Fortune is rarely kind to heroes.
Everybody knows you cannot risk
danger after danger and be safe.
Fate may spare you many times, she gets you in the end.
    But look, here comes Lycus, scowling, savage,
his violent stride as threatening as his face.               330
He is brandishing the sceptre that he stole.

LYCUS  I rule the wealthy regions around Thebes,
and all the fertile soil of sloping Phocis,
and all the places washed by Ismenus,
and all the valleys under high Cithaeron,
and the Isthmus which divides the double sea—
not lazily inheriting the kingdom

from my father's house. I have no fancy ancestors,
my family is not loaded up with titles.
I am famous for machismo.* Boasting of blue blood          340
means praising other people.—But if one's power is stolen,
maintaining it is hard. My only hope is force.
Remember how to keep your throne when people hate you:
with a drawn sword. Regimes are unstable when the ruler
does not belong.—But a nice big royal wedding,
and bed with Megara, will make our powers
flow together. Her famous forebears will paint
my unknown family a better colour. And I predict,
she will not reject me or turn down my proposal.
But if she should be stubborn and refuse,                  350
my plan is to uproot Hercules' whole house.
Should the people's gossip and resentment
hold me back? No: the first art of government
is putting up with hatred.—Time to try it.
A lucky opportunity: she is here, by the altar's protection.
Her head is veiled as if in mourning; at her side
clings Hercules' real father.*

MEGARA                        That man! He means ruin,
destruction to our family. What is his latest plan?

LYCUS  Princess, you bear a noble name by birth.
Let me talk to you, for just a little while:                360
listen patiently to what I have to say.
If people always bicker back and forth,
and never let their anger leave their hearts—
victors still clutching their weapons, losers getting them ready—
then wars will leave us nothing; farms will lie in ruin,
their fields laid waste. Homes will be torched;
the people will be buried deep in ash.
It is good strategy for victors to want peace;
necessity for the conquered. So come, share my rule.
Let us be partners together. Have this as proof of my faith:   370
take my hand.—Why so quiet? Why scowl?

MEGARA  Would I touch a hand stained with the blood
of my father and my brother, double murder? No!
The sun will rise in the west and set in the east,
snow and fire will make a pact of friendship,

and rocks will unite Sicily and Greece.
The strait Euripus* with its shifting tide
will sooner stand stock still on Euboea's shore,
before I touch you. You stole my father, my kingdom, my brothers,
my home, and my country—what else? I still have one
      thing left,                                                        380
dearer to me than brother, father, kingdom, or home:
my hatred for you. I resent that I have to share it
with the whole population. How little of it is mine!
Go ahead, be a tyrant, boast, puff yourself up with pride.
The avenging god follows close behind the proud.
I know all about Thebes. No need to mention
the crimes that mothers here have done and suffered.*
Why speak of that mixed-up man: husband, father, and son?*
Why bring up the brothers' two camps, and their separate
      funeral flames?*
That proud mother turned to stone from grieving,*           390
and her sad rock still drips on the Phrygian mountain.
Why mention even Cadmus himself,* his head transformed
to a crested snake, as he wandered in exile through Illyria,
leaving long tracks as he slithered his body along.
These precedents foretell your fate. Go on, be a tyrant—
as long as your story ends in the usual Theban way.
LYCUS  Crazy woman, enough of your wild talk.
Let Hercules teach you to put up with royal commands.
I know I stole the throne, but I won, and I have got it.
I will be king without fear of the laws.                         400
My arms defeated law. But let me say a little
to defend my case. Did your father die in war?
And your brothers? Weapons never keep to limits;
a sword drawn in anger cannot be made gentle,
nor easily repressed. War delights in blood.
You say he fought for his kingdom, while I was driven
by base desire? The reasons for war do not matter;
the main thing is its end. Now let us forget all that.
When the victor lays down his arms, it is right
for the loser to lay down her hatred. I do not ask you to kneel   410
and worship me as ruler. It is enough for me
if you accept your ruin with good heart.

You are a worthy consort for a king. Let us get married.
MEGARA  My blood runs cold in my veins, I feel myself shaking.
I can hardly believe my ears—such evil words!
I was not frightened when peace broke, the crash of war
sounded around my walls; I could bear it all, quite calmly.
But I tremble at this marriage. Now I know myself a slave.—
But let chains weigh my body down, let death come slow,
dragged out by long starvation; no force on earth          420
can conquer my fidelity. Hercules, I will die yours.
LYCUS  Can a husband drowned in Hell make you so brave?
MEGARA  He has gone down low in order to rise high.
LYCUS  An enormous mass of earth is weighing him down.
MEGARA  No weight can press him down; he held the sky.
LYCUS  I can force you.
MEGARA                    Only those who cannot die can suffer force.
LYCUS  Then tell me what royal gift you want from me
as dowry for this new marriage.
MEGARA                    Either your death or mine.
LYCUS  Crazy woman, you will die.
MEGARA                    And meet my husband.
LYCUS  Is that slave more powerful than my throne?          430
MEGARA  How many kings that 'slave' has put to death!
LYCUS  Then why does he serve a king and bear the yoke?
MEGARA  If there were no hard commands, what place for courage?
LYCUS  You think it courage, to be thrown to beasts?
MEGARA  Courage means conquering what everybody fears.
LYCUS  He talked big, but Hell's shades push him down.
MEGARA  There is no easy path from earth to heaven.
LYCUS  Who is his father, that he should hope for a home in the sky?
AMPHITRYON  Poor wife of mighty Hercules, be quiet now;
it is my job to give him back his father,          440
explaining his true heritage. After so many deeds
of legendary heroism, after he made peace
through all the lands the rising and the setting sun can see;
after so many monsters killed; after he scattered
the blood of the impious Giants, and defended the gods—
is his paternity still unclear? Are we calling Jove a liar?
At least believe in Juno's hatred.
LYCUS                    You blaspheme Jove!

Human beings cannot mate with gods.

AMPHITRYON  They can! Many gods were born that way.

LYCUS  And were they slaves before they became gods?          450

AMPHITRYON  Apollo served as a shepherd,* driving flocks.

LYCUS  But he did not wander all over the world in exile.

AMPHITRYON  Really? His exiled mother gave birth on a
    wandering island.*

LYCUS  Did Apollo face wild beasts and fearful monsters?

AMPHITRYON  A dragon* was the first to stain his arrows.

LYCUS  Have you forgotten what Hercules suffered as a baby?

AMPHITRYON  His father's thunderbolt pushed Bacchus from
    the womb;
  he soon stood tall beside that thundering father.*
  What about the god who rules the stars and shakes the clouds?
  Did he not lie hidden in a cavern* as a baby?          460
  The most important babies need most looking after;
  being born a god does not come cheap.

LYCUS  When a man suffers, be sure he is human.

AMPHITRYON  When he is brave, do not say that he suffers.*

LYCUS  Should we call him brave, when the lion skin fell
    from his shoulders,*
  a gift to a girl, and his club fell too, and his body
  shone bright with a gaudy dress from Tyria?
  Should we call him brave, whose shaggy hair
  dripped with perfume? Whose famous hands were quick
  to work to the womanish beat of the tambourine,          470
  wearing a foreign turban on his ferocious head?

AMPHITRYON  Delicate Bacchus did not feel any shame
  to toss his lustrous hair, and use his slender hands
  to shake light ivy wands, wearing his flowing dress
  adorned with gold as he pranced and minced along.
  After mighty exploits, heroes need to relax.

LYCUS  Yes, and ruin the house of Eurytus,
  and drag off flocks of virgin girls* like sheep?
  No Juno nor Eurystheus ordered this;
  these are his very own actions.

AMPHITRYON                    You do not know it all.          480
  It was his very own action to break the bully Eryx
  with his own gloves, and Antaeus just the same;

and to make the altars, which had sucked up strangers' blood,
drip with the righteous killing of Busiris;
it was his choice to force Cycnus to die,
although no wound nor sword could pierce his flesh.
Triple Geryon* was killed by his single hand.
You will join the list!—But these were better:
the women they raped were unmarried.

LYCUS                        A king may act like Jove;
    you gave one wife to Jove,* give another to the king.     490
    Your daughter-in-law will learn from you this ancient lesson:
    to take the better man, when even the husband says yes.
    But if she is stubborn and refuses to marry me,
    I can use force to get blue-blooded children from her.

MEGARA  By Creon's ghost, by the gods of the house of Labdacus,*
    by the sacrilegious wedding torch of Oedipus—
    now bless this marriage with the usual outcome.
    Now bloodstained daughters of King Danaus,*
    bring here your hands, polluted with mass murder.
    One bride missed the crime; I will make it up.     500

LYCUS  Since you are stubborn, refusing my hand,
    and you threaten your king, it is time for you to learn
    the extent of my royal power. Embrace the altars;
    no god will tear you from me, not even if earth could open
    and Hercules ride back victorious to the sky.
    Heap up more logs! Let the temple burn and fall
    on the suppliants within. Let a single fire
    consume his wife and all her flock of children.

AMPHITRYON  As Hercules' father, let me beg for just one thing—
    an appropriate request—that I may be first to die.     510

LYCUS  A man who uses death as punishment for all
    has not learnt true tyranny. Devise different penalties:
    forbid death to the wretched, force it on the happy.
    While the pyre grows big with tinder wood,
    I make my promised sacrifice to Neptune.

AMPHITRYON  By the highest power of heaven, by Jupiter,
    father and ruler of gods, whose thunderbolts
    shake us on earth, restrain the unholy hands
    of this tyrant! But why do I pray to the gods?
    Listen, son, wherever you are.—Why is the temple     520

suddenly tottering? Why this rumble from the earth?
A hellish crash sounds from the bottom-most depths.
He hears me! It is the sound of Hercules' steps.
CHORUS  Fortune, enemy to heroes, how unfairly
    you portion out the prizes of the good.
    Eurystheus can be king and take it easy;
    Alcmena's son must struggle all the time,
    fighting monsters with hands that held the sky.
    He keeps on cutting off the savage snaky heads;*
    he fools the sisters* and brings the apples back,      530
    when the dragon that guards the golden fruit
    allows his watchful eyes to fall asleep.
    He went as far as the Scythian nomads' home,
    and tribes that do not know where their fathers lived.
    He trod the icy backbone of the sea,
    along the silent ocean, on the quiet beach.
    The waters there are hard, there are no waves;
    where ships were once spreading their billowy sails,
    the Sarmatae are tramping with bare feet.
    The sea is still, but twice a year it moves:      540
    accommodating boats, then bearing horsemen.
    There he fought the queen of the Amazons.
    A golden belt was slung around her hips;
    she stripped it from her body, a lovely prize,
    along with her shield and the band from her snowy breasts.
    She went down on her knees, and looked up to her conqueror.
    What were you hoping for, what drove you down
    to the dizzying depths, when you took the risk of taking
    the path of no return, to the realm of Proserpine?
    No winds from south or west can blow down there,      550
    stirring the seas to rise with swelling waves.
    Down there no Castor and Pollux, helpful stars,
    come to guide the sailors in their fear.
    The sea is stagnant, thick with blackish water.
    Whenever pale Death champs his greedy teeth,
    bringing countless people down to Hades,
    a single ferryboat has borne them all.
        May you defeat the cruel Stygian laws,
    conquer the distaff of Fate, which will not wind back!

The king who rules so many souls down there,                560
while you were making war on Nestor's Pylos,
raised his destructive hands against you, brandished
his three-pointed trident at your heart;
but when he was slightly grazed, he ran away,
the lord of death was terrified to die.*
Burst fate with your hands. Let the gloomy shadowlands
have a view of the light. May the impassable gate
open up to give an easy journey to the sky.

    The songs and humble prayers of Orpheus
could move the pitiless rulers of the dead,                  570
when he was trying to get Eurydice back.*
The power that had brought rocks and trees alive,
summoned the birds and checked the flowing streams,
and made wild animals stop still to listen,
comforted the dead—not used to hear such sounds—
and rang out still more clearly in that insensate place.
Even the Furies weep for the Thracian bride;
even the gods who never weep are crying.
Even the judges on their thrones, with their stern brows,
who weigh up all the crimes of times gone by,               580
even they weep for Eurydice.
Finally the Lord of Death says: 'We give up.
Go out to the upper world. But one proviso:
Eurydice, follow behind your man.
Orpheus, you must not look back at her
until bright day unfolds the heavenly light,
and you are at the gate of Taenarus.'
True love hates delays, will not endure them.
When he hurried to look at his prize, he lost her.
But if these kingdoms can be won by song,                   590
these kingdoms can be won by violence.


# ACT THREE

HERCULES  O ruler of the lovely light, jewel of the sky,
    whose flaming chariot crosses both halves of the world,
    lifting your bright head across the breadth of earth:

Apollo, pardon me, if you have seen
anything you should not. I acted under orders,
bringing secrets up into the light. And you,
Jupiter, hide your gaze with your thunderbolt;
and you, king of the second realm,* the sea,
sink down to the ocean floor. Whatever gods                     600
look down on earthly things, and fear pollution
from new monstrosities—turn your eyes up to the sky,
avoid this horrible wonder.* Only we two should see it:
I who brought him here, and she* who made me do it.—
There is not earth enough for all my pains and labours
brought by Juno's hatred. I have seen the hidden places,
unseen by the sun, where the terrible Dark Lord
rules under that lower, blacker sky.
If I had wished to rule the underworld,
I could have. I have conquered that whole chasm              610
of night eternal, dark darker than night,
the gods of loss, and the Fates. I scorned death, and returned.
What else remains? I have seen Hell, and revealed it.
Juno, you have let my hands be idle for a while.
Give me a task, if you have any more. What else should I win?
    But why are foreign soldiers camped out by the temple,
besieging in full arms the holy seat?

AMPHITRYON  Do my eyes deceive me? Has my wish come true?
  Has the hero of Greece, world-conqueror,
  come back from the silent land of grief and shadows?            620
  Is it really my son? I feel my legs grow weak.
  Son! It is you! At last, for real, our saviour!
  Let me hold you! Are you back alive, or am I holding
  a ghost—a cruel trick? Is it you? I know your muscles,
  your shoulders and the long club in your hands.

HERCULES  Father, why is my wife dressed in dingy mourning?
  Why are the children covered in dirt? What is the matter?
  What disaster has come upon our house?

AMPHITRYON  Your father-in-law is dead, Lycus is tyrant,
  he wants to kill your children, wife, and father.                     630

HERCULES  Ungrateful land, did no one come to help
  the house of Hercules? Did the world I used to protect

stand by and watch this horror?—But why waste time
    complaining?
Slaughter the victim! Let my record bear this stain,
let Lycus be my final enemy.
I have to pour out streams of enemy blood.
Theseus, stay back, in case of a sudden attack.
More labours for me! Father, wife, I must wait
to hold you in my arms. Lycus will tell Dis*
that I have got back home.

THESEUS                    Queen Megara, do not cry.          640
And you, Amphitryon, your son is safe,
so stop your falling tears. If I know Hercules,
Lycus will pay the death he owes to Creon.
'Will pay' is slow. He pays. Still slow! He has paid already.

AMPHITRYON   May god's power help our wishes to come true,
abide with us in our troubles.—Friend and companion
of my heroic son, tell us all about his exploits.
How did he travel on that long journey down to the shades?
How did he manage to capture Cerberus?

THESEUS  You force me to recall things which my mind          650
shudders even to think of. Even now, I scarcely believe
in the life-giving air. My sight is weak, eyes fail;
they can hardly bear the unaccustomed day.

AMPHITRYON   Remnants of fear are still buried deep in your heart.
Defeat them, Theseus, do not cheat yourself
of the prize for all your pain: past suffering
is sweet in memory. Tell us your terrible adventures.

THESEUS  I pray by Natural Law,* and by you, King
of the Limitless Realm,* and you, Proserpine,
sought by your mother in vain across Mount Etna:*          660
may I safely reveal the secrets of the earth.

    In the land of Sparta there is a famous ridge,
where the thick woods of Taenarus loom over the sea.
Here is the mouth of the hidden house of Dis;
the high cliff gapes and an enormous gulf
opens its great jaws to show a mighty cave,
and reveals a broad path down for everyone.
It is not pitch-dark at the beginning;
from behind your back still shines a gleam of light;

the flickering glow of the weakened sun now fades,                    670
frustrating your vision; just as at early dawn,
or dusk, one sees light mixed up with night.
You come to a vast plain, a spreading emptiness.
All of humanity will sink and come to it.
It is no trouble to go there; the path itself leads down.
Just as often a current takes hold of resistant boats,
so the downward wind and the greedy force of Hell
drive you down and the clutching shades will never
let you turn back. When you get inside, you find
the mighty curve of Lethe's quiet waves,                    680
which take one's cares away; and to remove
all chance of going home, the river loops,
winding its heavy waters, just as Meander*
wanders with no fixed bed and retreats from itself,
doubting whether to flow to the sea or back to the source.
Here is the ugly marsh of stagnant Cocytus;
vultures and owls shriek with the sounds of grief,
and the ill-omened screech-owl's cries ring out.

    The leaves are black with shadow and they tremble
on the overhanging yew, where sluggish Sleep                    690
and desperate Hunger with her skinny lips,
cling, while Shame hides her guilty face, too late.
Fear and dark Terror and gnashing Pain,
black Grief and shaky Sickness follow them,
and War, girded with iron; trailing behind them
feeble Old Age comes leaning on a stick.

AMPHITRYON  Is any field there good for corn or vines?

THESEUS  There are no verdant fertile meadows there,
no ripe crops sway under the gentle breeze,
no orchards hang with fruit upon the branch.                    700
The underworld is barren emptiness,
its ugly earth untended for all time:
the mournful goal of everything, end of the world.
The air hangs motionless, and black night looms
over a lifeless world of universal grief;
the place of death is even worse than death.

AMPHITRYON  What about the king of that dark kingdom?
Where is his throne as he guides the ghostly people?

THESEUS  There is a hiding-place in Tartarus' shadows,
    engulfed in fog and heavy with dense mist.                               710
    Here from a single source two streams emerge,
    unlike each other: one flows with quiet waters
    down to Styx, the river by which gods swear their oaths.
    The other rushes with a mighty swell,
    rolling rocks around, to Acheron,
    the river nobody can cross back over.
    They form a double moat around the palace
    of Dis, shadowed by trees. Under a vast rock
    looms the tyrant's entrance. This is the way for the dead,
    the gate to the kingdom. A plain lies round the palace,              720
    where the god sits in terrible majesty,
    his face proud as he judges the new souls.
    His brow is stern, but he looks like his brother*—
    his lineage matches Jove, as does his face—
    the face of the Thunderer. Much of the horror of that world
    lies in its master, whose face is feared even by
    the fearsome.

AMPHITRYON  Is the story true that in Hades
    there is belated justice, and that sinners
    forgetful of their crimes, must still be punished?
    Who is the judge of truth and justice there?                          730

THESEUS  More than one chief justice sits on those high seats,
    passing retrospective judgement on trembling souls.
    Cretan Minos holds one court, another
    Rhadamanthus, and another Aeacus.
    Each soul suffers what he or she has done.
    Sins rebound upon the sinner, punishments fit the crime.
    I saw bloodstained kings locked up in dungeons,
    and peasants' hands whipping the backs
    of cruel tyrants. But those who were gentle rulers,
    who had the power of life and death, but still showed mercy,    740
    and wielded power without spilling blood,
    checking their own desires—they measure out
    long miles of happiness, then rise to heaven,
    or to the fields of joy, Elysium,
    to be judges themselves. O you who rule,
    hold back from human blood! Your crimes are judged

more harshly than on earth.

AMPHITRYON                    Is there a place
  set aside for sinners? Is it like the stories,
  the wicked suffer cruelly, held in eternal chains?

THESEUS  Ixion whirls round twisted on the wheel;                    750
  the heavy stone weighs down Sisyphus' neck;
  in the middle of the river, with dry lips,
  the old man* tries to get the water; it splashes his chin,
  but every time it promises fulfilment,
  the drink dies on his lips. The fruit mock at his hunger.
  Tityos forever feeds the bird,
  the Danaids carry their full urns in vain;
  the wicked Theban bacchants are still crazy,
  the ravening Harpy snatches Phineus'* food.

AMPHITRYON  Now tell about my son's heroic deeds.                    760
  Did his uncle give the dog? Or did he win it?

THESEUS  The deadly cliffs overhang the sluggish waves,
  where the waters hardly move, the sea stagnates.
  The hideous old man,* dressed all in rags,
  ferries the frightened spirits over the river.
  His beard is shaggy and uncombed, a knot of rope
  belts his shabby tunic; his cheeks are hollow.
  He is the ferryman, punting with his long pole.
  He lets the passengers off his boat, then turns
  to get more spirits. Hercules asked to be ferried.                    770
  The crowd drew back, and scary Charon shouted:
  'Stop right there, rash man! Where do you think you are going?'
  But Hercules brooked no delay. He seized the pole
  and mastered the boatman, forced him to surrender,
  and climbed in the boat. A vessel large enough
  for all the nations sank beneath one man.
  The Lethe-water splashed over both sides
  when he sat down. Then the monsters he defeated trembled,
  Centaurs and Lapiths driven to fight by drink;
  the Hydra retreats to the farthest reaches of the marsh,                    780
  sinking his ever-growing heads in the waters of Styx.

    After this you come to the house of greedy Dis.
  Here the cruel Hell-Hound terrifies the spirits,
  barking loud as he shakes all his three heads,

guarding the kingdom. Snakes lick his rotting face,
his long mane of fur is thick with vipers,
a serpent hisses down his twisty tail.
His looks befit his rage: soon as he hears
footsteps, his snaky fur stands up on end,
he pricks his ears to catch the passing sound—                790
he is practised at listening to ghosts. When Jupiter's son
gets nearer, the dog sits doubtful in his cave,
and shivers a little.—Now look! He barks and howls,
terrifying all the silent world. All over his back, the snakes
are hissing their hostility. The din of the terrible noise
from his three mouths makes all the spirits tremble,
even those in bliss. Then Hercules releases
the cruel jaws from his left hand, thrusts out
the enormous lion's head for a shield.
His conquering right arm lifts high his club.                  800
He whirls him here and there, battering blows,
striking again and again. The dog, defeated,
yields, becomes submissive, lowers all his heads,
granting access to the cave. The king and queen
shiver on their thrones, and say: 'Take him away!'
They gave me, too, to Hercules as a gift.

   Stroking the weighty shoulders of the beast,
he bound him in an adamantine net. The watchful guard
of that dark kingdom now forgot himself;
he shyly drooped his ears, submitted to the leash,          810
and recognized his master. Head down low
he followed him, wagging his snaky tail.
After we came to the borders of Taenarus,
his eyes bedazzled by the unfamiliar light,
he plucked up courage even in defeat,
and angrily shook his chains. He almost defeated his conqueror,
lowering his heads to drag him off his feet.
Then Hercules needed help even from me;
we joined our strength together and pulled the dog,
wild with rage and trying in vain to fight back,            820
up to the world. When he saw the light of day,
and lifted his eyes to the clear and shining sky,
night overwhelmed him, he lowered his face to the ground;

he shut his eyes, shut out the hateful light,
turned back his faces, and strained with all three necks
to go back under earth. Then he crept to hide his heads
beneath Hercules' shadow. But with a happy shout
out came a throng of spirits wearing laurel,
singing the praise of Hercules—well deserved.

CHORUS Eurystheus was hurried into birth,*                    830
and ordered you to delve down under earth.
Only this was missing from your labours:
robbing the ruler of the underworld.
You dared to go inside the hidden land,
where the path leads down to distant shades,
dark and dismal through the scary woods,
but crowded with a mass of company.

    As many as the people in the city,
greedy to see the games at a new theatre;
as many as rush to see Olympic Jove,                          840
when the fifth summer brings the festival;*
as many as when the nights grow long again,
and even-balanced Libra yearns to rest,
and holds Apollo's chariot in suspense:
the crowd attends the Mysteries of Ceres;
abandoning their homes, Athenian believers
hurry by night to perform the holy rites.*
So many are driven through the silent fields.
Some of them move slowly, bowed by age,
sad and sated from their long, long lives.                    850
Some are running, young and vigorous:
virgin girls, who were not yet yoked in marriage,
boys who had not had their hair cut yet;*
babies who have just learnt one word: 'Mamma.'
Children alone are granted a favour to lessen their fear:
they get to carry a torch to mitigate the night.
The others wander sadly through the dark.
How do you feel, when light is gone, and grieving,
each of you realizes for yourself
that the whole world is pressing on your head?              860
No change: thick emptiness, those awful shadows,
the awful colour of night, the nothingness

of a silent world and clouds that bring no rain.
　　May we grow old before we travel there!
But no one comes too late to the place from which
you never can return back to your home.
What good is it to hurry our hard fate?
This whole mass of people, wandering the world,
will go to death and sail those sluggish seas.
Death, all things that grow belong to you:　　　　　　　870
from east to west, all things that see the light.
Poor things! Life readies us to come to death.
Even if death is slow, we rush ourselves;
the moment which first grants us life, steals it.
　　This is a happy day for Thebes!
Show your respects at the altars,
kill fat victims there.
Come, all girls and boys together
do your traditional dance.
Farmers of the fertile fields　　　　　　　　　　　　880
put down your ploughs and dance.
Hercules has achieved a peace
between the Dawn and the Evening Star,
and where the Sun holds up the noon
and bodies cast no shade.
All the lands the ocean
washes with her wide waves
are tamed by Hercules' labours.
He crossed the river of Hell,
made peace there, and comes back.　　　　　　　　890
Now there is nothing to fear;
Nothing lies beyond the underworld.


# ACT FOUR

CHORUS  Cover your tangly hair with the leaves you love,
　　the poplar,* while you make your sacrifice.
HERCULES  My hand exacted vengeance upon Lycus: he has fallen
　　flat on his face on the ground. I also felled
　　everyone who helped the tyrant's crimes.

Now in triumph I sacrifice for father and the gods,
slaughtering the victims at the altars.

    I pray to you, the friend and helper of my labours,          900
Warrior Goddess Athena, whose Gorgon-headed aegis
threatens to turn your enemies to stone;
come, my Lord* who tamed Lycurgus and the Red Sea,
carrying your spear tipped with the leafy thyrsus;
come, Apollo, with your sister, powerful twins—
the sister skilled at archery, and Phoebus at the lyre—
and come, all you my brothers who live in heaven;
at least the ones not born from my stepmother.*
    —Summon here
droves of fattened beasts. Bring to the altars
all the perfumes of Arabian trees, and all the spices          910
of Indian fields, to make fat smoke pour out.
Let the poplar leaves adorn my hair,
and, Theseus, on your noble brow, you wear
a wreath of olive. I will worship Jupiter;
you go worship the founders of the city,
the woodland caves of wild-man Zethus, Dirce's fountain,
and the Tyrian palace* of the stranger-king.
Put the incense on the fire!

AMPHITRYON               Son, stop! First purify
    your hands! They are still dripping with your enemies' blood.

HERCULES  If only I could use the blood of his hateful head          920
    to pour a libation to the gods! No lovelier liquid
    could stain the altars; no victim could be fitter,
    more perfect as a gift slaughtered for Jove,
    than an unjust king.

AMPHITRYON           Let your father finish your labours;
    you need to allow some time for rest and quiet.
    You are tired.

HERCULES        No! I want to do it myself. I will pray
    as Jupiter and I myself deserve. May heaven stand still,
    and earth and sea; may the everlasting stars
    run smooth across the sky, may deep peace feed the people;
    may all the iron of the world be used for harmless farmwork,          930
    and may the sword be buried. May no rough storms
    shake the ocean. May fire not flash from heaven,

from angry Jupiter's hand. May no river, fattened on snow,
flood across the fields and ruin all the crops.
May there be no more poisons: may no plant
swell up in the night-time, heavy with that juice.
May no cruel tyrants rule the world. But if, even now,
earth still intends to produce more evil, if even now
horror is in the works—then let it be mine.—But what is this?
Darkness gathers at noon! The sun is overcast                    940
but by no cloud. What makes day run away,
driving it back to the east? Why does strange night
bring forth its black face? Why do so many stars
fill up the sky by day? Look, my first labour,
the Lion* shines across the sky, grows hot
consumed by rage, his teeth ready to bite.
Now he prepares to pounce on another star: threatening,
he stands there, vast jaws gaping, breathes out fire and glows
shaking his mane on his shoulders. He is ready to leap
over all the stars of sickly autumn, freezing winter,          950
in a single leap, hunting the Bull, the star of spring,
to jump and break his back.

AMPHITRYON                    What is this sudden trouble?
Son, why are you frowning and shaking your face to and fro,
why do you strain your eyes to see an illusory sky?

HERCULES  I have tamed the whole of earth, the sea has
        ceased to swell,
the kingdom of the dead has felt my power;
heaven has so far escaped: a labour worth my hand.
I will be carried up to the heights of the universe,
up to the aether; the stars are my father's promise to me.—
What if there is resistance? I am too big for earth,          960
she sends me back to heaven. Look, the whole assembly,
all the gods are calling me, they open wide the doors;
but one goddess says no. Open heaven, take me back!
Or shall I batter down the door of this stubborn world?
Why the hesitation? I will set free Saturn from his chains,*
I will set my grandfather against the wicked reign
of my treacherous father. Let the Titans make war,
I will whip them up to fight. I will carry mountains, forests,
my hands will seize the clifftops, thronged with Centaurs.

I will build two mountains into a path to the sky:          970
Pelion will see its Chiron under Ossa,
Olympus, set up in third place, will reach the heavens—
thanks to me.
AMPHITRYON  No more of these terrible plans!
Your great, heroic mind has fallen sick;
restrain yourself from this insane idea!
HERCULES  What is this? The wicked Giants take up arms.
Tityos* has escaped from Hell, the wound in his chest
still gapes open, but how near he stands from heaven!
Cithaeron topples, high Pallene shakes,
Tempe's valleys wither. One giant grabs Mount Pindus;          980
another, Oeta, while Mimas* goes into a terrible rage.
The Fury with her flaming torch swishes her whip,
and bringing burning brands straight from the fire
she thrusts them in my face. Cruel Tisiphone,
fenced in with snakes, slams shut the gate with her stick,
taking the place of the watchdog who was stolen.—
But look, my enemy's children are skulking here,
the nasty seedlings of the tyrant Lycus. I hate your father;
I will send you back to him with my own hands. Let fly
light arrows from the bow. This onslaught really is          990
Herculean.
AMPHITRYON  Mad! He self-destructs! How will it end?
He has curved together the ends of his mighty bow,
he opens his quiver, he launches the arrow, it flies
with a swoosh—now it pierces all the way through the neck,
and comes out the other side.
HERCULES                                    I have to drag out the others,
all the hidden children. What am I waiting for?
I still have to fight a bigger war: at Mycenae,
my hands must tear those walls the Cyclops built.*
Throw down the bolt, swing wide the palace doors,
burst through the bars, knock down the entrance-way.          1000
Let there be light on all the palace: here I see
the son that wicked father hid away.
AMPHITRYON                                    Poor thing!
He cries for mercy, holding on to your knees
with his tiny hands. What a dreadful crime, what a sight!

He grabs the crying child, and whirls him round
two or three times in the air, and cracks his head,
bursting his brains which spatter all over the roof.
Poor Megara enfolds her baby in her arms,
rushing like a madwoman to escape.

HERCULES  Fine, go hide in thundering Jupiter's arms;          1010
my hands will find you out wherever you are.

AMPHITRYON  Poor woman, where are you going? What hiding-
place can you find?
No place is safe when Hercules attacks.
So do not run; embrace him, plead with him
and try to calm him down.

MEGARA                    Husband, I beg you, stop!
You know me—Megara. This is your child;
he looks just like you. Can you see? He reaches for you.

HERCULES  Now I have you, stepmother! Time for your payback!
Set Jupiter free from his slavish, degraded marriage.
But before the mother, I will kill this monstrous baby.          1020

AMPHITRYON  Crazy! What are you doing? Shedding
your own blood!
The toddler, horror-struck at his father's fiery face,
dies unwounded, terrified to death.
Now he bashes his heavy club at his wife:
he breaks her bones, he tears her head from her body
annihilating it. Can I bear to watch? I am old;
I should not be alive. If grief is bitter, here is
death ready-made. Drive your sword into my heart,
or turn on me that club besmeared with blood
from so many monsters. Get rid of this fake 'father'          1030
who shames your name, in case I obstruct your fame.

CHORUS  Why do you seek death of your own accord, old man?
Are you crazy? What are you doing? Run away,
and save the hands of Hercules from this one last crime.

HERCULES  Good! The house of that evil king is demolished.
These animals I killed, I dedicate
to you, wife of great Jove. I gladly kept my promise,
just as you deserved. Argos will pay even more.

AMPHITRYON  Son, you have not yet atoned. Finish the sacrifice.
Another victim stands by the altar: Look!          1040

Neck bowed, he waits for you. Here I am, I am ready, I want it.
Slaughter me.—What is this? I cannot see straight;
grief makes my eyes weak. Or do I see
Hercules' hands tremble? He is falling asleep,
his head sinks down, his neck is bowed and weary.
Now his knees collapse, he falls to the ground,
like an ash cut down in the forest, or a mass of bricks hurled out
into the sea to build a pier. Are you still alive?
Or has the madness which killed your family killed you too?
He is just asleep: I can see the movement of breath.                    1050
He needs to rest a while: deep sleep can overcome
the sickness of his heart, and comfort him.
Slaves, take his weapons away, in case the madness comes back.
CHORUS  Heaven, grieve,
  and you, great Father of high heaven,
  and fertile earth,
  and the fluctuating waves of the sea,
  and you above all, who pour your light
  over the world and the spreading ocean
  whose shining face puts night to flight: flaming Sun—            1060
Hercules has seen as much as you—
  the east and west where you rise and set,
  and known both of your homes.
    Gods, release his heart from all these monsters, such great
        horrors;
  turn his mind around to better thoughts.
And you, Sleep, master of trouble, rest of the soul,
  best part of human life,
  winged child of starry night,
  gentle brother of cruel Death,
  you mix falsehoods with truth,                                        1070
  accurate prophet and the worst of all,
O peace of the world, harbour of life,
  rest from the light and friend of the night,
  visitor to kings and slaves alike,
  you force the human race, fearful of death,
  to practise for the longer night.
Comfort this weary man, be gentle to him,
  let heavy numbness weight him down and hold him;

sleep can bind this body, never tamed before:
and do not leave his fierce heart until                      1080
his mind returns again to its old ways.

    Look, as he sprawls on the ground,
nightmares whirl his wild heart:
the terrible sickness he suffered is not defeated yet.
He usually lays his weary head on his sturdy club;
his empty hand is reaching for its weight,
with a useless sweep of the arm.
The storm is not yet quiet in his heart,
as when a violent wave whips up the sea,
and even when the wind calms down,                           1090
the waters swell.
Banish the tide of madness from his soul;
bring back the man's heroic sense of duty.
Or if his mind is still aroused by madness, keep it so,
wandering in the dark as it began.
Only being mad
can keep you pure.
The closest thing to having innocent hands
is ignorance of your crimes.

    Now let Hercules' hands                1100
thump on his chest;
shower vengeful blows
on the shoulders that carried the world.
Let heaven hear his mighty groans
and the queen of the Dark World,
and Cerberus, who wears a collar of huge chains
hear it as he barks in his infernal cavern.
Let the deep ring out with his mournful cries,
and the spreading waves of the wide sea,
and the air—which in better days                            1110
has felt your weapons.
A chest so thronged with suffering
must not be beaten lightly;
let all three kingdoms sound with a single grief.

    Strong arrows, that hung so long
to decorate his neck,
and heavy quiver,

blast down blows on his untamed back;
let his oakwood club beat his strong shoulders,
and the stout stick load up his torso with its cruel knots.    1120
May all his weapons weep such agonizing pain.
     Go, you poor unlucky little boys,
marked by the shadow of your father's labour,
you will never grow to share your country's glory,
never strike a blow to cast out cruel tyrants,
never learn to exercise your limbs
in the wrestling-grounds of Argos,
growing strong with boxing-gloves or fighting hand-to-hand—
ready to aim light darts from Scythian quivers
and fire them with sure hands,                                 1130
and pierce the unsuspecting deer as they run away,
and the lion-cub whose mane has not yet grown.
Go, you ghosts, to the gates of the Styx;
go on, poor innocents,
whose father's murderous madness
destroyed on the threshold of life.
Go and see the angry kings of Hell.


# ACT FIVE


HERCULES   What is this place, what kingdom is this, what part of
           the world?
Where am I? In the land of the rising sun, or beneath
the pole of the frozen north? Is this the distant country       1140
that lies between the western sea and Ocean?*
What air am I breathing? What land do my tired feet tread?
Certainly I have come back: but why do I see
these bloody bodies and the house upturned?
Perhaps my mind is forming images of Hell?
Even after my return, I see the hordes of ghosts.
I am ashamed to speak, I am afraid; something,
I intuit some disaster, but what—I do not know.
Father, where are you? Where is my brave wife,
and all our children? Hey—on my left side                      1150
the lion's skin is gone! It served me as a cloak

and as a bed: for me, it was soft enough.
Where is it? Where are my arms? Where is my bow?
Who could take them from me while I live?
Who stole such treasures? Who was unafraid
of Hercules, even asleep? I want to see my conqueror:
up, courage. My father must have left heaven
and got a new son—who? At whose conception
did the night last even longer than for mine?*
What horror is here? My children's bloody bodies,          1160
murdered, and my wife dead. What Lycus has seized power?
Who has dared commit such crimes against Thebes,
when Hercules is back? O fellow-countrymen,
inhabitants of the Argive fields and of the lands
beaten by the double sea, the realm of Pelops,
come to help, reveal to me the wicked murderer.
My rage is turned on everyone: whoever does not show me
my enemy, is my enemy.—You defeated a hero: why hide?
Go on, make more conquests: try the fierce horses
of the bloody Thracian, or the herd of Geryon,          1170
or the lords of Libya;* now is the time to fight.
Look, here I am, stripped bare; you can use my own weapons
to attack me, unarmed.—But why do Theseus
and my father avoid my eyes and hide their faces?
Stop crying! Tell me, who has murdered them,
all my family at once? Father, why so quiet?
Theseus, tell me! Come on, by your faith!
Neither speaks, they look ashamed, and hide
their faces, their furtive tears. In such disaster
what place is there for shame? Was it the tyrant          1180
of Argos,* or did a troop get up in arms
against me for the death of Lycus, come to wreak destruction?
I beg you, by the glory of my labours,
father, and the power of your name—
second only to Jove—tell me: who ruined my home?
Who is my destroyer?

AMPHITRYON          Let it go. Do not speak of these horrors.
HERCULES  What, no revenge?
AMPHITRYON                    Revenge often does harm.
HERCULES  Who could lie back and take such terrible things?

AMPHITRYON  One who feared even worse.

HERCULES                              What could be feared
  worse or more hard to bear than this, my father?            1190

AMPHITRYON  How little you yet know about the tragedy!

HERCULES  Pity me, Father! I hold out my hands in prayer:
  what is this? He retreats from my hands? This is a clue:
  where does this blood come from? Why is this arrow
  dripping with children's blood? It was dipped in the
       Hydra's poison . . .
  Now I see my arrows, I need not ask who did it.
  Who could bend the bow, or whose right arm
  could flex the string—hard even for myself?
  Father, tell me now. Did I commit this crime?
  They will not speak. I did.

AMPHITRYON                     The grief is yours,            1200
  the guilt your stepmother's. Bad luck is not your fault.

HERCULES  Now, Father, thunder from the whole of heaven;
  forget me, but belatedly avenge
  your grandsons. Let the starry sky resound,
  let both poles send darts of fiery flames.
  Bind me to the Caspian rock, tear me apart,
  and let the hungry vulture peck my liver.
  Why are the rocks of Prometheus empty? Why is the Caucasus,
  sheer and barren cliff, home to wild beasts and birds,
  empty now? Or take me to Scythia,                           1210
  where the Symplegades* close in upon the sea,
  tie my hands stretched out across the deep,
  and when the rocks begin to clash against each other,
  spurting up the ocean to the sky,
  I will block the mountains with my restless bulk.
  Or should I make a pyre, heap up treetrunks and logs,
  and burn my body, tainted with blood I should have loved?
  Yes, that is the way: send Hercules back to Hell.

AMPHITRYON  His mind is not yet free from its wild frenzy,
  but his rage has shifted, and his madness turns             1220
  upon himself. That is how passion works.

HERCULES                              Terrible home
  of the Furies, hellish prison, and places set aside
  for throngs of sinners! If any place of exile

lies hidden beyond Hell, unknown to me
and Cerberus, hide me there; I will go to the bottom-most pit,
and stay there.—Oh, my heart has been too fierce!
Who could grieve enough for you, my children, scattered
over the whole of the house? I have not learnt to cry;
my face is hardened by my sufferings.—One boy
can have my bow, another have my arrows,                    1230
this one, my mighty club. For you I will break my weapons:
child, for you I will break my bow, and my club will burn
for you, my dead son. On your pyre, child, I will lay
my quiver full of arrows, tipped with Hydra-poison.
My weapons will be punished. And I will burn you too,
the ones that cursed my weapons: my stepmother hands.

AMPHITRYON  Who has ever called an accident, a crime?

HERCULES  Major accidents are often crimes.

AMPHITRYON  Now we need a Hercules: to bear this weight
    of pain.

HERCULES  Madness has not deprived me of all my sense
    of shame:                                              1240
nobody could bear to see my wicked face.
My arms have been stolen: Theseus, I demand
you give them back right now. If I am sane,
give them to my hands; and if still mad,
father, stand back; I will find a way to die.

AMPHITRYON  By all the sanctity of family, and by my rights,
    whether you call me 'guardian' or 'father',
by my white hair which should earn me respect,
I beg you, do not leave me lonely in old age,
tired out by life; you are the one support                 1250
of this ruined house, the one light for my pain;
protect yourself. I got no benefit
from all your labours; I was always scared
of treacherous seas and monsters; I feared the bloody hands
or bloody altars of every tyrant in the world;
You were always gone from me, my son. Grant me the joy
of seeing you and touching you, I beg you.

HERCULES  There is no reason I should linger out my life
    delaying this awful day. I have lost everything:
mind, arms, fame, wife, children, hands,                   1260

and even madness. Nobody could cure
a heart so tainted: sin must be healed by death.

AMPHITRYON  You will kill your father.

HERCULES                                I will die, so as not to.

AMPHITRYON  With your father watching?

HERCULES                                I have taught him to
     watch my crimes.

AMPHITRYON  No: remember all your world-renowned good deeds;
     forgive yourself for just this one bad act.

HERCULES  Shall I forgive myself, after forgiving no one?
     I did good under orders. Only this is mine.
     Help me, Father, think of family loyalty,
     or of my cruel fate, or of the ruined glory                    1270
     of my old courage. Bring me my arms, let my hands
     take revenge on Fortune.

THESEUS                        Your father's prayers
     ought to work, but let me also try
     to move you with my tears. Get up, burst through your troubles,
     with your usual energy. Take up again that spirit
     which can face any danger. Now is the time
     to use your heroic courage: Hercules must not stay angry.

HERCULES  If I live, I am a murderer. If dead, a victim.
     I need to hurry up and clean the earth; too long
     this wicked, cruel, wild, barbaric monster                     1280
     has wandered free before me. Come, right hand,
     try a mighty labour, bigger than the Twelve.
     Coward, do you hesitate? Are you only tough
     when facing children and their frightened mothers?
     Unless I get my arms, I will tear up all the woodland
     of Pindus, and the groves of Mount Cithaeron
     and burn the forests as my pyre; or else destroy
     the roof of every house on every household, all the temples
     along with all the gods, down on my body,
     and bury myself in the ruins of my city.                       1290
     If the city walls feel light on my strong back,
     and seven gates are not enough to weigh me down,
     I will pull down upon my head the total mass
     of the central firmament, the boundary of the gods.

AMPHITRYON  Here are your arms.

HERCULES                         Fit words for Hercules' father.
  Look, this arrow was the one that killed my son.
AMPHITRYON  Juno used your hands to fire this shot.
HERCULES  Now I will use it myself.
AMPHITRYON                         How my poor heart
  thumps with fear, and beats my troubled chest.
HERCULES  The arrow is on the string.
AMPHITRYON                      Watch out! This time you
      know                                                    1300
  what you are doing; this crime will be your choice.
HERCULES                                          Well,
      what should I do?
AMPHITRYON  I ask for nothing; my grief is secure;
  you alone can save my son for me,
  and you cannot rob me of him. My worst fear
  is over now; you cannot hurt me, but you can
  still make me happy. Make your decision, knowing
  your reputation hangs here in the balance:
  either you live, or kill me. My frail life
  is weary with old age, weary with pain;
  I hold it on my lips. How can you hesitate          1310
  to give your father life? I will not bear it longer:
  I will push my chest against the deadly sword:
  here, here is the crime of Hercules sane.
HERCULES  Stop it, Father, stop it now, take back your hand.
  Lie down, my heroism: endure your father's order.
  Let this labour now be added to my labours:
  staying alive. Theseus, lift my poor father,
  collapsed on the ground. My guilty hand cannot touch
  my loved ones.
AMPHITRYON     I am happy to hold this hand,
  I will walk and lean on it, and holding it close to my heart   1320
  I will find comfort for my sadness.
HERCULES                         In exile, where can I go?
  Where can I hide myself, or where can I be buried?
  What Tanais or Nile or turbulent Tigris
  in Persia, or what wild barbarian Rhine,
  or Tagus, flowing full with Spanish gold,
  could ever wash my hand? If icy Maeotis

poured its frozen waters over me,
and all the ocean ran across my hands,
still my guilt sticks deep. Sinner, where can you run?
Do you want to go to the east or west?                          1330
Both of them know me; I spoilt my chance of sanctuary.
The whole world flees from me, the stars have turned
revolving on perverted paths; even the Sun
was happier looking at Cerberus. O loyal friend,
Theseus, find me a distant hiding-place;
since when you witness other people's crimes
you sympathize with the guilty, pay me back
for what I did for you; I beg you, take me back
to Hell, back to the shades, and tie me up
in the chains you left; that place will keep me hidden—          1340
but even Hell knows me.

THESEUS                        My country awaits you.
There Mars had his hands washed clean of murder,*
and he got back his arms; to you that land is calling,
practised in giving innocence back to gods.

# THYESTES

*Tantalus killed his son, Pelops, and gave him as a feast to the gods. As punishment in the underworld he suffered eternal hunger and eternal thirst, with water and food forever just out of his grasp. The two sons of Pelops struggled for power over the throne of Mycenae. They agreed that whichever of them possessed the golden sheep from Atreus' herd should be king. Thyestes produced the sheep, and seized power, ousting Atreus. But Atreus accused his brother of plotting with his own wife, Aerope, to steal the fleece and the throne; he seized power in turn, and exiled his brother. Seneca's play shows what happened when Thyestes returned from exile.*

# DRAMATIS PERSONAE

GHOST OF TANTALUS
FURY
ATREUS
ATTENDANT
THYESTES
TANTALUS JUNIOR, older son of Thyestes
PLISTHENES, younger son of Thyestes; silent part
MESSENGER
CHORUS

# ACT ONE

GHOST OF TANTALUS  Who draws me from the cursed realm of
    Hell
  where I must gape my greedy mouth for food
  that flees my grasp? Who shows the homes of gods
  to Tantalus again—despite that past disaster? Is anything worse
  than to be always wet and always thirsty, worse than hunger
  yearning without end? Can the slippery stone of Sisyphus
  be coming for me, must my shoulders bear it?
  Or the wheel which whirls the limbs in all directions?
  Or the sufferings of spreadeagled Tityos,* whose belly is an
    empty cave,
  who feeds black birds on his own eviscerated flesh,          10
  and since night heals whatever day destroyed,
  his horizontal body gives fresh food for every beak?
  I am doomed to some new torture. What will it be?
  O cruel judge, whoever you are, that give new punishments
  to those already dead: now try to increase the pain
  at which even the guard* of this terrible jail trembles,
  which makes grim Acheron shudder,* and terrifies
  even me. Now from my family line a swarm of children
  creeps out, who will surpass their ancestors.
  They will make me look innocent. No one has dared
    such deeds.          20
  If any space lies empty in the world of sin,
  I claim it. Minos* has work to do
  as long as Pelops' house still stands.
FURY                        Go on,
  horrible Ghost, torment the wicked gods with all your rage.
  Let every crime participate, and let the sword
  be drawn by each in turn. Let anger know no limit,
  no shame, while darkening passion whips their hearts,
  Long live the father's fury, and let eternal sin
  enter the hearts of his offspring. Let nobody have the time
  to hate a bygone sin. Let new ones always rise,          30
  with more than one in every one, and let crime grow

until it is avenged. Let the arrogant brothers lose
their power, and get it back from exile.* While kings falter,
let Fortune's shifting wheel turn from that troubled house.
Let power turn to grief, and grief to power,
and wash away the kingdom in the eternal tide of chance.
When god* says: 'Now go home,' let those exiled
for crime, return for new crimes; let them be hated
by everyone—as much as by themselves. Let there be nothing
out-of-bounds for anger. Let brother fear brother,                    40
parent child, child parent; let children's deaths be terrible,
but even worse their births;* let wife be enemy
to husband, plotting against him;* let war cross the sea,
let blood drench every land, and let Desire
conquer the mighty leaders of the people;
let sexual wickedness be the least of sins;
let moral righteousness, and faithfulness,
and all law perish. Let even heaven be touched
by human wickedness; why do the stars still shine,
and give their usual fiery glory to the world?                        50
Let deep night come, let day fall from the sky.
No more household gods! Bring hatred, murder, death;
use them to fill up all house of Tantalus.
Adorn the pillars, let the doors look green and merry,
bedecked with laurel leaves; and light a fire
fitting for your return. Repeat that Thracian crime,*
but with more victims. Uncle,* why so slow?
[Is Thyestes not yet grieving for his children?]*
Will he ever strike? Now let the fires be lit,
to boil the cauldrons; chop up the bodies in pieces,                  60
let children's blood pollute the ancestral hearth,
let the tables be set. You will come as a guest to a crime,
but one you* already know well. Today you will have a vacation,
to free yourself from hunger at that table.
Fill up your empty belly; watch as he drinks that cocktail
of blood and wine. I have found a type of feast
which even you would avoid. Stop, where are you going?
TANTALUS  Down to the lakes, the rivers, the waters which flee me,
the tree whose laden branches escape my hungry lips.
If only I could escape to the black bed of my prison,               70

and if my punishment seems too light, I would change
to a different river: may I be plunged in fire,
trapped in the middle of Phlegethon's boiling water.*
I call to all who suffer punishments*
decreed by fate: to you, who lie in fear,
beneath the hollow cavern, always frightened
the mass will fall upon you; you who shudder
at the gaping jaws of the ravening lions, and the awful Furies
who tangle you in their nets; and you, half-burnt,
trying to ward off the approaching torches.                     80
Listen to what I have to say: believe me, I learnt the hard way:
love your punishments. When will I achieve
escape from those above?*

FURY                               First you must cause chaos,
bring evil to the house, create in the kings
the urge to fight and kill; stir up the heart
into a crazy commotion.

TANTALUS                    Punishment is something
I must accept, not become. Is it my mission to go
like deadly gas from a vent in the earth, or a plague
infecting the world? Will I bring my very own grandsons
to such a horror? Great Father of Gods—and my father*
        as well,                                               90
though you blush to admit it—you may judge that my tongue
talks too much and deserves the cruellest torture;
still I must speak of this: I warn you all, do not
pollute your hands with blasphemous murder, do not
infect the altars with a Fury's curse. I will stand by,
I will prevent this evil.—Why are you lashing your whip
in my face? Why the threat of these circling snakes? Why pierce
my belly with desperate hunger? My heart is burning,
alight with thirst; my half-charred stomach smokes.
I follow you.*                                                 100

FURY Good! Spread out your madness through the house.
Make them resemble you, make them hate, make them thirst
to drink their own blood. Now the palace feels
your coming and it trembles with your touch.
Well done! Now go back to your hellish lakes,
your old familiar water. Now earth grieves

to feel the burden of your feet. Do you not see
how water is pushed back* into the ground, and how the banks
stand dry, as a fiery wind drives the clouds away?
The trees grow white, the fruit falls from the branches,          110
and near at hand the Isthmus, roaring with the sound
of breaking waves dashing on both its sides,
as its slim strip of land divides the neighbouring waters,
now widens and hears the sound of distant tides.
Lerna* now moves back, and river Inachus
lies hidden, nor does sacred Alpheus
reveal its waters. Mount Cithaeron's heights
have shed their snow and all their white is gone.
The famous town of Argos fears its ancient thirst.*
See, even the Sun wonders whether to order the day,          120
whether to goad to life a day which is doomed to die.

CHORUS  If any of the gods loves Argos, in Achaea,
or Pisa famous for its chariot-race,
or the Corinthian realm around the Isthmus,
which divides the twin gates and the sea;
if any cares for the snows of Mount Taygetus,
frozen by Boreas in the winter-time
on the topmost mountain peaks, melted again
in summer by the winds that guide the sails;
or if Alpheus' icy stream, that shines          130
as it glides past the Olympic stadium
is loved by any god, let him smile on us, and stop
this endless cycle of catastrophe.
Do not allow each generation to get worse,
each son more evil than his father was.
Let thirsty Tantalus' wicked children grow
weary at last, and put aside their rages.
Enough wrong has been done. Goodness has done no good,
and those alike in evil hurt each other. Myrtilus*
deceived his master, was betrayed, and died,          140
driven with treachery like his own, and giving
his name to that infamous Myrtoan sea.*
No tale is more familiar to Ionian sailors.
The little boy* was run through with a sword—what
        wickedness!—

while he ran eagerly to his father's arms:
he fell, an unripe victim at the altar,
and Tantalus, you carved him up, to serve
as a feast for the visiting gods. Eternal hunger
follows as reward for such a meal;
eternal thirst, too—proper punishment                          150
for such a savage kind of dinner-party.
Tantalus lingers, empty-mouthed and weary.
Abundance hovers over his evil head,
snatched from his grasp more swiftly than by Harpies.*
The tree is weighted down with heavy leaves,
and bent by its own fruit; its swaying motion
mocks the gaping jaws of Tantalus.
But for all his desperate yearning hunger,
he refuses to reach for the tree. He has had already
so many disappointments. He turns away,                        160
clamps shut his mouth, and binds his hunger with locked teeth.
But then the whole wood moves its riches closer,
ripe fruit surrounded by the heavy leaves
jumps just above his head, and sets on fire
his hunger. Hunger tells his hands: 'Wake up,
and get to work.' But when he stretches them out
he sets himself up for failure. All the harvest
and all the nimble grove is snatched into the air.
Then thirst comes over him, as bad as hunger;
his blood grows hot, the fire sets him alight;                  170
poor man, he stands there hoping for the water,
which seems to flow towards his mouth; but it twists away,
leaving a barren, empty channel. The stream
abandons him; he tries in vain to follow.
He drinks the thick dust left from the rushing river.

# ACT TWO

ATREUS  You have no courage, will, or spirit! What is worse,
    in my view, for a tyrant in a crisis,
    you have not taken revenge. After such crimes, such lies,
    such brotherly betrayals, can you do nothing in your anger,

Atreus, but whine? The whole world ought already          180
to be ringing with your clashing arms, your fleet
should be lined up on both sides of the Isthmus,
country and town should blaze with fire, and swords
flash everywhere. Let the whole land of Argos
sound with the clatter of horsemen; let the forests
and mountain citadels provide the enemy
no safety. Come forth, people of Mycenae,
and blow the trumpet of war. If anyone tries to protect
that hated brother of mine, I will have him slaughtered.
I do not care if this great and glorious house          190
falls to ruin and kills me, as long as it kills him too.
Come on, my soul! Do deeds that history will condemn
but never cease to speak of. The crime that I must dare
is black and bloody—the kind of thing my brother
would wish he had done himself. To revenge a crime
you must go one better. Can any brutality outdo
the crimes of Thyestes? Does he ever give up?
His ambition knows no bounds when times are good;
no rest, when times are bad. I know the man:
persuasion and advice have no effect. He can be broken.          200
So now, before he has had time to gather his strength,
a pre-emptive strike is needed, to stop him attacking me
when I am off my guard. He will kill me, or I him;
the winner is the one who gets there first.

SERVANT                              Are you not afraid
the people will speak against you?

ATREUS                              The best thing about being king
is making folks accept whatever you do,
and even praise it.

SERVANT              If you force praise by fear,
hatred and fear come back around to you.
True glory, true respect, come from the heart
not from the lips.

ATREUS              Even a low-born peasant          210
can get true praise. But only the powerful
can get false praise. Let them want what they do not want.

SERVANT  A king should want the good, his wishes match his
          people's.

ATREUS  If rulers can only do good things, their rule
   depends on the people's consent.

SERVANT                If there is no honour,
   no reverence for law, no trust, no faith, no goodness,
   the kingdom cannot stand.

ATREUS            Trust, faith, goodness,
   are merely private goals; kings follow their own way.

SERVANT  Remember that harming a brother, even a bad one,
       is wrong.

ATREUS  Any wrong is right against a brother like that.     220
   What crime has he left undone, what has he spared
   to touch with sin? He seduced my wife, he stole her
   and stole my kingdom too; he used deceit
   to get the ancient mark of rule and to wreak havoc
   upon our family. In Pelops' lofty stables
   there is a famous magic ram, lord of a wealthy flock.
   A golden fleece flows over all his body.
   Every new king in turn from the race of Tantalus
   bears a sceptre gilded by that wool.
   The owner of the ram is king, he has the power     230
   over this mighty house. Safe in a distant meadow
   the holy animal grazes; the meadow is surrounded
   by a stone wall to protect the fateful beast.
   With brazen daring he made my wife his partner,
   betrayed my bed and stole away the ram.
   That was the source of all our pain, inflicted
   by each upon the other. In fear I wandered, an exile,
   through my own kingdom, threatened by all my family:
   my wife was corrupted, my throne shaken by betrayal,
   my house was sick, my blood in doubt.* I was sure of nothing   240
   except my brother's enmity. Why hesitate? Begin,
   at last, to raise up your spirits. Look to Tantalus and Pelops:
   my actions must be made to fit their model.
      Tell me how to slaughter this terrible man.

SERVANT  Let your enemy die by the sword, and breathe his last.

ATREUS  Death is the end of suffering. I want him to suffer.
   Only weak kings kill. Under my rule, people beg
   for the favour of death.

SERVANT               But are you not moved by morality?

ATREUS  Away, morality!—If in fact you ever came
  to our house. Let come the gang of ravening Furies,      250
  with violent Erinys, and Megaera, shaking
  fire in each hand. The rage that burns my heart
  needs to become more savage. I want to be filled
  with greater horror.

SERVANT                    You are mad! What is your plan?

ATREUS  Nothing that could accept the normal limits of pain;
  I will leave no crime undone, and none will be enough.

SERVANT  Death by the sword?

ATREUS                          Far too little.

SERVANT                          Burning?

ATREUS                                  Still too little.

SERVANT  Then what means can your huge resentment use?

ATREUS  The man himself: Thyestes.

SERVANT                              Too much! even for your rage.

ATREUS  Yes, I agree. A trembling frenzy shakes my heart,      260
  and stirs it deep inside; I am swept away—to where
  I do not know, but I am. Earth bellows from below,
  the day is calm but I hear thunder; through all its towers
  the palace crashes and seems to break. Shaken,
  the Lares* turn away. Let it be, let this evil come about,
  despite your terror, gods.

SERVANT                    So what are you planning to do?

ATREUS  My heart is swollen with some greater thing,
  something extraordinary, more than human.
  It stirs my idle hands. I know not what it is,
  but it is something huge. And let it be. Heart, take it up.      270
  Crime suits Thyestes, suits Atreus too;
  let both perform it.—The house of Thrace has seen
  feasts unspeakable*—of course, it is an atrocity,
  but rather too cliché. My resentment needs to find
  something more. Procne, inspire my heart,
  with Philomel—our motives are alike.* Help me,
  urge on my hands. Let the father carve and eat
  his children, and do it with greed, and even joy.
  Good, that is plenty; I like this type of punishment—
  for the moment. But where is it? Why is Atreus      280
  innocent so long? A vision appears before me,

of a bloodbath, of a father's bereavement, his loss devoured
by the father's mouth. My heart, why shrink again,
why sink before the thing itself? Come on, you have to be brave.
As to the worst obscenity in my evil plan,
it is: he will do it himself.

SERVANT                     But how will you deceive him
to put his foot into our net and be trapped?
He knows you hate him; he suspects you.

ATREUS                                        He could not be caught
unless he wished to be. He hopes to get my kingdom.
That hope will make him brave the threats of the stormy sea,     290
cross over the dangerous straits of Libyan Syrtis,
that hope will make him meet Jove's thunderbolt,
that hope will even make him face the worst of all:
his brother.

SERVANT      But who can make him trust you? Who
can make him believe it?

ATREUS                     Evil hope will swallow anything.
But I will send my sons to tell their uncle
his days of wandering in exile are finally over,
he can change misfortune for a kingdom, and rule Argos
sharing the power. If at first Thyestes stubbornly refuses
to listen, then his children—being naive, and tired     300
from all their troubles, easy to win over—
will yield first. Then his old ambition,
the bitterness of poverty and hardship,
will soften him, however hardened from misfortune.

SERVANT  But time has surely made his pain seem light by now.

ATREUS  Wrong! Every day he feels his suffering more.
It is easy to bear misfortune, hard to go on doing it.

SERVANT  Pick other agents* for your savage plan.

ATREUS  Young people are more obedient to bad orders.

SERVANT  If you teach them to turn on their uncle, they will turn
          on their father.     310
Crime often comes back round again to its teacher.

ATREUS  Even if nobody teaches the ways of crime and deceit,
power itself will teach it. Are you worried they will grow bad?
They were born that way. The plan you call so wicked,
which you think savage, brutal, blasphemous—

maybe Thyestes is plotting it already.

SERVANT                              Will the boys
be told of the plot?

ATREUS                  Children of tender years
cannot keep a secret; they could reveal my scheme.
Bitter experience teaches one to keep quiet.

SERVANT  Then you will trick the boys through whom you plan    320
to trick Thyestes?

ATREUS                    Yes; then they will be innocent.
Just think: why should I implicate my children
in my own crime? Our hatred is between us, let us solve it.
No, my heart! You are shrinking back. If you spare your boys,
you will spare his too. Let Agamemnon be
a knowing instrument of my plot; let Menelaus
be conscious of the crime. Let me get proof
of their paternity from this bad deed. If they refuse
to fight for hatred, if they call him, 'Uncle',
he is their father. Let them go.—But a fearful face          330
often reveals the truth; large plots betray
people against their will. Let them not know
the size of the scheme they serve.—And you must not tell.

SERVANT  I need no warning. Loyalty and fear—
but loyalty mostly—keeps your secret safe with me.

CHORUS  Now this noble house,
    descended from ancient Inachus,*
    has finally fixed* the brothers' quarrel.
        What rage incites you
    to shed each other's blood                                340
    and get the throne by crime?
    In your greed for power, you do not know
    where kingship really lies.
    Wealth does not make the king,*
    nor robes of Tyrian purple,*
    nor the diadem on the brow,
    nor ceilings bright with gold.
    A king is one who can set fear aside,
    who has no wickedness inside his heart.
    Neither the rashness of ambition, nor                     350
    the fickle favour of the populace

can ever sway him.
Not all the gold-mines of the west,
or all the wealth of Tagus
whose riverbed shines golden;*
nor all the wheat, ground by the threshing-floors
in the blaze of the Libyan harvest.*
The zigzag of the lightning's path
will never touch him, nor the wind
from the east, seizing hold of the sea;                           360
nor the savage swelling of the wild
Adriatic Sea.
No soldier's spear
nor drawn swords can subdue him.
From a place of safety,
he looks down on everything,
and willingly meets his fate.
He does not complain at dying.
    Let the rulers band together:
those who rouse the nomadic Dahae,*                               370
those who control the Indian Ocean,
whose waters are stained the colour of blood
by so many shining jewels;
or those who fight on the Caspian Mountains
the strong Sarmatian invaders.*
War is for those who dare to walk
on the frozen Danube, and those who wear
distinguished robes of silk:
the Seres,* who live beyond our maps.
A strong mind is more powerful.                                  380
There is no need of horses,
there is no need of arms and feeble weapons,
such as those the Parthian
shoots from a distance when he pretends to flee,*
no need to flatten cities
by bringing in siege weapons
to whirl the boulders through the air.
A king is a man without fear,
a king is a man without desire.
Everyone makes this kingdom for himself.                         390

Stand, if you wish, on the slippery
pinnacle of power.
But I am satisfied with sweet peace.
Let my place be humble, let me enjoy
quiet free time forever.
Let my life flow by in silence,
unmarked by the people of Rome.
When my days have passed in this way,
without noise, let me grow old,
but never rise in class, and let me die.                    400
Death weighs more heavily on those
who are all too well known to everyone
but who do not know themselves.


# ACT THREE

THYESTES  How I longed for my homeland, my house,
    and the wealth
of Argos! This is the greatest happiness for exiles, after pain,
to see their native earth and their ancestral gods—
if there are really gods—and the high and holy walls
built by the Cyclopes,* on larger-than-human scale.
I see it all at last—the racetrack thronged with boys,
where I often used to win the prize, in my father's chariot.     410
All Argos will rush to meet me, all the people—
but that includes Atreus. Go back to your exile in the woods,
the thickly tangled groves, and the life you led in the wild,
with animals, and like them. No reason to be dazzled
by the false, flashy brightness of royal power.
When you look at the gift, look at the giver too.
Just now, I had the kind of life that everyone would pity;
but I was brave and happy. Now, on the other hand,
I am dizzy with fear. My heart is stuck, and longs
to carry my body back. I find myself moving, unwillingly.      420
TANTALUS JUNIOR*  What is this? My father hesitates,
    he looks around, unsure of himself, uncertain.
THYESTES  My heart, why all this pondering? Why do you
    twist around

such an obvious course of action? When everything is in doubt—
the kingdom, and your brother—why would you fear more
  suffering?
Evil is conquered and tamed now: why run from misfortune?
Your pain has been well invested. Unhappiness now feels good.
Turn back and tear yourself away, while you still can.

TANTALUS J. Father, why are you driven to turn back from
  your home
as soon as you glimpse it? Why wrap your garments close      430
to avoid such marvellous benefits? Your brother is no longer
  angry;
he returns and restores to you part of the kingdom.
He sets the bones of the broken house, and gives you back
  yourself.

THYESTES Even I do not know quite why I am frightened.
I see nothing to fear, but I am still afraid.
I want to go, but my knees feel wobbly and weak,
I get carried somewhere different from where I meant.
Even if sails and oars spur on a ship,
a current may confront them and carry the ship away.

TANTALUS J. Overcome the obstacles that clutter up your mind,   440
and look at all the prizes you can get if you turn back.
Father, you can be king.

THYESTES                    I can, since I can die.*

TANTALUS J. Absolute power is—

THYESTES                         Nothing, if you have no desires.

TANTALUS J. Your children will inherit.

THYESTES                                The kingdom cannot hold
  two.

TANTALUS J. Can someone choose unhappiness when happiness
  is possible?

THYESTES Believe me, it is only language misapplied
that makes us want to be 'great', and fear to 'suffer'.
Lofty position brought me constant fear; I was afraid
even of my own sword. Ah, what a wonderful thing
to get in no one's way, to have a carefree picnic      450
relaxing on the ground! Crime does not enter hovels:
those who live in tiny homes can drain their cups in safety.*
Poison is drunk from gold. I know of what I speak.

It makes good sense to choose bad fortune over good.
The little low-lying town does not tremble at the house
that stands up high above it on the mountain peak,
nor does the ivory shine on the lofty ceilings;
no sentry guards my bedroom while I sleep.
I need no fleet to catch my fish, I do not need
to drive the sea away with piles of rocks,*                        460
nor glut my greedy belly with imported goods.
No distant field in Parthia or Geta need be ploughed
to feed me; I need no worship with incense or altars,
replacing Jupiter with myself. No treetops sway
up high upon my roof; no steaming baths that take
many hands to heat. My days are not passed in sleep,
I do not stay awake to drink all night.
Nobody fears me; I have no need of weapons to keep
     my house safe:
deep peace comes to those in modest circumstances.
The ability to do without a kingdom is a kingdom.             470

TANTALUS J.  If god gives power you should not turn it down,
  nor try to get it. Your brother asks you to rule.

THYESTES  He asks? There must be trickery of some kind.

TANTALUS J.  Family loyalty usually comes back again,
  the love we ought to feel will heal its long-lost strength.

THYESTES.  Could my brother love me? Before that happens,
  the sea will rise to drench the stars, the raging waves
  of the stormy Sicilian strait will stand stock still,
  ripe corn will grow on the Ionian waters, and black night
  will light the earth. A loyal pact will sooner             480
  join fire to water, death to life, or wind to sea.

TANTALUS J.  But why are you afraid? What do you suspect?

THYESTES  Everything. What limit should I put to my fear?
  His power is as great as his hatred.

TANTALUS J.                                What power does he have
        against you?

THYESTES  I fear nothing for myself now; but you, sons,
  make me fear Atreus.

TANTALUS J.               But you are on guard; why fear?

THYESTES  When trouble comes it is too late to be careful.—
  Let it go. But I declare to you, my son, just this one thing:

I follow you, it was not my idea.

TANTALUS J.                              God will

smile on good thinking. Go, no hesitation.                    490

ATREUS  The beast is tangled in the nets I laid.

I see his offspring with him, all that hateful family
joined together. Now my hatred lives
safely; at last Thyestes is in my hands,
he comes to me, he comes, and all of him.
I can hardly control my feelings, my vengeance strains
      at the leash:
just like an Umbrian hound* held on a long rope,
as he tracks his prey with his keen nose, his face
close to the ground; while he sniffs the lingering scent of the boar
from a distance, he runs quietly, and listens,                    500
but when the prey gets nearer, then he strains
with his whole neck, and shouts with all his lungs:
'Hurry, Master!' and he tears himself from the collar's grip.
While my anger hopes for blood it cannot hide:
but I must hide it. Look how his hair is matted
with dirt and long enough to cover his sad face.
Look at his horrid beard. My loyalty must be perfect:
How nice to see my brother!* Come to my arms!
I missed you. Whatever quarrels we had are over now.
From this day forward let us pay respect for family;                    510
let us say no to hatred! No more being enemies!

THYESTES  If you were not like this, I could have refuted
      all charges.
But Atreus, I confess. I committed all the crimes
you thought I did. My case looks black in the light
of your brotherly love today. A man who could hurt
so good a brother seems a total scoundrel.
It is time for tears. For the first time you see me a suppliant;
never before have I begged, but now I kneel before you.
Let all our anger be set aside, all rage
be wiped clean from our hearts. Take these sweet children                    520
as pledges of my good faith.

ATREUS                              Stop hanging onto my knees!

Stand up and come into my arms instead! And you,
protectors of our old age, all you boys,

come and embrace me!—Take off these dirty clothes;
it hurts me to see you like this. Dress up in garments
as rich as my own. Be ready to take your share
of your brother's kingdom. This is my greatest glory:
returning my father's crown to my brother safe and sound.
Having a kingdom is only luck; to give it away is virtue.

THYESTES   Brother, may the gods reward you fairly,                    530
   with blessings to match such kindness. But the royal crown
   would not suit my rough appearance, and my hands
   are too tainted to take the sceptre. I would prefer
   to be lost in the midst of the crowd.

ATREUS                                     This kingdom allows
      two rulers.

THYESTES   I see all that is yours as mine, dear brother.

ATREUS   When Fortune pours out gifts, who would refuse?

THYESTES   The man who knows how fast they flow away.

ATREUS   Do you forbid your brother to get glory?

THYESTES   Your glory is achieved, mine is to come;
   my mind is set, I will reject the kingdom.                          540

ATREUS   I will leave my share unless you take yours.

THYESTE   I will accept it. I will bear the name of kingship;
   but you will have the law, the army and myself.

ATREUS   Accept and bear the bindings on your noble head;
   I will sacrifice the designated offerings* to the gods.

CHORUS   Would anyone believe this? Fierce Atreus,
   so wild and violent, so lacking self-control,
   stopped dead, stunned, at his brother's face.
   There is no greater power than true devotion;*
   strangers' quarrels may endure long years,                         550
   but true love always holds those it has held.
   When major grievances stir anger up,
   to rupture friendship and sound the sign for war,
   when light-armed troops are clattering their reins,
   and shining swords swing out from all directions,
   wielded by Mars who longs for more fresh blood,
   raging as he swipes again and again—
   loving duty overcomes the sword
   and joins the fighters' hands in peace, to their chagrin.
      What god has made this sudden truce, after                      560

so great a conflict? Just now throughout Mycenae
rang out the dreadful noise of civil war.
The mothers, faces pale, clutched hold of their babies,
the wives were fearful for their armoured husbands;
their swords unwillingly obeyed their hands,
rusty and ruined from the time of peace.
One struggles to restore the falling walls,
another to rebuild the shaken turrets,
another locks the gates with iron bolts,
and terrified, up on the battlements,                           570
the guardsman keeps awake the whole long, anxious night.
For fear of war is even worse than war.
But now the threats of cruel swords subside;
now the deep rumble of the trumpets sounds no more;
now the shrill bugle's screech no longer rings;
deep peace has been restored to the happy town.
   So, when the waves are swelling from the deep,
when the north wind whips up the Sicilian sea,
the monster Scylla roars as her caves are battered,
and sailors in the harbour fear the sea,                        580
vomited out by ravenous Charybdis.*
The savage Cyclopes, who live on top
of molten Etna, fear their father's* work:
in case the waters poured on top put out
the fire that sizzles in the ever-burning furnace.
Ithaca trembles and Laertes fears
his own poor kingdom will be under water.
But if the winds grow weak and lose their strength,
the sea subsides more gently on its bed,
the waters which the fleet had feared to cross—                 590
even the splendid ships with sails unfurled—
lie calm and open to the playful skiff.
You can pause and count the swimming fish
where recently beneath the giant storm
the shaken Cyclades* were trembling at the sea.
   No situation lasts. Pleasure and pain
give way in turn; but pleasure is more brief.
A fleeting hour exchanges high and low.
The man who can give crowns to other men,

before whom people kneel on trembling knees, 600
whose nod can make the sun-dark Indians,
the Medes, and the Dahae, whose horsemen fight the Parthians,
all at an instant lay aside their wars—
that man is worried as he wields his sceptre,
fearfully trying to tell the future, the chances
which whirl the world around, and fickle time.

　　You to whom the lord of sea and land
has given the great power of life and death,
set aside your proud and puffed-up face.
Whatever your subordinates fear from you, 610
your master may in turn inflict upon you:
for every kingdom lies beneath another.
If daybreak when it comes sees someone proud,
that day's departure will see him lie low.
　No one should trust too much in his good fortune,
no one should give up hope of better luck.
Clotho mixes good with bad and stops
Fortune from standing still; each man's fate rolls round.
No one has supporters rich enough
that he can guarantee himself tomorrow. 620
God moves our lives around on his swift spindle
and turns them upside-down.


# ACT FOUR

MESSENGER  What wind can whirl me sky-high through the air,
　　and wrap me in dark clouds, to tear my eyes away
　　from such abomination? This house would make blush
　　even Pelops and Tantalus.
CHORUS　　　　　　　　　　What is your news?
MESSENGER  What place is this? Is it Argos, Sparta,
　　inheritance of two good brothers,* bordering
　　the twin sea-spouts of Corinth? Or is this where
　　the savage nomads run in flight on the frozen Hister; 630
　　or Hyrcania, deep with snow, or Scythia, home to wanderers?
　　What place is witness to so great a horror?
CHORUS  Tell us, reveal the evil, whatever it is.

MESSENGER  If my heart stops fluttering, if my body, stiff with fear,
can let my limbs be free. The vision of that crime
will not go from my eyes. Storm-winds, carry me
to where the day is taken far away.
CHORUS  Do not keep us suffering in suspense!
Tell us what you shudder at! Reveal the criminal!
I ask not 'Who?' but 'Which of them?' it was. Out with it!      640
MESSENGER  On top of the citadel, one side of Pelops' castle
is turned towards the south. Its farthest side
rears high as the mountain, shadowing over the city.
If the people grow rebellious, kings can reach
to strike them. An enormous hall inside
shines bright, its woodwork all adorned with gold,
its marvellous columns spotted with different colours.
After this public area, known and revered by all,
the palace spreads out into many rooms:
a hidden space lies in the farthest part,                      650
an ancient grove buried in a deep valley,
at the centre of the kingdom, where no tree
blossomed or put forth fruit; no gardener pruned them.
The yew and cypress and the black holm-oak
swayed in that shadowy wood. Above them all
the oak tree dominates the grove from its great height.
From here the sons of Tantalus begin their reigns
from here they ask for help when things look bleak or doubtful.
Gifts hang from the trees; there is the trumpet,
the broken chariot,* spoils of the Myrtoan Sea;               660
the wheels hang down from the pole that deceived the king.
All the family's history is here. Here Pelops
attached his turban to the tree, and the enemy spoils,
and a cloak embroidered with triumphs over foreigners.
Under the shadows is set a dismal fountain,
stuck in a black and stagnant pool; most like
the ugly water of terrible Styx, by which the gods swear faith.*
They say the spirits groan here in the dead of night,
the grove resounds with the clattering of chains,
and the ghosts howl. All things that make one shudder        670
even to hear, are there made visible. Old tombs break open,
releasing hordes of wandering dead. Everywhere spring

unprecedented wonders. Indeed, throughout the wood,
flames sparkle, and the tallest trunks shine, without fire.
Often the wood rings out with triple barking,
often great phantoms terrify the house.
Fear is not soothed by dawn: night-time belongs to that grove;
even in full daylight, the place is ruled by awe.
True oracles are given here to those who ask,
when from the inmost place, with a great crash,                    680
fates are set free, the whole wood gives a roar
when god unfurls his voice. This was the place
where angry Atreus dragged his brother's children.
The altars are adorned—how can I say this?—
the little princes have their hands tied back;
he binds their poor little heads with a purple band.
Incense was not forgotten, or the holy juice of Bacchus,*
and with the knife he daubed the victims with salted grains.
All due ritual was observed, in case such a horrible crime
be done improperly.

CHORUS                     Who held the sword?                        690

MESSENGER  He was the priest himself, he was the one
who gabbled out the deadly prayers, the rites of murder.
He stood there at the altar, he checked the victims' bodies,
and he himself arranged them for the knife,
and acted as the audience.* No part of the rite was lost.
The woods were trembling, the whole ground was shaken,
making the courtyard totter: it seems to hesitate,
unsure where it can set its weight. A shooting star
rushes with a black trail on the left part of the sky;
the dedicated wine is changed to blood                             700
and flows into the fire. His royal crown
kept falling down. In the temples the statues wept.
All were aghast, but Atreus himself
alone remained unmoved, and was the one
to scare the gods that tried to threaten him.
Without delay he stood at the altar and scowled.
Just as in the forests of the Ganges
a hungry tigress prowls between two bullocks,
wanting to seize them both, but wonders which
to pounce on and bite first; she turns her jaws                    710

this way and that, keeping her hunger waiting—
so dreadful Atreus watches the boys whose lives are due
to his unholy rage. He wonders which
to slaughter first, and which to butcher second.
It makes no difference, but he ponders, and enjoys
order in brutality.

CHORUS                    So which did he strike?

MESSENGER  Do not imagine he lacked family feeling:
first to be killed was his father's namesake, Tantalus.

CHORUS  How did the boy behave or look as he was killed?

MESSENGER  He stood there unconcerned and he refused          720
to waste his voice on prayers. But the wild murderer
buried his sword in a deep thrust, and pressing down
he fixed his hand on his throat; when he drew out the sword
the corpse still stood; it was unclear for a while
where it should fall, but it fell on the uncle.
Then that barbarian dragged Plisthenes to the altar,
and added him to his brother. He cut through his neck;
the body without its head flopped to the ground,
while the head rolled down, protesting indistinctly.

CHORUS  After the double murder what did he do?          730
Did he spare the little one, or heap more crime on crime?

MESSENGER  Just as the long-maned lion in Armenia
lies on his heap of victims after slaughter,
his jaws dripping with blood, his hunger assuaged,
he does not set aside his anger, everywhere
he still pursues the cattle, snarling with tired teeth—
so Atreus rages and swells with his rage,
holding out the sword drenched in the two boys' blood,
careless where his fury leads him, cruelly,
he drives the blade in the chest of the child, right through,          740
and all at once it pokes out from his back.
He fell and put the fires out with his blood,
wounded on both sides, he died.

CHORUS                              What savagery!

MESSENGER  Are you horrified? If the crime stopped there,
Atreus would be holy.

CHORUS                    But can nature allow
a worse atrocity?

MESSENGER          You think this the end of his crime?
It was the first step.
CHORUS                    What more could he do? Did he throw
the bodies to wild beasts to tear, refuse cremation?
MESSENGER  If only he had! If only they lay unburied,
uncremated corpses, dragged away                                    750
to be a dismal dinner for wild beasts.
This man makes normal pain desirable:
if only the father could see his children unburied!
Incredible evil! Historians will deny it.
The entrails ripped from the living children's bellies
quiver, their veins throb, the heart still beats in fear;
but he sorts through the innards, checks the omens,
and scans the still-hot markings of the veins.
Once he was happy with the victims, he devoted himself
to his brother's dinner. He himself carved up                       760
the body into segments, chopped the broad shoulders
down to the trunk, sawed through the biceps, laid bare
the limbs and chopped the bones—the cruel monster!
He only left the heads and hands—hands given in good faith.
He sticks the organs to the spits, and over the furnace
they slowly burn and drip; the boiling water
tosses them as the pot glows hot. The fire jumps over
the meat he gives it, and repeatedly
throws it back to the trembling hearth, resisting
its orders to stay still; it burns against its will.              770
The liver hisses on the spit; I can hardly say
whether the bodies or the flame groaned louder. The fire turned
to pitch-black smoke, and the smoke itself, heavy with smog,
could not drift upwards, could not move up high;
the malformed cloud covered even the household gods.
O all-enduring Sun, though you retreated
and drowned the broken day in the middle sky,
you set too late!* The father rips apart his sons,
putting into his murderous mouth his own dear flesh and blood.
His hair is wet and shiny with perfume, his body heavy          780
with wine; his mouth is overstuffed, his jaws
can hardly hold new morsels. O Thyestes,
your only blessing is your ignorance.

But you will lose that too. If only Titan
could turn his chariot, meeting his own face,
and heavy night sent from the dawn usurp the day,
to cover up this black deed with new darkness.
But we must see this evil; all is now revealed.

CHORUS  Why, Lord of Earth and Sky?

Why is all beauty gone, why is dark night                          790
risen at noon? Why this change of yours,
why destroy day in the middle of day?
Why, Phoebus, do you rob us of your face?
The messenger of night, the Evening Star,
has not yet called the night-light out;
the turning of the western wheel
has not yet set to rest its tired horses;
day had not yet switched to afternoon,
the trumpeter had not sounded the ninth hour;*
the oxen were not weary yet—the ploughman                          800
stopped, astonished, at the sudden dinner-time.
What drove you from your heavenly path?
Why were your horses flung away
from their usual track? Is Hell's dungeon opened
to reveal the conquered Giants, in a new
attempt at war? Is Tityos, though his torso
is weary of wounds, renewing his ancient rage?
Is Typhoeus throwing the mountain off his body,
and stretching out his bulk? Have the enemies
from the Phlegraean Field built up a highway                        810
and is Pelion pressed by Thracian Ossa?*
Are the usual cycles of the sky all gone?
Will there be no more dawn and no more dusk?
The rosy mother of first light, the Dawn,
who normally hands the horses' reins to Phoebus,
stops in bewilderment:
her kingdom's entryway
is all gone wrong;* she does not know
how to damp the tired horses or to soak
their manes, which smoke with sweat, into the sea.*                 820
The setting Sun is quite surprised to see
Aurora, an unusual guest to him;

he tells the shadows to grow long although
night is not ready yet:
the stars have not inherited the sky,
no fire lights up the heavens,
the heavy Moon does not arrange the shadows.
    But whatever it is, let it be night!
Our hearts go pitter-patter, struck with such dread
fearing that everything is shaken and may topple          830
into disaster, chaos come again,
to overwhelm humanity and gods; Nature
again may cover up the earth and circling sea
and all the spangles of the painted sky.
No longer will the Sun, leader of stars,
raise his eternal torch and usher in
the seasons, pointing out the proper times
for summer and winter. The Moon, whose light reflects
the flames of Phoebus, will no longer take
terror from night, beating her brother's horses         840
as she runs her shorter race.
The mass of gods
will be heaped away into a single chasm.
The Zodiac, bearing the constellations,
the pathway of the sacred orbs, dividing
zones at a sideways angle, as it turns the years
now will slip and see its stars have fallen.
Aries, who brings back the gentle winds
to ships, when spring has not yet become kind,
will plunge down headlong underneath the waves,     850
through which he carried Helle,* terrified.
The Bull too will be lost, whose shining horns
display the Hyads; after him fall the Twins
and the curving claws of the Crab.
The Herculean Lion, burning and flaming with heat,
will fall from heaven now a second time;
the Virgin will fall down to the abandoned earth,
as will the weights of the level, truthful Scales,
taking with them cruel Scorpio.
Old Chiron* holding feather-tipped arrows         860
to his Thessalian bow

will break his string and the arrows will be lost.
The icy Goat, who brings numb winter back,
will fall, and break your urn, Aquarius—
whoever you are.* With you will disappear
the last stars of the sky,
Pisces the Fish.
The wonders never washed in waves before
will be drowned in the whirlpool which will cover the world.
The slimy Snake which divides the Bears in half          870
like a river, and cold Ursa Minor
covered with hard ice, and joined to the larger Snake,
and the slow guardian of the Great Bear,
Arctophylax will topple and rush to ruin.

    Were we from all humanity the ones
who earned destruction, crushed by the overturning
of the hinges of the world?
Will the last days come in our time?
We were born for a cruel lot,
whether we, poor things, have lost the sun,                880
or forced him into exile.—
Enough complaints, enough of fear;
one would have to be greedy for life not to want
to die when the world is dying.

# ACT FIVE

ATREUS  My steps are level with the stars, I rise above the world
    touching heaven's axis with my exalted head.
    Now royal power and my father's throne are mine.
    No need of gods! Now all my prayers are answered.
    It is good, it is plenty, it is enough, even for me—
    but why, enough? I will go on, and fill the father up          890
    with his children's death. Shame need not stand in my way:
    the day is over: go on while the sky is empty.
    If only I could prevent the gods from leaving,
    drag them down and force them all to watch
    this vengeance feast!—But let the father see it, that is enough.
    Though day resists, I will shake off the shadows,

under which your misery is hidden.
You have been lying there eating, looking safe and cheerful,
for far too long. You have had enough food, enough wine.
I need Thyestes sober for this horror.                          900
Slaves! All of you! Undo the doors of the palace!
I want the whole house open; party time!
    How sweet to watch him looking at his children's heads,
how sweet to see his altered face, to hear him
as his first grief gushes out. Look, he is dazed;
he stands there stiff and breathless. This is my work's harvest:
I want to watch the onset of his pain.
The open halls are bright with many torches;
he flops around on the gold and purple sofa,
propping his head on his left hand, befuddled with wine.        910
He belches. Yes! I am God! Highest of all the powers,
and King of Kings! This is better than I dreamed of.
He is full up. Now he sips from the silver cup.
Drink! No holding back! There is still plenty of blood;
there were so many victims. The vintage wine
camouflages the blood. May this drink, right here, right now,
round off his meal—a cocktail of his children's blood.
He would have drunk my children otherwise. Look, now
he calls for festive music. He is wasted, out of his mind!
THYESTES  Long suffering has numbed my heart.                   920
    Now set aside your cares!
Away with grief, away with fear,
away with that companion of my exile:
bitter poverty, and shame which weighs
heavily on the poor. The sense of loss
is worse than suffering.—Good for me!
I fell from a great height, but fixed my feet
firmly on the ground. Good for me!
I was oppressed by such calamities,
but bore the burden of my shattered power;                      930
I did not break. I was faithful to my royal blood:
unconquered, upright in the midst of pain,
I bore the imposition of disaster.
But now—cast off the clouds of cruel fate,
away with all the marks of my bad times;

time for a happy face to greet my joy.
The old Thyestes is no longer here.

    Unhappy people tend to have this fault:
never believing happiness has come.
But good luck can come back again, although     940
those who have suffered distrust celebrations.—
Pain, you rise up inside me for no reason!
Why call me back and tell me not to revel
in this happy day, why say that I should weep?
Why do you stop me from binding up my hair
with lovely flowers? It stops me, stop now, stop!

    The spring-time roses topple from my head,
my hair, so wet from all this spicy perfume,
stands up on end with sudden shock.
I had not meant to weep; I find my cheeks are wet.     950
My words are interrupted by my cries.
Sorrow loves tears—she is used to them.
Unhappy people have a strange desire to cry:
I feel like letting out unlucky groans,
I feel like tearing up my fancy clothes, deep-dipped
in Tyrian purple dye. I feel like screaming.

    The mind gives indications of a grief to come,
prophet of its future pain.
Sailors know a major storm is coming
when the calm waters swell without a wind.     960
Madman, what are you imagining?
What griefs or storms? Be trustful in your heart
towards your brother. At this point, whatever happens,
either your fears are groundless, or too late.

    Poor me! I do not want to feel this way:
but terror wanders in me and my eyes
gush with sudden tears. There is no cause.
Is it grief or fear? Or does great pleasure
make me cry?

ATREUS  Brother, let us celebrate together     970
    this happy day. Today my throne is solid,
    and we are bound in solid trust, sure peace.

THYESTES  I am full of food and full of wine.
    The only thing that could increase my pleasure

is if my boys could join me in my joy.

ATREUS  Your boys are here, believe me—held by their father.
They are here and always will be; no part of your children
can ever be taken from you. I will give you the faces
you long to see, I will fill you full with them all.
Do not worry, you will be satisfied. They are mingling          980
with my own boys, and enjoying a holy meal.
But they will be summoned. Have a drink.
This is a family cup.

THYESTES                    Thank you for the gift,
and here's to brotherhood. Pour a libation first
to the gods of our fathers; then drink. But what is this?
My hands refuse me, the cup is too heavy to hold;
the wine slips from my very lips and pours
away from my open mouth. How very frustrating!
Look, even the table is shaking, the ground trembles;
the fire flickers out; even the heavy sky          990
is empty, stupefied: not night or day.
What is this? The mighty dome of heaven slips,
struck over and over; darkness grows more dense;
night hides herself in night. All stars are gone.
Whatever it is, I pray the storm may spare
my brother and my children. Let it strike
only my wretched head. Now give my children back!

ATREUS  I will. And they can never be taken from you.

THYESTES  My stomach feels upset. What is this rumbling inside me?
What is trembling? I feel a restless weight:          1000
my belly moans with someone else's moan.
Come here, children! Your poor father wants you.
Come here! When I see you, I will be fine.
Where are their voices coming from?

ATREUS                              Get ready to hug your
    children.
They are here already. Do you not recognize them?*

THYESTES  I recognize my brother. Earth, can you allow
such an atrocity? Will you not break and sink
into the Styx and shadows of Hell, rip open and tear away
the kingdom and the king down into empty chaos?
Will you not uproot this Mycenean palace          1010

from its foundations? We should both already
have been with Tantalus. If anything lies lower
than Tartarus—and our grandfather—then, Earth,
    break your bonds,
create a massive chasm, cast us down there,
bury us and cover us both up
with all of Hell. May the souls of the damned
wander above our heads, and the river of fire,
Phlegethon, burning, burning, roasting its toasted sands,
surge roughly over my place of exile.
Earth, why do you lie there, still, a useless lump?                    1020
The gods have gone away.

ATREUS                Now be happy! You missed
  your children; here they are! Brother, no need to wait.
  Enjoy them, kiss them, multiply your hugs by three.

THYESTES  Is this trust? Is this friendship? Is this a brother's word?
  Is this how you end your hatred? I do not even ask
  to get my children safely back. I only want
  something which cannot hurt your hatred or your crime.
  I ask you as a brother: let me bury them.
  Let them be cremated, right away. Give me my children,
  not to keep, but lose.

ATREUS           You have all that remains                    1030
  of your children—and even what does not.

THYESTES  Are their bodies food for birds of prey?
  Are wild beasts ripping them apart and eating them?

ATREUS  You are the one who feasted on your sons.

THYESTES  This is what made the gods ashamed, this drove
  the day back to the east. Ah, what can I say,
  how can I even mourn? What words could fit?
  I see their heads cut off, their hands dismembered,
  their feet torn from their broken bodies.
  These are the parts that even their greedy father                    1040
  did not have room for. Inside my belly they heave,
  the horror struggles to escape; there is no exit.
  Brother give me your sword—it has already
  gorged on my blood. That way, I can journey to my children.—
  But the sword refuses. I will beat my chest,
  batter my body with grief—but now stop, poor hands:

be gentle to the dead. Who has seen such horror?
What pirate in the rocky, barren land
of Caucasus? What menacing highwayman
in Attica? Look, my children and I                              1050
weigh down one another. The crime at least is balanced.

ATREUS  Balance the books of crime when you commit it,
not when you pay it back. Even this is too little for me.
I should have poured hot blood into your mouth
direct from their wounds, to make you drink them alive.
My impatience cheated my rage. I used my sword
to stab them. I rushed at the altars. I satisfied
the holy fires with slaughter. Chopping up
their lifeless bodies, I pared their limbs
to little scraps, which I plunged in the boiling pots,          1060
and had them simmered on a gentle heat.
I cut the arms and legs and muscles off
while they were still alive, and skewered them
on nice slim spits. I saw them groan, and brought
fresh fires with my own hands.—But all of this
could have been better done by their own father.
My vengeance is a failure. The wicked father
munched up his sons, but did not know it; nor did they.

THYESTES  Listen to this sin, seas shut in your winding shores,
and you, gods, listen too—wherever you have hidden.          1070
Listen, Lower World, and listen, Earth; and Night,
heavy with darkness: pay attention to my words.
Only you, Night, are left to comfort me;
you too have been abandoned by the stars.
My prayers will be good and unselfish—in fact now
what could I ask for myself? I pray only for you.
Great King of the Sky,* Lord of the Hall
of Heaven, wrap the universe in clouds,
make all the winds wage war, and bellow thunder
from every part of earth; and do not use                        1080
the gentle hand with which you touch the homes
of innocent men. Strike as you did when the mass
of the triple mountain fell, along with the Giants*
who stood as high as mountains. So prepare
to fight and hurl your fires; avenge this ruined day,

shoot flames; make up the light robbed from the sky
with lightning. Do not pause to judge the case:
we both deserve damnation.—Or do it for my sins:
come find me, let your trident pierce
my heart with fire. My last hope for my sons          1090
is that I may cremate them with due rites.
Then I myself must burn.—If nothing moves the gods,
if there are no powers above to hunt for sinners,
let night remain eternal, covering up
my giant sins with growing darkness. Sun,
if you stay back I have no more complaints.

ATREUS Hurrah for me! Now I have my real prize.
Without this pain, my crime would have been wasted.
Now I believe I have my sons, I have my marriage back.*

THYESTES What had my sons done to deserve this?          1100

ATREUS                                        They were yours.

THYESTES But giving children, to a father...

ATREUS                                        Yes! And best of all,
legitimate sons.

THYESTES          I call the gods, the guardians of the good!

ATREUS And the gods of marriage?

THYESTES                              Who pays back crime with crime?

ATREUS I know your complaint: you mind me doing it first!
You are not hurt because you gulped that ghastly meal,
but because you did not serve it. You had the plan
to lay out the same menu for your credulous brother,
to make their mother help attack the children
and kill them the same way. Only this stopped you:
you thought they were yours.

THYESTES                        The gods will take revenge;          1110
I give you to their care for punishment.

ATREUS And for your punishment, I give you to your children.

# EXPLANATORY NOTES

The references are to the line numbers in the translation.

## PHAEDRA

5 *Cecrops . . . Parnethus . . . Thriasian dales*: all sites in Attica, the south-east promontory of central Greece, whose chief city was Athens.

8 *Riphaeus*: series of mountain ridges in Scythia, now identified with the Urals.

11 *Zephyr*: the west wind.

35 *Molossians . . . Cretans . . . Spartan dogs*: the Molossians, who lived in the mountains of NW Greece, had dogs known for their aggression. Cretan hounds are a famous type of hunting-dog. Spartan dogs were well known for their quickness and keen scent.

55 *masculine goddess*: Diana (Artemis), virgin goddess of the hunt.

92 *his usual faithfulness*: Theseus had already abandoned his former lover, Ariadne (see note to l. 760).

103 *loom of Pallas*: Pallas Athena was the inventor of weaving and the loom.

104 *the wool slips down . . . hands*: reminiscent of Sappho, fragment 102 —an account of a woman distracted by love from her work: 'Mother, I cannot tend my loom.'

107 *witnessing the silent rites*: refers to the Elysinian Mysteries, a secret religious ritual.

109 *the goddess*: Athena.

113 *the fateful trouble of my poor mother*: Phaedra's mother, Pasiphaë, fell in love with a white bull and gave birth to the half-man, half-bull Minotaur.

120 *What Daedalus . . . love*: Daedalus constructed a fake cow so that Pasiphaë could conceal herself inside it and mate with the bull.

122 *the terrible monster*: the Minotaur, shut up in the labyrinth created by Daedalus.

125 *the Sun, whom she detests*: Pasiphaë was the daughter of the Sun, who told Vulcan (Hephaestus) about Venus' adulterous affair with Mars.

149 *your father*: Minos.

154 *your grandfather*: the Sun.

157 *the father of the gods*: Jupiter.

174 *your brother's*: the Minotaur, killed by Theseus.

185 *one tyrant god*: Cupid, god of love.

192 *The sturdy Warmonger . . . the Blacksmith god . . . even Phoebus himself*: Phaedra lists in turn three gods mastered by Cupid: Mars, Vulcan, and Phoebus Apollo.

222 *Dis*: another name for Hades, king of the Underworld.

223 *Stygian*: 'hellish' (from the Styx, one of the rivers of the underworld). The dog is Cerberus, guard-dog of the underworld.

226 *former wife*: Theseus killed Hippolytus' Amazon mother, Antiope.

240 *love has conquered even wild beasts*: Phaedra alludes to the bull, conquered by love for her mother Pasiphaë.

244 *Pirithous' companion?*: suggests that Theseus, who has gone to the underworld to help his friend Pirithous steal someone else's wife (Persephone, wife of Hades), would be a hypocrite to condemn Phaedra's feelings.

245 *he indulged Ariadne*: Minos did nothing about Theseus' abduction of Ariadne, and therefore can be assumed to be tolerant towards his daughters' extramarital affairs.

247 *the breasts which were dear to you*: the Nurse was once Phaedra's wet-nurse.

275 *twice born*: there are two mythical accounts of Cupid's paternity: he may be the son of Venus by Mars, or, according to a less common tradition, Mercury.

286 *Hesperides*: a legendary garden tended by nymphs at the western end of the world.

298 *he called the cattle home*: Phoebus Apollo transformed himself into a human serf to work for Admetus; in earlier traditions, the labour is a punishment for Apollo's killing the Cyclopes, but in Hellenistic poetry it becomes service for love.

300 *great ruler . . . inferior beings*: Jupiter, who disguised himself many times in order to have love affairs with human women.

301 *he is a bird*: Jupiter changed himself to a swan to have sex with Leda.

303 *a young bull*: Jupiter changed into a bull to abduct Europa.

309 *the shining goddess*: the moon-goddess Diana, who fell in love with Endymion; the Chorus imagines that Diana must have had her heavier brother, Apollo (l. 316), take over her chariot while she spent time with her lover.

317 *set aside his quiver*: Hercules subjected himself to Queen Omphale, dressing as a woman and spinning wool.

389. *Tyrian dye . . . silk*: Phoenician (Tyrian) dye was used for splendid clothes; silk was wrongly believed to grow from trees.

401 *a woman from Tanais or Maotia*: Phaedra wants to model herself on the Amazons.

404 [CHORUS]: some editors attribute lines 404 and 405 to the Nurse.

405 *the Virgin*: Diana.

406 [NURSE]: some editors attribute this speech to Phaedra.

412 *Hecate*: a moon-goddess, often represented as 'triple': she presides over three realms (earth, sky, and underworld), and has three incarnations: Diana, Moon, and Hecate the witch.

421 *charms of Thessaly . . . sky*: Thessalian witches were said to use magic to try to draw the moon down from the sky.

422 *no shepherd*: the moon (Diana) fell in love with a shepherd, Endymion.

445 *Bacchus*: Roman god of wine (equivalent to the Greek Dionysus); here used as metonymy for alcohol.

447 *Venus*: Roman goddess of sex (equivalent to the Greek Aphrodite).

452 *God's rules*: 'God' is used in the singular, for some unspecified deity. This does not necessarily suggest monotheism. But Seneca, or the Nurse, could be drawing on Stoic belief in a universe permeated by a single divine spirit (see Introduction).

456 *rejoicing*: the Latin word *laetus* means both 'happy' and 'fertile'. The Nurse plays on the double meaning, suggesting that happiness and sex might be the same thing.

465 *Mars*: Roman god of war (equivalent of the Greek Ares).

475 *seize*: the verb used, *carpere*, is the same used in Horace's famous dictum, *carpe diem*, 'Seize the day' (*Odes*, 1. 11). The word cleverly reinforces the Nurse's *carpe diem* message: Hippolytus must seize his youth, before death seizes him.

478. *Styx*: the River of Pain, one of the four rivers of the underworld. It is here used to stand in for the whole underworld.

481 *follow nature*: alludes to the central Stoic precept that one should live a 'life following nature'. The Nurse perverts Stoic language: she means something very different by 'following nature' from the Stoic wise-man's life of restraint and emotional moderation (see Introduction).

504 *Ilissus*: a river in Attica, near Athens. The conversation in Plato's *Phaedrus* takes place by the Ilissus, represented as an idyllic spot.

505 *Alpheus*: a river that flows through Arcadia—a real place in central Greece, but also, in literature after Virgil's *Eclogues*, the location of a fictionalized pastoral world.

507 *Lerna*: the river by which Hercules killed the Hydra, in the Greek city of Argos.

527 *the first great age of man*: Hippolytus draws in this passage on the famous myth of the Golden Age, our earliest source for which is the archaic Greek poet Hesiod. The story that humanity has gone through a series of separate races, each more degenerate than the last. Modernity is always the worst age, the Age of Iron; before that, there were (in some versions) the Heroic Age, the Silver Age, and, earliest and best, the Golden Age.

528 *no blind desire for gold*: it is a conventional paradox that the Golden Age was characterized by people's lack of interest in literal gold.

530 *no trusting ships . . . deep*: the invention of seafaring is often said to mark the end of the Golden Age: it is the beginning of human domination of nature by technology, the end of natural symbiosis. Jason was supposedly the first to build a ship, for the voyage of the Argonauts.

560 *lays siege*: military language is applied to the world of erotic seduction.

564 *Medea*: after killing her children by Jason the Argonaut in revenge for his infidelity, Medea escaped to Athens. Aegeus, king of Athens, protected and married her. They had a child, Medus, and when Theseus, son and heir of Aegeus by an earlier union with another woman (Aethra), returned to Athens, Medea plotted to kill him. The allusion to Aegeus and Medea is a reminder that a stepmother has threatened a stepson in the previous generation; now history repeats itself, with a new, erotic twist.

567 *reason, nature, or passion*: Hippolytus makes a contrast between three concepts central to Stoic thought: *ratio* ('reason', 'rational good sense'), *natura* ('nature'), and *furor* ('violent passion').

571 *Hesperian Tethys*: the sea-goddess Tethys was the wife of Oceanus, god of the sea, and they lived in the farthest west (the land of Hesperus, hence Hesperian). Here normal events are reversed, so that the sea raises the sun from the west, rather than the sun sinking into the western ocean.

576 *Amazons*: a race of women who excluded men from their society and who fought battles like men. Their name may be from the Greek *amazos*, 'breastless', from their supposed practice of cutting off their right breast in order to throw javelins or shoot arrows better.

*they submitted to the yoke of Venus*: they were willing to have sex.

577 *you are the proof of that*: according to legend, Amazons killed their sons; theirs was an all-female community. Hippolytus was brought up by his father, Theseus.

605 *what I desire*: an incomplete line in the original.

627 *stole his wife*: Theseus helped his friend Peirithous steal Hades' wife Proserpine (Persephone) from the underworld.

650 *wound the long thread on the twisting path*: a reference to Theseus' first adventure, his journey to Crete, where Ariadne guided him through the Labyrinth and he killed the Minotaur.

654 *my Apollo*: as granddaughter to Helios, the Sun-god, Phaedra lays claim to the Olympian Sun-god, Apollo.

656 *even his enemy's heart*: Ariadne, Phaedra's sister, who should have been Theseus' enemy, fell in love with him.

663 *heavenly vault*: Ariadne became a star.

671 *Great ruler of gods*: Jupiter, king of the gods, who controls thunder and lightning.

688 *your mother's*: see note to line 113.

697 *the Colchian*: Medea, who was from Colchis, on the eastern side of the Black Sea.

709  *Diana of the crossbow*: the huntress goddess was famous for her skill at archery.

715  *Tanais . . . Maeotis*: rivers (in modern Russia, and on the Black Sea) that mark the ultimate eastern boundaries of the Roman empire.

718  *not even Neptune . . . a sin*: Shakespeare uses this passage in *Macbeth*: 'Will all great Neptune's ocean wash this blood | Clean from my hand? No, this my hand would rather | The multitudinous seas incarnadine, | Making the green one red' (II. ii. 59–62).

752  *Hesperus . . . Lucifer*: the Evening Star, which is also the Morning Star.

753  *thyrsus*: the ivy wand traditionally carried by Bacchus (Dionysus) and his followers.

756  *horned head*: in Hellenistic times Bacchus was often represented with horns, perhaps because of his association with bulls.

760  *loved somebody more than Bacchus*: Theseus. In the more usual version of the story, Phaedra's sister, Ariadne, was abandoned by Theseus on Naxos, and only then rescued by Bacchus. Seneca's Chorus seems to adopt an alternative version, in which Ariadne abandons Bacchus for Theseus.

781  *who have a habit of catching pretty boys*: a reference to Hylas, boy lover of Hercules, who was abducted by water nymphs on an island stopover while on the voyage of the *Argo*.

792  *cymbals*: traditionally believed to counteract witchcraft.

810  *Cyllarus*: the horse of Castor, brother of Pollux (the twin Dioscuri). In Virgil, *Georgics*, 3. 90, the horse is represented as belonging to Castor; Seneca corrects Virgil, since traditionally Castor was the horseman, Pollux the boxer.

838  *Eleusis . . . gift*: a reference to the rites held at the shrine to Ceres and Proserpine, goddesses associated with the harvest. Corn was said to have been given to Triptolemus, king of Eleusis, by Ceres. This is a highly allusive way of saying 'after four years', i.e. after four harvest-times.

839  *weighed out day to match the night*: at the equinox day and night are the same length.

904  *the second lot*: alludes to the tradition that the three parts of the world—sky, sea, and underworld—were assigned to the three brother gods by lot: Jupiter got the sky, Poseidon the sea, Hades the underworld.

927  *Antiope*: Theseus' first wife, Hippolytus' Amazon mother. If he had not killed her, Theseus suggests, then Hippolytus might have slept with her.

942  *my ocean father*: Neptune (Poseidon).

1014 *Auster . . . Corus . . . Leucate*: Auster is the south wind, Corus is the north-west wind. Leucate is a promontory of the island of Leucas, in the Ionian Sea—an area known for its storminess.

1022 *Asclepius*: son of Apollo, the god of healing.

1023 *Sciron*: a highway robber who made people bathe his feet and, while they were doing it, kicked them over a cliff where they were killed by a giant tortoise. He was killed by Theseus, and Ovid tells the story that his bones turned into the crags (*Metamorphoses*, 7. 444–7).

1024 *promontory of land*: the Isthmus of Corinth.

1067 *My father's job is conquering wild bulls*: Theseus killed the Minotaur (half-bull, half-man), and the Bull of Marathon.

1092 *Phaethon*: son of the Sun. He begged his father to let him drive his chariot one day, but the boy could not control the horses and was thrown down to his death.

1136 *Mother Goddess*: Cybele. The woods on Mount Ida, in the Troad, contained a place dedicated to Cybele.

1153 *the books are balanced*: because Hippolytus has replaced Theseus in the underworld.

1165 *you always bring disaster*: when Theseus went to Crete to kill the Minotaur, his father, Aegeus, told him to raise white sails on his ship on its return, to show that he was still alive. Theseus forgot to do this, and Aegeus killed himself when he saw the ship.

1167 *in love or hatred for your wives*: Theseus killed his first wife, the Amazon mother of Hippolytus, in hatred. He has now destroyed his home again because of his love for Phaedra.

1170 *Sinis . . . Procrustes . . . Cretan bull*: various villains and monsters killed by Theseus. Sinis used trees to pull apart his victims (see note to line 1224). Procrustes murdered his guests by hammering them to a bed. The Cretan Bull is the Minotaur, trapped in the Labyrinth created by Daedalus.

1180 *the fiery river*: Phlegethon, one of the four rivers of the underworld.

1181 *I want to do right by the dead*: Phaedra combines two traditional religious practices: she cuts and tears her hair as if in mourning for the dead, but she simultaneously prepares herself for death (as Iris in Virgil's *Aeneid*, Book 4, prepares Dido for death by cutting her hair).

1201 *Taenarus*: an entrance to the underworld.

1202 *Lethe . . . Cocytus*: Lethe was one of the rivers of the underworld, whose waters caused forgetfulness (which is welcome to the unhappy dead). Cocytus is another underworld river, known for its sluggish waters.

1205 *Proteus*: sea-god known for his ability to change shape at will.

1207 *Father*: Neptune (Poseidon), Theseus' divine father, who also helped him to abandon Ariadne on Naxos.

1212 *all three kingdoms*: sea, sky, and underworld, won by the three divine brothers, Poseidon, Jupiter, and Hades (see note to line 904).

1224 *Should a pine tree be bent . . . branches*: Theseus suggests that he should be killed by one of those whom he defeated in his heroic past. Murder-by-pine-tree was characteristic of Sinis. Seneca conflates two different legends about how exactly the killing worked. One version suggests that the hands of the victim were bound to one tree, legs to another, and the victim was thus torn apart. Alternatively, a single tree was used: the victim was catapulted into the air by the tree, and died from his fall. Seneca includes both the catapulting and the tearing apart.

1228 *I know what punishment I will get, and where*: because Theseus has already been to the underworld.

1237 *Sisyphus . . . Let the water mock . . . Tityos . . . the wheel*: the passage cites four of the most famous punishments of the underworld. Sisyphus had to push a rock up a hill, and every time it almost reached the top it rolled to the bottom again. Tantalus was always thirsty, always hungry: he had a stream of water and a bunch of grapes always just beyond his grasp. Tityos had his liver pecked out every day by a savage bird: every night it grew back and the same thing happened again. Ixion, father of Pirithous, was bound to a wheel and whirled around forever.

# OEDIPUS

29 *Cadmus*: the legendary founder of Thebes. After Cadmus' daughter, Agave, killed her own son, Pentheus, who had rejected the rites of Bacchus (Dionysus), Cadmus was driven out of the city and turned into a snake.

44 *Apollo's sister*: Diana, the moon-goddess.

119 *Parthians . . . fly*: Parthian archers used to fired arrows over their shoulders while riding away from the enemy (the 'Parthian shot').

129 *seven gates*: the city of Thebes had seven entrances.

166 *ferryman*: Charon, who carried the dead across the river Styx to the land of Hades.

171 *the Dog*: Cerberus, guard-dog of the underworld.

192 *Holy Fire*: i.e. *ignis sacer*, a skin disease similar to erysipelas, 'St Anthony's Fire'.

250 *and you*: the gods in the following list are: Jupiter, lord of the sky; Apollo, the sun-god; Diana, his sister, the moon-goddess; Neptune, god of the sea; and Pluto/Hades, lord of the underworld (who provides dark homes for the dead).

282 *double seas*: Corinth; the double seas are those on either side of the Isthmus of Corinth.

298 *I would let the god possess me*: i.e. if he were younger Tiresias would allow the god to speak directly through his body and voice, like a spirit medium, instead of using divination.

315 *Iris*: goddess of the rainbow.

335 *scatter the salted meal*: in Roman religious ritual the sacrificial victim was purified by having its head sprinkled with a mixture of brine and spelt, traditionally prepared by vestal virgins.

363  *the bad side*: diviners divided entrails into two areas: the lucky and the unlucky sides.

393  *Erebus*: Hell.

420  *pretending to be a blonde-haired teenage girl*: Juno was jealous of Jupiter's love-affairs with mortals. When Bacchus, son of Jupiter, was born from Semele, he was hidden disguised as a girl.

441  *after mangling Pentheus*: Pentheus, king of Thebes, refused to accept Bacchus as a god. In revenge, Bacchus drove Agave and her companions mad as they worshipped him on the mountains, and they tore apart Agave's son Pentheus, under the belief that he was a wild animal.

444  *Ino*: after Bacchus' mother Semele was killed by the thunder of her lover, Jupiter, Semele's sister Ino raised the boy. She was later transformed into a sea-goddess.

447  *Palaemon*: also known as Melicertes, son of Ino, who became a sea-god.

448  *barbarian pirates*: Bacchus, captured by pirates, turned himself into various wild animals, including a lion and a tiger; he also turned the masts and oars into snakes, and covered the ship with vines; the sailors went crazy, jumped overboard, and were turned into dolphins.

486  *daughters of Proetus*: in Argos, Bacchus drove the daughters of King Proetus mad, and they wandered in the woods thinking they were cows. The city of Argos then accepted the god—despite the fact that the city belonged to Juno (Hera), Bacchus' resentful stepmother.

489  *the girl*: Ariadne, abandoned on Naxos by Theseus, rescued by Bacchus.

498  *The new bride*: Ariadne, installed as a constellation in the sky.

502  *hates the thunder*: Bacchus' mother Semele asked to see her lover in his true form, but when Jupiter complied she was destroyed by his thunder; Jupiter rescued her foetus and carried him to term in his own thigh.

540  *through the vast ocean*: alder was used for making boats.

560  *Guardian of the Lake of Lethe*: Cerberus, guard-dog of Hell.

588  *the soldier brothers . . . teeth*: Cadmus sowed dragon's teeth, which sprang up as armed men.

611  *Zethus . . . Amphion*: twin sons of Jupiter, who built the city walls of Thebes. Dirce, wife of the tyrant Lycus, had treated their mother cruelly for many years; when the brothers grew up they tied her to the horns of a bull. Amphion was a great musician, and his music was powerful enough to lift the rocks to build the walls.

615  *Niobe . . . her ghosts*: punished for boasting that she had borne more children than Leto—mother of Apollo and Diana—by having all her children killed, Niobe now, in the land of the dead, is reunited with them.

616  *Agave . . . crazy*: daughter of Cadmus; inspired with divine madness by Bacchus, she killed her son Pentheus (see note to line 29).

712 *Cadmus came from Sidon*: searching for his sister Europa, abducted by Jupiter.

713 *Dirce's waters*: the fountain in Thebes.

714 *Tyrians*: Cadmus' companions, people of Tyre.

716 *his sister*: Europa, abducted by Jupiter in the form of a bull.

718 *that same god*: Jupiter.

719 *An oracle*: the Delphic oracle told Cadmus to follow a heifer until it lay down, and to make his home in that place.

722 *Boeotia*: from Greek *bous* (Latin *bos*) meaning 'cow' or 'ox'.

730 *Chaonian treetops*: oaks.

731 *still resting much of his body on the ground*: these lines refer to the legend that Cadmus, arriving at the location of the future city of Thebes, encountered a dragon which guarded the fountain of Dirce, sacred to Ares/Mars, god of war. He killed the dragon, and was told by the goddess Athena to sow its teeth in the ground. From the teeth sprang up a throng of armed men, who immediately began fighting each other. Only five survived, and these helped Cadmus build the city.

741 *Lucifer*: literally, 'the light-bearer', another name for the Morning Star, the planet Venus.

751 *the hunter*: Actaeon, grandson of Cadmus. He saw the goddess Diana bathing naked. In revenge, the goddess turned him into a stag and he was killed by his own hounds.

763 *goddess*: Diana.

813 *You got your name . . . feet*: the exposed baby had his feet pierced, to prevent him from toddling away. One of the etymological legends about the name 'Oedipus' suggests that it comes from the Greek words *oidao*, 'to swell', and *pous*, 'foot': so the name means 'Swollen-footed', as in Shelley's *Swell-foot the Tyrant*. The other traditional interpretation is that it comes from *pous*, 'foot', and *oida*, 'to know': Oedipus is then 'Know-foot', the one who knows enough about feet to solve the riddle of the Sphinx.

825 [JOCASTA]: the manuscripts attribute these lines to the Old Man. Zwierlein and other scholars attribute this intervention, and the follow-up remarks, to Jocasta, because in Sophocles' *Oedipus Tyrannus* it is she who tries to prevent Oedipus from discovering the full truth.

893 *the mad boy*: Icarus, who tried to fly on wings made by his father Daedalus, when escaping from the king of Crete. He flew too close to the sun, causing his wax wings to melt, and fell into the sea and drowned; the sea was renamed the Icarian Sea.

986 *Lachesis*: one of the three Fates, who spin the destinies of all people.

995 [*Epilogue*]: unlike most of Seneca's tragedies, *Oedipus* is structured in six sections, not five. The final section can be seen as a kind of epilogue.

## MEDEA

3 *the first ship*: the *Argo*.

5 *Titan*: the sun-god.

7 *Hecate triple-formed*: goddess associated with witchcraft and the moon. She is 'triple-formed' because her power extends to heaven, earth, and the underworld.

11 *master of the melancholy realm, and queen*: Hades, god of the underworld, and Persephone.

12 *abducted . . . but he kept his word to you*: Persephone was stolen by Hades to be his wife, and she still rules the underworld for six months of the year; Hades was thus a more honourable rapist than Jason, who stole Medea and now abandons her.

17 *you stood round my marriage bed*: Medea imagines that the Furies must have been in attendance at her doomed marriage.

29 *my grandfather*: Medea is the daughter of Aeetes, son of the Sun.

43 *your own cruel home*: the mountain-range of the Caucasus, which bordered on Medea's home city, Colchis, was famous for its harshness; the inhabitants of the Caucasus were believed to be particularly fierce and inhospitable.

60 *the royal Thunderer*: Jupiter.

63 *the goddess who restrains . . . Mars*: the goddess of peace, Pax.

67 *you, who bless all legal weddings*: Hymen, god of marriage.

71 *the messenger of double times*: Lucifer, who heralds 'double times' because he is both the Morning and the Evening Star.

79 *the city without a wall*: Sparta. Spartan women notoriously exercised like men, unlike the women of other Greek cities.

81 *Alpheus*: a river that runs through the Peloponnese. It was sacred to Jupiter.

83 *Aeson's son*: Jason.

84 *the child of thunder*: Bacchus (Dionysus), son of Jupiter, the thunder-god; Bacchus' mother, Semele, was struck by a thunderbolt when Jupiter appeared to her in his true form.

87 *the fearsome virgin's brother*: Apollo, who shakes the tripods of the oracles; he is the brother of the virgin goddess, Diana (Artemis).

89 *Castor . . . Pollux*: twin sons of Jupiter; Castor was known for his horse-riding, Pollux for his boxing.

97 *Phoebe*: Diana, the moon-goddess.

109 *Abusing masters . . . allowed*: licensed mockery was a traditional element in both Greek and Roman marriage celebrations.

131 *The golden glory . . . stolen*: the Golden Fleece, stolen by Jason with the help of Medea.

132 *the wicked girl's young playmate . . . sword*: the 'wicked girl' is Medea herself; her 'playmate' is her brother Aspyrtus, whom she dismembered,
scattering the pieces behind the *Argo*, as she and Jason escaped, to delay
the pursuit of her father, Aeetes.

134 *Pelias . . . pot*: Jason's hostile uncle, whom Medea killed by persuading his
daughters that they could make him immortal by putting him in a pot of
boiling water.

148 *Malea*: one of the three southern promontories of the Peloponnese.
Medea implies that her revenge will be so enormous that it will be seen
even in very distant places.

169 *earth-born soldiers*: a reference to the dragon's teeth which Jason threw
into the ground, and they sprang up as armed men. On Medea's advice,
Jason threw a stone into the middle of the army, and the men began
attacking each other.

215 *women warriors*: the Amazons, who lived on the river Thermodon.

257 *Acastus*: the son of Pelias. After Medea tricked his sisters into killing their
father, Acastus tried to take revenge on both her and Jason.

315 *the slow old man . . . controls*: the Plough (the Big Dipper) was supposed
to be steered by another set of stars, Bootes, the old ploughman.

351 *Scylla*: the mythical sea-monster, who lived between Sicily and Italy; she
had six heads and the voice of a dog, and she ate sailors—including some
of Odysseus' men (*Odyssey*, 12. 85–100).

378 *Thule*: land lying north of Britain, perhaps Iceland or Norway, traditionally believed to be the farthest northern part of the world.

408 *Charybdis*: a monstrous whirlpool, located opposite the rocks of Scylla,
which threatened Odysseus and his men.

409 *Titan*: one of the Titans, either Typhoeus or Enceladus—was imprisoned
under Mount Etna.

456 *the Clashing Rocks*: two rocks that moved together, crushing ships
between them. The *Argo* had to pass between them.

457 *your uncle's lands*: Pelias, king of Iolchos (see note to line 201).

466 *the bull*: the first test set for Jason by King Aeetes, in order to earn the
Golden Fleece, was yoking his fire-breathing oxen.

467 *a never-conquered race*: the people of Colchis, known for their wildness.

468 *the field of armoured men*: see note to line 169.

471 *Phrixean ram*: Phrixus, with his sister Helle, was going to be sacrificed by
their father, but a golden ram saved them; when Phrixus reached Colchis
he sacrificed the ram to Zeus, and hung its fleece in a tree.

472 *the sleepless monster*: the dragon that guarded the Golden Fleece; Medea
put it to sleep by her magic.

473 *my brother*: see note to line 132.

476 *that old man*: Pelias (see note to line 134).

477 [*I left my realm behind . . . someone else's.*]: some editors omit this line on the grounds that it interrupts the sequence of thought.

512 *Phoebus . . . Sisyphus*: Medea is descended from the Sun (Phoebus Apollo, god of the sun). Sisyphus, notorious for his wickedness, was the founder of Corinth, the forefather of Creon and his daughter.

577 *Hecate*: see note to line 7.

579 [CHORUS]: this choral ode is in sapphics; I have tried to echo the metrical pattern in English.

584 *Hister*: the lower Danube.

590 *Haemus*: a mountain-range in Thrace.

599 *that boy*: Phaethon, who tried to drive the chariot of his father, the Sun.

607 *that daring vessel*: the *Argo*.

609 *Pelion's mountain glades*: the *Argo* was built of wood from Mount Pelion.

617 *Tiphys*: the steersman of the *Argo*. Seneca, unlike other authors, implies that he was king of Aulis.

625 *Orpheus*: child of the Muse Calliope and Apollo, another hero on the *Argo*. He tried to rescue his wife, Eurydice, from the underworld. Hades had ruled that he must not look back at her until they reached the sunlight, but Orpheus did look back, and she was lost again, forever. Later Orpheus was torn apart by Maenads, and his head drifted, still singing, down the river Hebrus.

634 *the two sons of the North Wind*: Calais and Zetes, killed by Hercules because they had persuaded the other Argonauts to leave him behind after he left the ship to search for his lost lover, Hylas (see note to line 647).

635 *the sea-god's offspring*: Periclymenus, killed by Hercules in his attack on Pylos.

640 *the cruel furnace*: after he was poisoned by the agonizing shirt of Nessus, Hercules built his own funeral pyre on Mount Oeta and threw himself on it.

641 *two destructive poisons*: the poison shirt, given to Hercules by his wife Deianira (under the mistaken belief that it was a love-potion), was tainted with two different poisons: the blood of the centaur Nessus and that of the Hydra (see note to line 776).

643 *Ancaeus*: another Argonaut, killed by the Calydonian boar.

644 *Meleager*: killed his uncles when they tried to seize the hide of the Calydonian boar. His mother, Althea, killed him by putting on the fire a magic log which held his life.

647 *the young boy*: Hylas, Hercules' lover, seized by water nymphs on a stop-over on the journey of the *Argo*.

652 *Idmon*: the seer on the *Argo*.

654 *Mopsus*: another Argonaut with prophetic powers.

656  *Thetis' husband*: Peleus, exiled several times.

658  *Ajax*: the 'lesser' Ajax—not the 'great' Ajax, son of Telemon—was the son of Oileus, an Argonaut; Seneca's Chorus suggest that Ajax's death was expiation for his father's participiation on the *Argo* journey.

660  *Nauplius*: another Argonaut; he tried to attack the Greeks in revenge for the death of his son, Palamedes.

662  *wife*: Alcestis agreed to die in exchange for her husband, Admetus, king of Pherae.

695  *the Bears*: Medea lists a series of constellations: Ursa Major, Ursa Minor, Ophiuchus, Hydra.

699  *Python*: the serpent who threatened Leto when she was pregnant with Apollo and Diana; Apollo killed it in revenge.

707  *Eryx's rocks*: a mountain in Sicily.

709  *Prometheus' blood*: Prometheus was chained to a rock in the Caucasus, and every day an eagle pecked out his liver.

720  *Athos*: a mountain in northern Greece.

721  *Pangaeus' ridges*: Pangaeus is a mountain in Thrace.

724  *Hydaspes*: a tributary of the river Indus. It is said to be 'bejewelled' because India was thought to be rich in gems and treasure.

726  *Baetis . . . country*: Baetica was a Spanish province.

741  *Dis*: another name for Hades, god of the underworld.

742  *Tartarus*: strictly, the area under the underworld; here it seems to be used by metonymy for the rivers of the underworld.

745  *Ixion . . . Tantalus*: famous sinners tormented in the underworld: Ixion was bound onto a wheel forever, Tantalus was eternally thirsty but never allowed to drink. Pirene is a fountain in Corinth, so Medea implies that he can come and visit in Corinth.

747  *Sisyphus*: ancestor of Creon and Creusa; he is tormented in the underworld by having to push a stone up a hill forever.

749  *Danaids*: the daughters of Danaus, fifty girls, all but one of whom murdered their husbands on their wedding night. They were condemned to fill leaky urns in the underworld forever. Their experience in husband-killing will prove useful in Medea's revenge against Jason.

751  *all three*: the moon, associated with the goddess Hecate, has three faces because Hecate is often portrayed with three faces.

769  *the Hyades*: a cluster of five stars in Taurus, associated with rain.

770  *Diana*: the moon-goddess, also identified with Hecate, the dark magical moon-goddess.

773  *Typhon*: the monster who attacked Jove (Jupiter), and was imprisoned under Mount Etna. He had snakes growing from his body; these are probably the 'limbs' that Medea uses.

776 *Nessus*: a centaur who carried Deianira across the river Evenus. He tried to rape her but was mortally wounded by Hercules, her husband. He gave Deianira the poison that would kill Hercules.

777 *Oeta*: Hercules built his own funeral pyre on Mount Oeta (see note to line 640).

780 *Althaea*: killed her son, Meleager, after he had killed her brothers (see note to line 644).

782 *Zetes*: Calais and Zetes chased away the Harpies when they were tormenting the blind prophet, Phineus.

783 *Stymphalian bird . . . Lernaean arrows*: killed by Hercules as one of his labours. He used arrows tipped with poison from the Lernaean Hydra.

791 *Thessalian witches*: said to use magic to draw down the moon.

795 *cymbals of bronze*: thought to counteract the effects of magic. They could restore the moon to normal if its path was affected by witchcraft.

798 *turf*: used as a makeshift altar.

804 *like corpses wear*: the corpse was traditionally draped with a headband.

806 *Maenad*: a crazed female worshipper of Bacchus (Dionysus).

824 *Prometheus*: stole fire for mankind, and was punished for this by an eagle who pecked out his ever-regenerating liver.

*Mulciber*: Vulcan (Hephaestus), god of fire.

826 *Phaethon*: Medea's cousin once removed, because the Sun was his father, Medea's grandfather(see note to line 599).

828 *Chimaera*: a monster with a head like a lion, tail like a snake, and in the middle a goat's body from which came fire.

830 *the bulls*: the fire-breathing bulls that Jason used to sow the dragon's teeth, with Medea's help.

831 *Medusa*: a snake-headed Gorgon, killed by Perseus.

913 *ancestral treasure*: the Golden Fleece.

914 *the old man*: Pelias (see note to line 134).

954 *proud Niobe*: boasted that she had more children (fourteen) than the goddess Leto, who had only two, Apollo and Diana. Apollo and Diana took revenge by killing all her children; she wept so much that she turned to stone.

## TROJAN WOMEN

14 *Pergamum*: Troy.

29 *my lord . . . Phrygia*: Priam, Hecuba's husband, the dead king of Troy and its surrounded region (Phrygia).

31 *the hero . . . fall*: Hector. See note to line 189.

34 *Cassandra*: Hecuba's daughter, was cursed with the ability to foresee the future but never be believed.

37 *I was the first to prophesy in vain*: when Hecuba was pregnant with Paris she dreamed she gave birth to a firebrand—foreshadowing Paris' role in bringing about the Trojan War and the destruction of the city.

38 *the cunning Ithacan hero and his friend*: Ulysses and Diomedes, who raided Troy at night (as described in Book 10 of the *Iliad*).

39 *Sinon's lies*: the Greek who used trickery to persuade the Trojans to take the Wooden Horse into the city.

44 *a king*: Priam.

61 *somebody*: Agamemnon, who took Cassandra home.

62 *they fear*: Hecuba was fated to turn into a dog.

66 *that terrible judge*: Paris, exposed as a baby on Mount Ida, and raised by shepherds there. He is the judge because he judged between the three goddesses (Venus, Athena, and Juno). He chose Venus (Aphrodite), goddess of love and sex, and was rewarded with the opportunity to carry off Helen, the most beautiful woman in the world—which started the Trojan War.

71 *Amyclae*: the birthplace of Helen.

134 *twice defeated*: Troy had earlier been captured by Hercules.

137 *the bow of Hercules*: brought back to Troy by Philoctetes.

164 *the Greeks are always stuck in a harbour*: the first of many allusions in this play to the time at the beginning of the war when the Greek fleet was becalmed at Aulis, unable to sail for Troy. The winds came only when Agamemnon sacrificed his daughter, Iphigeneia.

177 *its own Achilles*: Achilles' mother, Thetis, was a sea-goddess; hence Achilles' power over the ocean. Lines 176 and 177 are marked as spurious by Zwierlein.

181 *the lord of Thessaly*: Achilles, who came from Thessaly.

184 *Neptune's . . . son*: Cycnus, choked to death by Achilles.

186 *Xanthus*: Scamander, the river in Troy, which Achilles filled with Trojan corpses.

189 *Hector*: Achilles killed Troy's best champion, Hector, and dragged his corpse around the city behind his chariot.

211 *avoid the war*: Achilles' mother, Thetis, dressed him as a girl in the hope that the disguise would prevent him from being taken to Troy, where she knew he would be killed.

213 *Nestor*: one of the Greek leaders in the *Iliad*, famous for his great age.

215 *Telephus*: king of Mysia in Asia Minor, was wounded by Achilles, but later healed by the rust from his spear.

219 *Etion*: father of Andromache.

222 *Briseis and Chryseis*: the captured Trojan women over whom Achilles and Agamemnon argue in the *Iliad*. Agamemnon is forced to return his original concubine, Chryseis, to her father, and takes Achilles' girl, Briseis, instead. This is the cause of Achilles' rage.

227 *Lyrnesos . . . The homes . . . Tenedos . . . Scyros . . . Lesbos . . . Cilla*: all places sacked by Achilles.

228 *Caycus*: a river in Mysia, where Achilles wounded Telephus.

239 *Memnon*: nephew of Priam and son of Dawn (Aurora); killed by Achilles.

242 *even the sons of goddesses*: Achilles' mother was the goddess Thetis.

243 *the savage Amazon*: Penthesilea, queen of the Amazons, with whom Achilles fell in love as he killed her in battle.

248 *a daughter*: Iphigeneia, killed by Agamemnon in order to launch the Greek fleet against Troy (see note to line 164).

317 *via Ajax and Ulysses*: Priam came to Achilles in person to beg for the body of his dead son Hector (*Iliad*, Book 24). Agamemnon sent an embassy, including Ajax and Ulysses, to beg Achilles to return to fight for the Greeks (*Iliad*, Book 9).

331 *It is too late . . . wrong*: refers again to Agamemnon's killing of his daughter Iphigeneia.

333 *Punishing them is legal*: this was true under Roman law.

339 *Scyros arrogance*: Scyros is the island from which Achilles and Pyrrhus came. The point at issue, here and throughout the passage, is how much Pyrrhus resembles his father. Agamemnon accuses him of being proud and wilful, like Achilles.

*Brothers are brotherly there*: a dig at the lack of brotherly love in the relationship of Agamemnon's father, Atreus, and his uncle, Thyestes. Atreus killed and cooked Thyestes' children and served them up to him at a feast; the story is the subject of Seneca's tragedy *Thyestes* (below).

340 *my cousin, the sea*: Achilles' mother, Thetis, was a sea-goddess, so Pyrrhus is related by family ties to all the ocean. He implies that his family background is much more distinguished than that of Agamemnon.

342 *a virgin's secret rape*: Achilles seduced Deidamia, the daughter of the king, who gave birth to Pyrrhus.

346 *Hell from Aeacus, sky from Jove*: Aeacus, Achilles' grandfather, became a judge of the dead; Jupiter (Jove) was the father of Aeacus, great-grandfather of Achilles.

348 *whom gods feared to fight*: in Book 20 of the *Iliad* Apollo and Poseidon (Neptune) resist fighting with Achilles.

358 *a heavy price for me*: another allusion to the sacrifice of Agamemnon's daughter (see note to line 164). Calchas was the seer who proposed the killing.

387 *the lord of the stars*: the sun.

388 *Hecate*: the moon-goddess (see note to *Medea*, line 7).

391 *lake . . . swear their oaths*: the Styx in the underworld.

402 *Taenarus*: location of an entrance to the underworld.

414 *my body*: Andromache identifies herself with her husband's corpse.

439  *two watches . . . Plough*: these details identify the time as just past mid-night.

445  *igniting those Greek ships*: Hector sets fire to the Greek ships in the *Iliad*, Books 15–16.

447  *the fake Achilles . . . armour*: in Book 16 of the *Iliad* Achilles' friend Patroclus borrows his armour and goes into battle wearing it; Hector kills him and takes the armour.

455  *If only the whole city had been flattened*: Astyanax, the baby son, will be thrown from the one remaining tall tower of Troy.

521  *laid down*: the word used—*depositum*—is a kind of pun, since it also connotes a person who is 'dead' or 'buried' (from *depositus*, lit. 'put down').

555  *Orestes*: Agamemnon's son. The point is that the son of the losing hero would always have had to be killed; if the Greeks had lost, Agamemnon's son would have been the one.

     *Agamemnon did*: Agamemnon has already had to endure the loss of his child—Iphigeneia—whom he killed himself.

570  *even divine ones*: the reference is to Thetis, divine mother of Achilles, who tried to pretend that her son was a woman, to protect him from the war (see note to line 211). Her trick was exposed by Ulysses, who offered armour as a present to Achilles; he eagerly accepted, as (supposedly) no woman would.

664  *But you sold him to us*: Achilles and the other Greek leaders 'sold' the body of Hector to Priam, when he came to give ransom for his son's corpse.

670  *even those that blessed you*: refers to the temple of Minerva (Athena), desecrated by the rape of Cassandra by Ajax.

705  *Come out here*: there is a shift to lyric metre here; Andromache is singing as she calls her son out.

720  *Priam . . . threats of fierce Hercules*: Priam's father, Laomedon, promised to give a gift of mares to Hercules in exchange for building his city's walls. Laomedon reneged on the promise, and Hercules came to kill him—but, in Seneca's version of the myth, spared the boy Priam's life (a detail which does not appear in early versions of the story).

753  *you killed even Greeks*: Ulysses plotted the death of Palamedes, a Greek.

755  *fighting by night*: Ulysses was famous for his night-time expedition into the Trojan camp with Diomedes, described in the *Iliad*, Book 10.

778  *Trojan Games*: a Roman institution, which supposedly originated at Troy.

782  *honour foreign temples . . . dance*: refers to the games held in honour of Cybele, the mother-goddess from Asia Minor.

824  *twice over*: Hercules' bow, made on Mount Oeta, was used by Hercules himself in the first destruction of the walls of Troy, and then by Philoctetes in the final sack of Troy by the Greeks.

830  *Chiron*: the centaur who acted as tutor to the boy Achilles.

843  *Mysteries*: a secret religious cult in honour of Ceres (Demeter) and Persephone.

857  *Sparta . . . Argos . . . Mycenae . . . Neritos . . . Zacynthos . . . Ithaca*: Sparta was the home of Helen; Argos and Mycenae were the kingdom of Agamemnon; Zacynthos, Neritos, and Ithaca belonged to Ulysses.

976  *The boy from Scyros*: Pyrrhus.

978  *the king of kings*: Agamemnon.

991  *who got Achilles' spoils*: Ulysses, who was awarded Achilles' armour after his death.

1003  *you like my family's blood*: Pyrrhus has already killed Hecuba's old husband, Priam.

1034  *Phrixus . . . Helle*: a brother and sister who ran away from their jealous stepmother on a golden ram sent by Jupiter (see note to *Medea*, line 471).

1039  *Pyrrha and her husband*: the only survivors of a great flood sent by Jupiter to punish the human race.

1103  *the boy jumped down to Priam's kingdom*: the Latin line is metrically incomplete—a rare phenomenon in Seneca. The feeling of a gap clearly mirrors the sense: Astyanax is suddenly broken off. 'Priam's kingdom' is both Troy and, now, the land of the dead.

1104  *Colchis*: the kingdom of Medea, who killed her children: here it forms the first in a series of three famously barbaric places—none of which have seen behaviour as barbaric as that of Ulysses.

1106  *Busiris*: an Egyptian king who sacrificed on his altars all strangers who entered his kingdom.

1108  *Diomedes*: a Thracian king who fed his horses on human flesh.

1109  *your body*: Andromache suddenly addresses her dead son.

1117  *Still so like his father!*: because Hector's body, too, was mangled after death.

1134  *Hermione*: daughter of Helen.

## HERCULES FURENS

1  *only his sister*: one of Juno's grievances is that Jupiter has cheated on her so often that she is now only his sister, not his wife.

6  *the Bear*: Ursa Major, who is identified with the nymph Callisto, who was seduced by Jupiter then turned into a bear by Juno. All the constellations cited by Juno here are reminders of Jupiter's extramarital affairs.

9  *the Bull*: Taurus, identified with the mythical bull—Jupiter in disguise—who carried Europa to Crete.

10 *Pleiades*: three of the Pleiades, daughters of Atlas, slept with Jupiter.

12 *Orion*: not traditionally said to be a son of Jupiter, so his inclusion here is puzzling.

13 *Perseus*: the son of Zeus by Danae, conceived by a shower of gold: hence, 'golden'.

14 *Gemini*: Castor and Pollux, sons of Zeus by Leda.

15 *those whose birth made the wandering island stop*: allusion to the birth of Apollo and Diana: their mother, Leto, gave birth on the island of Delos, which had hitherto had no fixed place in the ocean; it stopped for her to give birth.

16 *Bacchus*: the child of Zeus by Semele, Bacchus became one of the Olympian gods.

18 *Ariadne's crown*: Ariadne, abandoned by Theseus, was found and loved by Bacchus, who put a crown of stars for her in the sky.

22 *Alcmena*: the mother of Hercules. Jupiter had promised that Hercules would win immortality after performing the labours.

24 *the night he was conceived*: on the night of Hercules' conception, Jupiter ran three nights into one.

33 *He wins!*: Seneca delays the actual name of the monster-killing hero whom Juno hates: Hercules.

38 *the two dark-painted peoples*: refers to the tradition—which goes back to Homer, *Odyssey* 1. 23—that there are two lands of Aethiopia: one situated where the sun rises and one where it sets; both peoples supposedly had dark skins because they were near to the sun.

46 *the Lion and the Hydra*: Hercules wears the skin of the Nemean Lion and uses arrows dipped in the poison of the Hydra—both monsters he has defeated.

48 *prizes back to earth*: the twelfth labour of Hercules—in many versions of the story—was to capture Cerberus, the guard-dog of the underworld, and bring him back up to the upper world.

52 *Hades' brother*: Jupiter, Hades, and Neptune are all brothers.

54 *Styx*: one of the rivers in the underworld, Styx is also used metonymically for the whole underworld kingdom.

71 *He raised . . . the world*: Hercules temporarily took over the task of bearing up the world from Atlas, who usually carried it.

82 *the monstrous giant*: Typhoeus, who was imprisoned under Mount Etna (the volcanic activity of that mountain was supposedly caused by his struggles).

83 [*And let the lofty moon . . . monsters.*]: this line is omitted by some editors, on the grounds that it contradicts Juno's earlier: 'No more monsters!'

132 *Ursa Major . . . Plough*: the Great Bear is actually the same constellation as the Plough (known in the United States as the Big Dipper).

134 *Mount Oeta's heights*: the place where Hercules will die, as described in Seneca's *Hercules Oetaeus*.

135 *Pentheus' death*: the king of Thebes, who was killed by his own mother when she was worshipping Dionysus on Mount Cithaeron—an instance of family murder under divinely imposed madness which foreshadows Hercules' own actions.

137 *Apollo's sister*: Diana, the moon-goddess.

139 *the Thracian king*: alludes to the story of Philomela, raped by her sister's husband Tereus, in Thrace; she was turned into a nightingale.

182 *The brutal sisters . . . spinning*: the three Fates, sisters who spin the threads of destiny or fate for all mortals.

215 *as a newborn baby*: Juno sent snakes to kill Hercules while he was still in his cradle.

223 *the speedy hind*: one of Hercules' labours was to capture the Ceryneian hind, sacred to Diana.

224 *The terrifying lion*: Hercules killed the Nemean lion, another monstrous animal.

226 *those awful Thracian stables*: Hercules had to capture the man-eating horses of the Thracian giant-king, Diomedes. Seneca's formulation suggests that Hercules also fed the king to the horses.

228 *the bristly wild boar*: another labour: the capture of the wild Erymanthian boar.

230 *the bull*: monstrous Cretan bull.

232 *triple-bodied shepherd*: Hercules killed Geryon, a giant with three heads and three bodies, and stole his cattle.

236 *countries singed by the noon-time heat*: Hercules visited Libya and Gibraltar.

238 *highway for the rushing ocean*: the Straits of Gibraltar.

240 *golden spoils*: the apples of the Hesperides, guarded by a hundred-headed dragon or snake.

241 *in Lerna*: the Lernaean Hydra had nine heads, which grew back when cut off; Hercules killed it by scorching each neck after decapitation.

243 *the birds*: the Stymphalian Birds were man-eating birds with poisonous dung; Hercules shot them down with his arrows.

245 *ever-virgin queen*: Hercules took the girdle of the Amazon queen, Hippolyta.

248 *Augean stable*: Hercules' most disgusting labour was to muck out the dung-encrusted Augean stables in a single day.

261 *an army jumped up*: Cadmus, founder of Thebes, planted dragon-teeth, and soldiers sprang up (see note to *Medea*, line 169).

262 *Amphion*: the singer who restored the walls of Thebes through the power of music (see note to *Oedipus*, line 611).

269  *this stranger*: Lycus.

285  *Mount Tempe*: Hercules supposedly opened the Vale of Tempe, cracking the mountains apart.

293  *self-forgetful dead*: the dead have forgotten themselves because they have drunk the waters of Lethe, river of forgetfulness.

300  *Ceres*: the mother-goddess associated with the harvest, who had a mystery cult at Eleusis.

319  *the dry beach*: Amphitryon seems to allude to an otherwise unknown incident in Hercules, life: apparently he managed to escape from the notorious quicksands of Syrtes.

340  *machismo*: Lycus uses the word *virtus* 'manly courage', 'heroism', which is also a primary characteristic of Hercules himself. The play is, among other things, a sustained meditation on what *virtus* really is.

357  *Hercules' real father*: a gibe at Hercules, suggesting that he is not really the son of Jupiter but of his adoptive human father, Amphitryon.

377  *Euripus*: the changeability of the shifting waters of Euripus was proverbial.

387  *mothers . . . suffered*: reference to Jocasta, mother of Oedipus; Ino, who plotted against Phrixus; and Agave, who killed her son Pentheus.

388  *that mixed-up man . . . son*: Oedipus.

389  *the brothers' two camps . . . flames*: this refers to the two sons of Oedipus, Polyneices and Eteocles, who fought and killed one another in a dispute over the throne of Thebes. When their bodies were put on the funeral pyre the flames divided, so that even in death the brothers could not be reconciled.

390  *That proud mother*: Niobe, daughter of Tantalus (see note to *Medea*, line 954).

392  *Cadmus himself*: founder of the Theban dynasty, changed to a snake by Bacchus.

451  *Apollo served as shepherd*: Apollo was enslaved to Admetus, and worked as his shepherd at Pherae.

453  *on a wandering island*: see note to line 15.

455  *A dragon*: according to some versions of the myth, Juno sent the dragon Python after Leto when she was pregnant; Apollo took revenge by killing the dragon.

458  *father's thunderbolt . . . thundering father*: Bacchus' mother, Semele, was burned up by Jupiter's thunderbolt (see note to line 16), but Bacchus 'soon' stood beside his father in battle, to fight against the Giants. Amphitryon's point is that vulnerability in babyhood does not prevent later heroism, or later deification.

460  *lie hidden in a cavern*: Jupiter's mother, Rhea, hid him in a cave on Mount Ida as a baby to protect him from his father Cronos, who had a habit of swallowing his children.

464  *do not say that he suffers*: Amphitryon's position is similar to the central Stoic tenet that virtue alone is sufficient for happiness. A perfectly wise, brave, and virtuous man must, in Stoic thought, be happy—regardless of the misery or torment of his external circumstances.

465  *the lion skin fell from his shoulders*: this refers to the story that Hercules was enslaved by the queen of Lydia, Omphale, and she made him wear women's clothes while she dressed in his lion skin.

478  *virgin girls*: Hercules raped Eurytus' daughter, Iole. This part of the legend is usually put chronologically later, after Hercules is married to his second wife, Deianira. There are many other stories of Hercules' sexual exploits; for instance, he had sex with all fifty daughters of Thespius (a feat sometimes called the thirteenth labour).

487  *Eryx . . . Antaeus . . . Busiris . . . Cycnus . . . Geryon*: Amphitryon lists tyrants and oppressors defeated by Hercules. Most of the characters on the list were cruel and violent to strangers. Antaeus challenged strangers to fight, and always won; Eryx did the same; Cycnus also killed strangers. Busiris sacrificed strangers at his altar. The three-headed monster Geryon was killed by Hercules when he went to steal his cattle (on Eurystheus' orders).

490  *you gave one wife to Jove*: Amphitryon 'lent' his wife Alcmena to Jupiter, on the night Hercules was conceived.

495  *Labdacus*: grandson of Cadmus, and grandfather of Oedipus; a king of Thebes, often treated as representative of the Theban royal family.

498  *daughters of King Danaus*: the fifty Danaids (see note to *Medea*, line 749).

529  *snaky heads*: refers to the Hydra, the many-headed serpent killed by Hercules.

530  *the sisters*: the Hesperides; Hercules stole their apples.

565  *The king who rules so many souls . . . terrified to die*: During Hercules' attack on the city of Pylos the gods Neptune, Apollo, and Hades tried to defend the city. The Chorus suggests that, having defeated Hades once, Hercules can do so again.

571  *Orpheus . . . Eurydice back*: the mythical singer and son of Apollo and the muse Calliope tried to win back his dead wife Eurydice by singing for Hades and Persephone (see note to *Medea*, line 625).

599  *king of the second realm*: Neptune.

603  *this horrible wonder*: Cerberus, the guard-dog of the underworld, whom Hercules has brought up to the light with him.

604  *she*: Juno.

639  *Lycus will tell Dis*: the conceit is that Lycus himself will soon be dead, and can pass the news on to the king of the underworld (Dis).

658  *Natural Law*: an unusual invocation—*fas omne mundi*, lit. 'all right of the world'.

659 *King of the Limitless Realm*: Hades, lord of the underworld—which constantly expands to contain new inhabitants.

660 *your mother . . . Etna*: Proserpine's mother, Ceres, searched for her all over the world when she was stolen by Hades; she used the fires of Mount Etna to light torches so as to continue searching by night.

683 *Meander*: a river in modern Turkey, famous for its many turns—hence 'meander'.

723 *his brother*: Hades and Jupiter/Jove are brothers; Jove looks stern only in some aspects, when he thunders, whereas Hades/Dis looks stern all the time.

753 *the old man*: Tantalus.

759 *Ixion . . . Sisyphus . . . Tityos . . . the Danaids . . . Phineus*: a list of all the usual mythological punishments of the underworld. See note to *Phaedra*, line 1237, and for the Danaids, *Medea*, line 749. The Theban bacchants are the women driven mad by Dionysus (see note to *Oedipus*, line 441). Phineus, a prophet, revealed the secrets of the gods and was punished by harpies (women with wings), who stole his food before he could eat it.

764 *hideous old man*: Charon.

830 *Eurystheus was hurried into birth*: when Hercules was about to be born, Jupiter vowed that the child born from his house that day would rule Mycenae. Juno, out of envy, hurried up the birth of Eurystheus, so he was born before Hercules, and became the king—and thus able to order Hercules to carry out the labours.

841 *the festival*: the Olympic Games, held in honour of Jupiter; by ancient inclusive counting, the 'fifth' summer is what we would call the fourth, because the games were, then as now, held every four years.

847 *the holy rites*: the Great Mysteries, a ritual celebration at Eleusis of the fertility goddess, Ceres; it was held at the autumn equinox, when the day and night are equal.

853 *hair cut yet*: boys' hair was cut at puberty.

894 *poplar*: particularly associated with Hercules, to whom these two lines are addressed.

903 *my Lord*: Bacchus. Lycurgus attacked the god and his servants, and the god took revenge. Later, apparently, Bacchus performed a miraculous crossing of the Red Sea and Persian Gulf, perhaps parting the waters like Moses.

908 *at least the ones . . . stepmother*: other sons of Jupiter not by Juno who live in heaven include Bacchus and Phoebus Apollo, and also Orion, Perseus, and Castor and Pollux.

917 *caves . . . fountain . . . Tyrian palace*: alludes to the major tourist-sites of Thebes, a city which had multiple founders: first the city was founded by Cadmus, and then the walls were built by Zethus and his brother Amphion, sons of Antiope by Jupiter, who were raised in a cave when

their mother was forced to expose them on Mount Cithaeron. Dirce, wife of Lycus, was cruel to Antiope; the sons, Zethus and Antiope, killed her by tying her to the horns of a bull. Bacchus marked the spot of her death with a fountain. The stranger-king is Cadmus, who came from Tyre.

945 *the Lion*: the first monster killed by Hercules, the Nemean Lion, is equated with the constellation Leo. Leo prepares to pounce on Taurus, the Bull.

965 *Saturn . . . chains*: identified with the Greek Titan Cronos, the father of Jupiter, whom Jupiter imprisoned in the underworld. Hercules is the grandson of Saturn because he is the son of Jupiter.

977 *Tityos*: see note to *Phaedra*, line 1237.

981 *Mimas*: one of the giants who rebelled against the Olympian gods, named by Horace (*Odes*, 3. 4).

998 *Mycenae . . . Cyclops built*: the kingdom of Eurystheus, Hercules' enemy. The monumental city walls were said to have been built by the Cyclopes.

1141 *the distant country . . . Ocean*: Gibraltar, which lies on the furthest point of the Mediterranean.

1159 *night . . . longer than for mine*: on Hercules' conception see note to line 24.

1171 *lords of Libya*: Hercules suggests that his enemy could repeat his own labours: defeating the horses of Diomedes, the Thracian (who used to be fed on Diomedes' guests); capturing the cattle of the monster Geryon; and defeating the tyrants Antaeus and Busirus (in Africa/Libya).

1181 *the tyrant of Argos*: Eurystheus.

1211 *Symplegades*: the Clashing Rocks (see note to *Medea*, line 456).

1342 *Mars had his hands . . . clean of murder*: Mars killed Halirrhothius after he raped his daughter, Alcippe; the trial after the murder took place on the Athenian Areopagus—the first murder trial held there.

## THYESTES

9 *the wheel . . . Tityos*: for these famous sufferers in the underworld see note to *Phaedra*, line 1237.

16 *the guard*: Cerberus, guard-dog of Hades.

17 *Acheron*: one of the rivers of the underworld, but here used to describe the whole underworld.

22 *Minos*: the judge of the dead.

33 *exile*: both Atreus and Thyestes, at different times, are exiled and then return to power.

37 *god*: this can be taken as general or unspecific (like 'the gods' or 'fate'), or as a reference to the god Apollo—whose oracle told Thyestes that he could only get revenge by incest.

42  *even worse their births*: the deaths of Thyestes' children, murdered by Atreus, will not be as bad as the conception of Aegisthus, by the incest of Thyestes and his daughter.

43  *plotting against him*: Atreus' wife, Aerope, plotted against him with Thyestes; Clytemnestra plotted with Aegisthus to kill her husband Agamemnon.

56  *Thracian crime*: Procne's murder of her son Itys, as revenge on her husband Tereus for his rape of her sister Philomela. The crime will be repeated, because again children will be killed as revenge on their father; this time it will be three children, not one.

57  *Uncle*: Atreus.

58  [*Is Thyestes . . . children?*]: the square brackets indicate that I think the line is probably spurious (as do many editors). It seems to interrupt the sequence of thought.

63  *you*: addressed to Tantalus.

73  *Phlegethon's . . . water*: Phlegethon, one of the four rivers of the underworld, flowed with fire not water.

74  *punishments*: this list of underworld punishments is based on Virgil, *Aeneid*, 6. 548–627. The sinners who suffer these things are not famous characters.

83  *those above*: the word used here—*superi*, lit. the 'upper ones'—could connote either the world above the underworld, or the gods. Tantalus hopes to evade both.

90  *my father*: Jupiter.

100  *I follow you*: this is a rare instance of an incomplete line in Seneca. In the original it is just one word (*sequor*).

108  *water is pushed back*: the trees and water replicate on earth Tantalus' underworld punishment: fruit dies and waters withdraw.

115  *Lerna*: a watery swamp, famous as the abode of the Hydra (a monster killed by Hercules). Alpheus is a river in the Peloponnese.

119  *Argos . . . ancient thirst*: Argos was parched of water before the legendary figure Danaus built wells for it.

139  *Myrtilus*: a charioteer, who betrayed his master, Oenomaus, for Pelops, who promised him half his kingdom if he sabotaged Oenomaus' chariot. Pelops then went back on his word, and drowned Myrtilus on his way home.

142  *infamous Myrtoan sea*: this stretch of the Aegean Sea was particularly dangerous. The implication is that the sea is treacherous, like its namesake.

144  *The little boy*: Pelops, whom Tantalus tried to serve up to the gods.

154  *Harpies*: birds with women's faces punishing Phineus, king of Thrace (see note to *Hercules Furens*, line 759).

240 *blood in doubt*: refers to Atreus' suspicion that Thyestes may have fathered his children, Agamemnon and Menelaus.

265 *Lares*: the household gods.

273 *house of Thrace . . . feasts unspeakable*: Thrace is the location of the Procne, Tereus, and Itys story: Procne fed Tereus his own son, Itys—an obvious precedent for Atreus' plan (already cited by the Fury, lines 53–4).

276 *our motives are alike*: Atreus claims that Procne's anger at her sister's rape is similar to his own anger at Thyestes' supposed rape of his brother's wife.

308 *other agents*: i.e. other than Atreus' own sons.

337 *Inachus*: a river-god, was the first king of Argos.

338 *fixed*: there is an ambiguity in the verb (*composuit*): the Chorus think that the quarrel is settled or resolved (i.e. finished), though the audience knows that the worst of it is just begun.

344 *Wealth does not make the king*: the Chorus here expound the Stoic principle that only the wise man is king.

345 *Tyrian purple*: an expensive dye associated with royalty.

355 *Tagus . . . golden*: Roman gold came mostly from Spain. Tagus is a river in Spain (modern Tejo), which was known for its gold deposits.

357 *Libyan harvest*: Roman wheat mostly came from Libya (North Africa).

370 *Dahae*: a barbarian tribe on the outer edges of the Roman empire, known for their archery.

375 *Sarmatian invaders*: refers to the area of Armenia, protected by the ridges of the Caucasus (the Caspian Mountains) from the nomadic tribes from the east; the Sarmatae ranged through modern Ukraine and Georgia.

379 *Seres*: a people who lived in the south-west part of modern China. Seneca emphasizes their distance from the known world (lit. 'in whatever place they lie').

384 *Parthian . . . pretends to flee*: see note to *Oedipus*, line 119.

408 *built by the Cyclopes*: see note to *Hercules Furens*, line 998.

421 [TANTALUS JUNIOR]: Thyestes' son is, as was common practice, named for his grandfather.

442 *since I can die*: i.e. the power to die implies total control over the world—a similar notion to the redefinition of kingship in Stoic terms, in the previous choral ode.

452 *drain their cups in safety*: the implied contrast is with kings and emperors, whose food and drink may be poisoned.

460 *piles of rocks*: refers to the Roman practice of building out into the sea.

497 *Umbrian hound*: a breed known for their keen sense of smell.

508 *How nice to see my brother!*: Atreus' soliloquy presumably ends here. 'How nice to see my brother' is addressed to Thyestes, but of course with

a double meaning; it is genuinely nice for Atreus to see Thyestes in such a bad state.

545 *the designated offerings*: Atreus constantly uses puns and dramatic irony against Thyestes. Here, for instance, the 'bindings' are the crown, but also suggest that he has succeeded in binding his victim in the net. The 'offerings' will include Thyestes' children, soon to be killed.

549 *devotion*: the word used here, *pietas*, could also be translated as 'family' or 'duty' or 'loyalty'.

581 *Scylla . . . Charybdis*: Scylla the sea-monster and Charybdis the whirlpool (see note to *Medea*, lines 351 and 408).

583 *their father*: the Cyclopes are one-eyed giants, metalworkers, who feature in the *Odyssey*; their father is Poseidon, god of the sea.

595 *the shaken Cyclades*: there is an allusion here to the legend that Delos, an island in the Cycladic group, once literally moved around, without a fixed place in the sea (see note to *Hercules Furens*, line 15).

628 *two good brothers*: Castor and Pollux, brothers of Helen; their devotion to one another is implicitly contrasted with the relationship of Thyestes and Atreus.

660 *the trumpet, the broken chariot*: the trumpet (for starting the chariot-race) and the chariot itself were dedicated by Pelops, after he successfully got the charioteer to sabotage the vehicle of his rival, King Oenomaus, in order to win the hand of Hippodamia. On the way home, Pelops killed the charioteer, Myrtilus, and threw him into the Myrtoan Sea (see note to line 139).

667 *Styx . . . swear faith*: river of the underworld, by which the gods swear their oaths.

687 *juice of Bacchus*: wine, since Bacchus is the god of wine.

695 *audience*: Atreus plays all the parts in the sacrifice, including that of observer—the person who had to watch for any bad omens during the ritual.

778 *you set too late*: the sun set at midday, but only after the dreadful dinner had already been eaten.

799 *the ninth hour*: lit. the 'third' quarter of the day, i.e. around 3 p.m.—the time when most Romans ate dinner. In Rome, trumpeters sounded the hours.

811 *Tityos . . . Typhoeus . . . Pelion . . . Ossa*: these lines trace a series of questions about whether the old battle of the gods and the Giants (Tityos and Typhoeus) will be renewed. The Giants supposedly piled mountains one on top of the other, Pelion on to Ossa, in their attempt to storm Olympus.

817 *all gone wrong*: Aurora, goddess of the dawn, is apparently upset that Phoebus Apollo, god of the sun, arrives to bring the day at some unusual time.

820  *into the sea*: usually the sun's horses are taken into the ocean by Tethys, goddess of the sea.

851  *carried Helle*: Aries is identified with the Golden Ram, who carried Helle and her brother over the Hellespont (see note to *Medea*, line 471).

860  *Old Chiron*: the centaur, tutor of Achilles, identified with the archer constellation, Sagittarius.

865  *whoever you are*: there were competing scholarly ideas about who Aquarius, the Water-Carrier, was: possibilities included Ganymede, cupbearer to the gods, and Deucalion, the survivor of the world's great flood.

1005  *Do you not recognize them?*: at this point Atreus reveals the children's heads.

1077  *King of the Sky*: Jupiter.

1083  *triple mountain . . . Giants*: see note to line 811.

1099  *I have my sons . . . marriage back*: Atreus crazily asserts that he has proved his paternity of his sons, and undone Thyestes' adultery with Atreus' wife, by his act of revenge.

A SELECTION OF   **OXFORD WORLD'S CLASSICS**

**Classical Literary Criticism**

**The First Philosophers: The Presocratics and the Sophists**

**Greek Lyric Poetry**

**Myths from Mesopotamia**

APOLLODORUS          **The Library of Greek Mythology**

APOLLONIUS OF RHODES **Jason and the Golden Fleece**

APULEIUS             **The Golden Ass**

ARISTOPHANES         **Birds and Other Plays**

ARISTOTLE            **The Nicomachean Ethics**
                     **Physics**
                     **Politics**

BOETHIUS             **The Consolation of Philosophy**

CAESAR               **The Civil War**
                     **The Gallic War**

CATULLUS             **The Poems of Catullus**

CICERO               **Defence Speeches**
                     **The Nature of the Gods**
                     **On Obligations**
                     **Political Speeches**
                     **The Republic** and **The Laws**

EURIPIDES            **Bacchae and Other Plays**
                     **Heracles and Other Plays**
                     **Medea and Other Plays**
                     **Orestes and Other Plays**
                     **The Trojan Women and Other Plays**

HERODOTUS            **The Histories**

HOMER                **The Iliad**
                     **The Odyssey**

## A SELECTION OF OXFORD WORLD'S CLASSICS

HORACE                  The Complete Odes and Epodes

JUVENAL                 The Satires

LIVY                    The Dawn of the Roman Empire
                        Hannibal's War
                        The Rise of Rome

MARCUS AURELIUS         The Meditations

OVID                    The Love Poems
                        Metamorphoses

PETRONIUS               The Satyricon

PLATO                   Defence of Socrates, Euthyphro, and Crito
                        Gorgias
                        Meno and Other Dialogues
                        Phaedo
                        Republic
                        Selected Myths
                        Symposium

PLAUTUS                 Four Comedies

PLUTARCH                Greek Lives
                        Roman Lives
                        Selected Essays and Dialogues

PROPERTIUS              The Poems

SOPHOCLES               Antigone, Oedipus the King, and Electra

STATIUS                 Thebaid

SUETONIUS               Lives of the Caesars

TACITUS                 Agricola and Germany
                        The Histories

VIRGIL                  The Aeneid
                        The Eclogues and Georgics

XENOPHON                The Expedition of Cyrus

A SELECTION OF    **OXFORD WORLD'S CLASSICS**

THOMAS AQUINAS    **Selected Philosophical Writings**

FRANCIS BACON    **The Essays**

WALTER BAGEHOT    **The English Constitution**

GEORGE BERKELEY    **Principles of Human Knowledge** and
       **Three Dialogues**

EDMUND BURKE    **A Philosophical Enquiry into the Origin of
       Our Ideas of the Sublime and Beautiful**
   **Reflections on the Revolution in France**

CONFUCIUS    **The Analects**

DESCARTES    **A Discourse on the Method**

ÉMILE DURKHEIM    **The Elementary Forms of Religious Life**

FRIEDRICH ENGELS    **The Condition of the Working Class in
       England**

JAMES GEORGE FRAZER    **The Golden Bough**

SIGMUND FREUD    **The Interpretation of Dreams**

THOMAS HOBBES    **Human Nature** and **De Corpore Politico**
   **Leviathan**

DAVID HUME    **Selected Essays**

NICCOLÒ MACHIAVELLI    **The Prince**

THOMAS MALTHUS    **An Essay on the Principle of Population**

KARL MARX    **Capital**
   **The Communist Manifesto**

J. S. MILL    **On Liberty and Other Essays**
   **Principles of Political Economy** and
       **Chapters on Socialism**

FRIEDRICH NIETZSCHE    **Beyond Good and Evil**
   **The Birth of Tragedy**
   **On the Genealogy of Morals**
   **Thus Spoke Zarathustra**
   **Twilight of the Idols**

A SELECTION OF     **OXFORD WORLD'S CLASSICS**

---

THOMAS PAINE     **Rights of Man, Common Sense, and Other**
                     **Political Writings**

JEAN-JACQUES ROUSSEAU     **The Social Contract**
                     **Discourse on the Origin of Inequality**

ADAM SMITH     **An Inquiry into the Nature and Causes of**
                     **the Wealth of Nations**

MARY WOLLSTONECRAFT     **A Vindication of the Rights of Woman**

A SELECTION OF     **OXFORD WORLD'S CLASSICS**

**Bhagavad Gita**

**The Bible** Authorized King James Version
    *With Apocrypha*

**Dhammapada**

**Dharmasūtras**

**The Koran**

**The Pañcatantra**

**The Sauptikaparvan (from the
    Mahabharata)**

**The Tale of Sinuhe and Other Ancient
    Egyptian Poems**

**The Qur'an**

**Upaniṣads**

ANSELM OF CANTERBURY     **The Major Works**

THOMAS AQUINAS     **Selected Philosophical Writings**

AUGUSTINE     **The Confessions
On Christian Teaching**

BEDE     **The Ecclesiastical History**

HEMACANDRA     **The Lives of the Jain Elders**

KĀLIDĀSA     **The Recognition of Śakuntalā**

MANJHAN     **Madhumalati**

ŚĀNTIDEVA     **The Bodhicaryàvatàra**

A SELECTION OF    **OXFORD WORLD'S CLASSICS**

**An Anthology of Elizabethan Prose Fiction**

**An Anthology of Seventeenth-Century Fiction**

**Early Modern Women's Writing**

**Three Early Modern Utopias (Utopia; New Atlantis; The Isle of Pines)**

FRANCIS BACON    **Essays**
                 **The Major Works**

APHRA BEHN       **Oroonoko and Other Writings**
                 **The Rover and Other Plays**

JOHN BUNYAN      **Grace Abounding**
                 **The Pilgrim's Progress**

JOHN DONNE       **The Major Works**
                 **Selected Poetry**

BEN JONSON       **The Alchemist and Other Plays**
                 **The Devil is an Ass and Other Plays**
                 **Five Plays**

JOHN MILTON      **The Major Works**
                 **Paradise Lost**
                 **Selected Poetry**

SIR PHILIP SIDNEY **The Old Arcadia**
                  **The Major Works**

IZAAK WALTON     **The Compleat Angler**

# A SELECTION OF   OXFORD WORLD'S CLASSICS

|  | Travel Writing 1700–1830 |
|---|---|
|  | Women's Writing 1778–1838 |
| WILLIAM BECKFORD | Vathek |
| JAMES BOSWELL | Life of Johnson |
| FRANCES BURNEY | Camilla |
|  | Cecilia |
|  | Evelina |
|  | The Wanderer |
| LORD CHESTERFIELD | Lord Chesterfield's Letters |
| JOHN CLELAND | Memoirs of a Woman of Pleasure |
| DANIEL DEFOE | A Journal of the Plague Year |
|  | Moll Flanders |
|  | Robinson Crusoe |
|  | Roxana |
| HENRY FIELDING | Jonathan Wild |
|  | Joseph Andrews and Shamela |
|  | Tom Jones |
| WILLIAM GODWIN | Caleb Williams |
| OLIVER GOLDSMITH | The Vicar of Wakefield |
| MARY HAYS | Memoirs of Emma Courtney |
| ELIZABETH INCHBALD | A Simple Story |
| SAMUEL JOHNSON | The History of Rasselas |
|  | The Major Works |
| CHARLOTTE LENNOX | The Female Quixote |
| MATTHEW LEWIS | Journal of a West India Proprietor |
|  | The Monk |
| HENRY MACKENZIE | The Man of Feeling |

A SELECTION OF  **OXFORD WORLD'S CLASSICS**

| | |
|---|---|
| ALEXANDER POPE | **Selected Poetry** |
| ANN RADCLIFFE | **The Italian** |
| | **The Mysteries of Udolpho** |
| | **The Romance of the Forest** |
| | **A Sicilian Romance** |
| CLARA REEVE | **The Old English Baron** |
| SAMUEL RICHARDSON | **Pamela** |
| RICHARD BRINSLEY SHERIDAN | **The School for Scandal and Other Plays** |
| TOBIAS SMOLLETT | **The Adventures of Roderick Random** |
| | **The Expedition of Humphry Clinker** |
| LAURENCE STERNE | **The Life and Opinions of Tristram Shandy, Gentleman** |
| | **A Sentimental Journey** |
| JONATHAN SWIFT | **Gulliver's Travels** |
| | **Major Works** |
| | **A Tale of a Tub and Other Works** |
| JOHN VANBRUGH | **The Relapse and Other Plays** |
| HORACE WALPOLE | **The Castle of Otranto** |
| MARY WOLLSTONECRAFT | **Mary and The Wrongs of Woman** |
| | **A Vindication of the Rights of Woman** |

# A SELECTION OF    OXFORD WORLD'S CLASSICS

|  |  |
|---|---|
| | Late Victorian Gothic Tales |
| JANE AUSTEN | Emma |
| | Mansfield Park |
| | Persuasion |
| | Pride and Prejudice |
| | Selected Letters |
| | Sense and Sensibility |
| MRS BEETON | Book of Household Management |
| MARY ELIZABETH BRADDON | Lady Audley's Secret |
| ANNE BRONTË | The Tenant of Wildfell Hall |
| CHARLOTTE BRONTË | Jane Eyre |
| | Shirley |
| | Villette |
| EMILY BRONTË | Wuthering Heights |
| ROBERT BROWNING | The Major Works |
| JOHN CLARE | The Major Works |
| SAMUEL TAYLOR COLERIDGE | The Major Works |
| WILKIE COLLINS | The Moonstone |
| | No Name |
| | The Woman in White |
| CHARLES DARWIN | The Origin of Species |
| THOMAS DE QUINCEY | The Confessions of an English Opium-Eater |
| | On Murder |
| CHARLES DICKENS | The Adventures of Oliver Twist |
| | Barnaby Rudge |
| | Bleak House |
| | David Copperfield |
| | Great Expectations |
| | Nicholas Nickleby |
| | The Old Curiosity Shop |
| | Our Mutual Friend |
| | The Pickwick Papers |

# A SELECTION OF    OXFORD WORLD'S CLASSICS

| | |
|---|---|
| CHARLES DICKENS | A Tale of Two Cities |
| GEORGE DU MAURIER | Trilby |
| MARIA EDGEWORTH | Castle Rackrent |
| GEORGE ELIOT | Daniel Deronda |
| | The Lifted Veil and Brother Jacob |
| | Middlemarch |
| | The Mill on the Floss |
| | Silas Marner |
| SUSAN FERRIER | Marriage |
| ELIZABETH GASKELL | Cranford |
| | The Life of Charlotte Brontë |
| | Mary Barton |
| | North and South |
| | Wives and Daughters |
| GEORGE GISSING | New Grub Street |
| | The Odd Women |
| EDMUND GOSSE | Father and Son |
| THOMAS HARDY | Far from the Madding Crowd |
| | Jude the Obscure |
| | The Mayor of Casterbridge |
| | The Return of the Native |
| | Tess of the d'Urbervilles |
| | The Woodlanders |
| WILLIAM HAZLITT | Selected Writings |
| JAMES HOGG | The Private Memoirs and Confessions of a Justified Sinner |
| JOHN KEATS | The Major Works |
| | Selected Letters |
| CHARLES MATURIN | Melmoth the Wanderer |
| JOHN RUSKIN | Selected Writings |
| WALTER SCOTT | The Antiquary |
| | Ivanhoe |

A SELECTION OF  **OXFORD WORLD'S CLASSICS**

WALTER SCOTT            **Rob Roy**

MARY SHELLEY            **Frankenstein**
                       **The Last Man**

ROBERT LOUIS           **Strange Case of Dr Jekyll and**
STEVENSON                  **Mr Hyde and Other Tales**
                       **Treasure Island**

BRAM STOKER            **Dracula**

JOHN SUTHERLAND        **So You Think You Know Jane Austen?**
                       **So You Think You Know Thomas Hardy?**

WILLIAM MAKEPEACE      **Vanity Fair**
THACKERAY

OSCAR WILDE            **The Importance of Being Earnest and**
                           **Other Plays**
                       **The Major Works**
                       **The Picture of Dorian Gray**

ELLEN WOOD             **East Lynne**

DOROTHY WORDSWORTH     **The Grasmere and Alfoxden Journals**

WILLIAM WORDSWORTH     **The Major Works**